DAPHNE

ALSO BY JUDITH COOK

FICTION
The Waste Remains
Lady from the Lake

SOCIAL–POLITICAL
Apprentices of Freedom
Close to the Earth
Portrait of a Poison
The Price of Freedom
Who Killed Hilda Murrell?
Red Alert
An Accident Waiting to Happen
Dirty Water

THEATRE
Directors' Theatre
The National Theatre
Women in Shakespeare
Shakespeare's Players
Backstage and At the Sign of the Swan
Shakespeare's contemporary playwrights
Directors' Theatre II

PLAYS
Who Killed Christopher Marlowe?
The Fate of Jeremy Visick
Unlawful Killing

Adapted from Daphne du Maurier
The King's General
Jamaica Inn

DAPHNE

A PORTRAIT OF
DAPHNE DU MAURIER

JUDITH COOK

BANTAM PRESS

LONDON · NEW YORK · TORONTO · SYDNEY · AUCKLAND

TRANSWORLD PUBLISHERS LTD
61–63 Uxbridge Road, London W5 5SA

TRANSWORLD PUBLISHERS (AUSTRALIA) PTY LTD
15–23 Helles Avenue, Moorebank, NSW 2170

TRANSWORLD PUBLISHERS (NZ) LTD
Cnr Moselle and Waipareira Aves,
Henderson, Auckland

Published 1991 by Bantam Press
a division of Transworld Publishers Ltd
Copyright © Judith Cook 1991

A catalogue record for this book is
available from the British Library.

ISBN 0593 020839

Typeset in 12/14pt Garamond by
Falcon Typographic Art Ltd, Edinburgh and London.
Printed in Great Britain by
Mackays of Chatham, PLC, Chatham, Kent.

This book is dedicated to two people:

My mother

A. L. Rowse, guide, mentor and friend

ACKNOWLEDGEMENTS

I would like to thank Victor Gollancz Ltd, for permission to quote from the works of Daphne du Maurier, in particular *Growing Pains* and *The Rebecca Notebooks* and to use lines from her poem, *Another World*. Also, Hodder and Stoughton for permission to quote from *Gerald du Maurier* by James Harding and Hamish Hamilton for the use of the extracts from *A Bridge Too Far* by Cornelius Ryan. I must also thank Miss Angela du Maurier for permission to quote from her book, *It's Only the Sister*. All other, briefer, quotations are fully acknowledged in the text.

I am indebted to Doubleday USA for information with regard to both the *Rebecca* plagiarism case and *A Successora* by Caroline Nabuco.

CONTENTS

PREFACE

There is one certain fact that any biographer of Daphne du Maurier, official or unofficial, has to face: that is that she intensely disliked the idea of anyone writing her biography. When I visited her not long after she had moved to her last home, Kilmarth, and she was showing me some family papers, I said, idly, that they would come in useful when someone came to write her biography. She made it quite clear that she was totally against the idea and the notion that someone would try and seek out what had motivated her, what she had felt at any given time in her life, let alone pick over her personal correspondence, truly appalled her. She was a very private person.

Yet she must have known that her notable success was such that potential biographers would find her intriguing, for she had become, in her own lifetime, a literary phenomenon. Her books sold in their hundreds of thousands, her devoted readership was, and still is, worldwide; and those who brought about her success were bound to want to know more about their author.

In 1988 Roger Redfarn, artistic director of the Theatre Royal in Plymouth, commissioned me to undertake a stage adaptation of Daphne's novel, *The King's General*. This followed a conversation we had had the previous year when I had suggested that it might transfer very well to the stage. It turned out to be a mammoth undertaking, especially in these financially restricting times, as it required a large cast, elaborate direction and epic staging. Rehearsals were long and arduous. On 19 April 1989, in the middle of our final dress-rehearsal, I was dragged out into the foyer to find a BBC Television unit waiting to interview me. For Daphne du Maurier had died in the early hours, news which had not reached us, locked away as we were in the theatre.

On the whole, I think that what I said then about her work is what I believe still, after a great deal more thought: that she was an exceptional story-teller and that we are currently very short of such writers; that she had a sense of place and could describe a landscape in such a way that it remains in the mind, and that she was never a formula novelist. I was not prepared to be prompted into saying that she was one of the greatest writers of the twentieth century, or that I thought every one of her books was exceptional.

Shortly after the play had finished its run, Dr A.L. Rowse, a much esteemed friend who has helped me in the past with my books on Elizabethan and Jacobean drama, suggested I write her biography. He thought I should do it because I had known her a little, because I was a writer myself and, perhaps, most of all, because I have Cornwall in my blood, although my Cornwall, like that of Dr Rowse, was never that of Daphne du Maurier. This, then, is the result.

I first met Daphne du Maurier in the 1960s. I had been working as a freelance researcher for Westward Television, the regional independent television company based in Plymouth. One of the subjects I covered was Civil Defence. At that time her husband, the late Lieutenant-General Sir Frederick Browning, was in charge of the defence arrangements for Cornwall and I was asked to interview him and then arrange for him to appear in a studio discussion. After the programme was over, we argued in a friendly way over the concept of civil defence in a nuclear age (I did not believe it possible) and before he left he said that he would contact me and invite me over to Menabilly for lunch. I thought at the time he was merely being courteous, but a short time later he rang and invited my then husband and myself for lunch, 'to meet Daphne', and continue the discussion.

I had been reading Daphne's books since my schooldays and was delighted to have the opportunity to meet her, although it was with some trepidation, as her reputation for disliking visitors was well known even then. In the event, she was quite charming. They both showed us over Menabilly and Sir Frederick pointed out where they thought a skeleton of an unknown Cavalier had been found, in the early part of the nineteenth century, bricked up in a wall. He also took us up to the ancient Iron Age fortification known as Castle Dor, and explained its strategic importance, both during the Iron Age (the time of the legendary Tristan and Iseult) and later, to Sir Richard Grenville's Royalist forces during the Civil War. In 1989 when I was grappling with the strategy of the Civil War in the West in general, and that very battle at Castle Dor in particular, I wished I had taken more notice of what he had said!

After that first visit, I went to Menabilly several times and, following a gap after Browning's death, I saw Daphne on her own, both there and then at Kilmarth, the house which featured in her final – and in my own estimation, best – historical novel, *The House on the Strand*. Our last two meetings I remember vividly. On the first occasion, I had been asked to interview her about *Rule Britannia*. I was suffering from a marriage on the point of breakdown and was emotionally and physically exhausted, so much so that sitting on her sofa, with the sun pouring in through the long windows, I went to sleep. She woke me later with a tray of tea . . . On the last, I was on holiday in Cornwall from London, where I was working, and I told her how I had just reread *Vanishing Cornwall* and how desperately homesick it had made me. 'You'll be back,' she told me. 'You'll see. It's in the blood.' I never saw her again.

I would have loved to have discussed the adapting of *The King's General* with her but, by that time, I knew she was too frail and confused for there to be any point. At least some of those who knew her, as well as those who had enjoyed her books, found it faithful to the original.

When Gerald du Maurier read a biography of someone he had known in the theatre, he said to Daphne that it was untruthful, and that he hoped that if anyone should write his one day, that they would show him 'warts and all'. Daphne agreed and in her own moving and revealing biography of Gerald, showed him as he really was. This is not the 'official' biography of Daphne du Maurier; it is an honest attempt to tell the story of someone who became a literary phenomenon as a hagiography would do her a disservice. She was a strange, self-contained and introverted woman, a woman who had suffered an emotional onslaught in her early years, the blighting effect of which never left her, ensuring that she was happiest retreating physically behind the walls of the house which obsessed her for most of her life, and mentally into the personae of her heroes and heroines and the fantasy world of fiction.

Two events marred the beginning of what has been a happy and fulfilling project. A few days after Transworld/Bantam Press had commissioned the book, my father, who had always been supportive of my work, died suddenly. Two days later he was followed, equally suddenly, by my dear agent, James Reynolds; negotiating *Daphne* was the last deal he struck and I had driven up to Northamptonshire less than a week before he died, with a bottle of champagne. I hope I have done them both justice.

I would like to thank all the people who have helped me with this book by providing recollections, papers and a variety of information. Of these I must single out Dr A.L. Rowse whose encouragement – indeed, prodding – made me undertake it in the first place. I am more than grateful, too, to Mrs Veronica Rashleigh of Menabilly and other members of her family, not only for letting me have access to information on the role of the family during the Civil War, but for letting me visit Menabilly again, and for explaining its history, ancient and modern. Others who gave specific assistance include Sir Alec Guinness, and Mr Richard Carew-Pole of Antony House. Special thanks, too, to Christine Alexander of 'Bookends' in Fowey, who obtained for me all those du Maurier books which are out of print and was particularly helpful in giving me an insight into Daphne du Maurier's continuing popularity, from the point of view of the bookseller.

I received a great deal of help from the courteous staffs of the British Library, its newspaper section at Colindale, the British Theatre Association – now, tragically, closed down as a result of the Government's policy on the Arts – the Press Association Library and that of the *Western Morning News*.

On a personal level, I enjoyed, throughout, the support and encouragement of my husband, Martin Green. It has also been a particular joy to work with my son, Simon Cook, who has taken most of the photographs; a strange link with Daphne who also collaborated with her photographer son. I also owe a debt to Mark Barty-King of Transworld/Bantam Press who has been kindness itself – something I badly needed following the death of Jim Reynolds.

Judith Cook
Plymouth 1990

CHAPTER I

Family Origins

Daphne du Maurier came from a fascinating back-ground, descending from the mistress of a royal duke and a family of French master craftsmen glass-blowers (with Revolutionary sympathies), through the artist and cartoonist George du Maurier to her father, the actor Gerald. It was a background to which she was to return continuously throughout her life.

It was fortunate that the various families seem to have kept so many records, the diaries, letters, papers that often disappear without trace.

To understand something of the world into which she was born it is necessary to look, however briefly, at some of the people who influenced her and to whom she was to return over the years in her books. The most colourful, without doubt, was Mary Anne Clarke.

Mary Anne was born in the slums of London probably during the mid-1770s – precise times, places and dates are missing. Her mother, widowed early, married a printer and compositor called Bob Farquhar and possibly her daughter, the young Mary Anne did, as is suggested in the book of that name, read radical pamphlets and gossip-ridden scandal sheets brought home to be proof read. At barely sixteen years old, she married an apprentice mason, Joseph Clarke, who had been lodging with her mother (after Farquhar had left her for another woman). Mary Anne had five children by Clarke;

two are known to have died in infancy; one – a namesake Mary Anne – who disappears from the chronicles as a young girl; and the two youngest, Ellen and George. It is through Ellen that the line was to descend to Daphne.

Clarke was a drunkard and a waster and it is hardly surprising that the strong-minded Mary Anne decided relatively quickly that she had had enough. By all accounts she was extremely engaging and very attractive, although not conventionally pretty. There was not a great deal of choice for a woman in her position at the end of the eighteenth century. She seems to have earned small amounts of money writing gossip for the half-penny scandal sheets, but her most marketable asset was her personality and she did not hesitate to use it. While it seems that she had at least one long-term lover for whom she felt a real affection, she indulged in a round of affairs with members of the aristocracy and the military who were to keep her in clothes, jewellery and accommodation, and provide some kind of security for her children.

If this had been all, then no more might have been heard of her than a passing reference in the contemporary gossip. But it was not. In 1806 she was introduced to the Duke of York, who was then Commander-in-Chief of the British army, and she became his mistress. Like his brother the Prince Regent, he ran to fat and existing portraits show him as an unattractive, pot-bellied figure. However, it is unlikely that his physical attraction, or lack of it, meant very much to Mary Anne, but his status and position patently did. Certainly at the beginning of their relationship he seems to have been besotted with her, showering her with luxuries and taking a house for her in Gloucester Place. Later she was to say that he never gave her enough money for the life-style she was supposed to keep up in order to do him credit.

Whether the idea was her own or whether she was used by unscrupulous people is not clear, but within a year of entering into her relationship with the Duke, she was beginning to act as a 'dealer' in army commissions and in arranging for people

2

to become recruiting officers (where they could earn so much a head for every man they persuaded to enlist). Mary Anne had had two stepbrothers, both of whom had been killed at sea when they were very young. Her real brother, Charlie, was desperate for a commission and his was the first she persuaded the Duke to arrange. He was gazetted cornet in the 13th Light Dragoons on 25 February 1804.

With the Napoleonic Wars at fever pitch, the competition for promotion among young army officers was intense. Mary Anne swiftly moved on to obtaining commissions first for friends, then acquaintances and then, simply, for cash. Eventually there was a tariff – a full major cost £900, a company could be purchased for £700 and a lieutenancy for £400. Mary Anne was paid strictly in cash for her efforts. The Duke asked no questions but was delighted not to be continually asked for money. Like all of the royal princes he was heavily in debt and most of his income went to keep up his official royal residence at Oatlands where his wife lived.

Mary Anne's activities became increasingly overt and she was warned by friends on a number of occasions to stop while the going was good, to use her influence with the Duke if she must but not to take money for doing so. It looked far too much like bribes. She did not take the advice, however, and continued fixing, dealing and writing indiscreet letters headed 'burn this'. Not surprisingly, after a time things began to go badly wrong. She had told the Duke she was a widow and, indeed, had claimed to have been one for years before she met him. In 1805 the long-lost Joseph Clarke surfaced and decided he, too, would have a share in his wife's good fortune, so he began writing a series of blackmailing letters. Finding Mary Anne insufficiently generous, he wrote an 'anonymous' letter to the Duke of York explaining that far from being a widow, Mary Anne had a husband who was alive and prepared to make trouble unless he was sufficiently well paid off.

It came at a bad time. The Duke was becoming rapidly disenchanted with Mary Anne and had acquired a second mistress, an opera dancer called Mrs Cary. When Joseph

Clarke decided to take matters a stage further and attempted to bring a suit in court naming the Duke of York as an adulterer, the Duke sent one of his equerries round to Mary Anne to tell her their liaison was over and that the Duke never wanted to see her again. She would be allowed £400, payable quarterly, in return for her good conduct, although the Duke did not consider he had any obligation to honour this agreement. Mary Anne had debts running into thousands of pounds, she was to say later, which she had accumulated by keeping his household going and providing him with the entertainment he demanded. She left Gloucester Place taking with her, as insurance, some sixty indiscreet letters that the Duke had written to her over the years.

She might still have remained anonymous had there not been an unforeseen series of events over the next eighteen months. In 1807 her brother Charlie, the first person for whom she had used her influence with the Duke, was court-martialled on two serious charges, the first of going absent without leave, and the second, fraud. In spite of her making every effort to help him with his defence, he was found guilty on the first charge but acquitted on the second. He was sentenced to be cashiered from the Army, a sentence confirmed by the Duke of York himself on 24 May 1808 in a letter to Lieutenant-General Lord Chatham, his commanding officer. Mary Anne determined upon taking her revenge.

Her first move was a heavy threat to the Duke's household that she held the indiscreet letters. This was countered by the appearance of a sheriff's officer arresting her for debt. The case came to court and was successfully fought by Mary Anne, after which it was made plain to her that if she ever threatened the Duke again with the publication of the letters she would certainly go to prison. It is unlikely ever to be known for certain who contacted whom, but one way or another she became involved with a radical MP called Colonel Wardle, the member for Okehampton. The British government had, so far, successfully held off the threat of any real revolutionary tendencies spreading to Britain, but it

4

remained a real fear. The Royal Family was far from popular in many circles and after discussions with Mary Anne, Wardle saw his chance to strike at them in the House of Commons. On 27 January 1809 Wardle raised the matter of the conduct of the Duke of York in the House with regard to the sale of promotions, the disposal of commissions and the raising of new levies for the Army.

He said: 'To stand forth the public accuser of a man of such high rank as the Commander-in-Chief may be deemed an arduous and presumptuous undertaking. However arduous and presumptuous it may be, nothing shall divert me from the performance of my duty; and I trust he will feel that, however high he may stand in point of rank and influence, the voice of the people, stated through their representatives, will prevail over corruption, and that justice will be done to a suffering nation. Unless corruption be attacked, and attacked strongly too, this country will fall an easy prey to an inveterate enemy.'

A special House of Commons Committee was set up to look into the matter and Mary Anne was brought before it as a witness, 'dressed as if she was going out to an evening party in a light blue silk gown edged with white fur, a white muff, white cap and veil, her dazzling smile, slightly *retroussé* nose and lively blue eyes entirely captivated the House', according to the *Morning Post*.

Although the Peninsula War was by this time at its height, the Clarke case stayed on the front pages of the newspapers for weeks, and provided a field day for cartoonists, lampooners and pamphleteers. 'It was', as Daphne du Maurier was to tell me herself, 'the Profumo scandal of its day, but even more so because of the involvement of the Royal Family. You couldn't possibly imagine anyone nowadays daring to publish the kind of cartoons Rowlandson produced about Mary Anne and the Duke.' She had a number of them in her house at Kilmarth.

It soon became apparent that Mary Anne had indeed taken bribes but the big question was, did the Duke know? The

Conservative government of the day did everything possible to play down the issue as they were frightened of anything which might smack of radicalism and revolution. Mary Anne proved to be the star of the show, answering any question put to her with wit. More of the Duke's letters turned up, this time left carelessly in a lodging house. A host of distinguished witnesses were called on both sides, but not the Duke himself. He wrote to the House expressing his deep concern that his name had been, 'coupled with transactions of the most criminal and disgraceful, and I must ever regret and lament that a connection should ever have existed which has thus exposed my character and honour to public animadversion.

'With respect to my alleged offence, connected with the discharge of my official duties, I do, in the most solemn manner, upon my honour as a Prince, distinctly assert my innocence, not only by denying all corrupt participation in any of the infamous transactions which have appeared in evidence at the bar of the House of Commons or any connivance at their existence, but also the slightest knowledge or suspicion that they existed at all.'

Mary Anne's answer to that was to threaten to write her memoirs. The other side tried to prove her letters had been forged but to no avail. The Enquiry itself ran until 22 February 1809 and was followed by a debate which ran for three solid weeks, ending late on 16 March with a division which the Government won by eighty-two votes. But it was a pyrrhic victory. Although, ostensibly, the vote acquitted the Duke both of personal corruption or connivance at what went on, in the public eye and in that of the Opposition, the Duke was guilty. Mary Anne became a national heroine and Colonel Wardle a public hero. When she took her seat at the Haymarket Theatre that night the audience rose to its feet and applauded her. By the end of the week the Duke of York had resigned as Commander-in-Chief of the British army and Colonel Wardle was voted a Freeman of the City of London.

Unfortunately, after that matters progressed badly. Mary

Anne was persuaded not to publish her memoirs. The publisher would receive £150 for every copy destroyed and, in exchange for handing over *all* her letters from the Duke, Mary Anne would receive a payment of £10,000 plus an annuity of £400 for life and £200 for each daughter, her annuity passing to them on her death. Wardle and the other Radicals involved could not understand why she did not refuse the offer and publish, but she told them she would not do so for the sake of her children's security. She then apparently turned right against Colonel Wardle and decided to put pressure on him to provide her with money in exchange for the help she had given him in bringing down the Duke. When he did not pay up she took him to court for debt and won that case too.

Although she did not publish the original memoirs, she wrote a pamphlet called *The Rival Princes* which she published in January 1810 which consisted of scandalous stories about all the Radicals who had taken part in the campaign against the Duke. To begin with, she appeared to do exactly as she had promised with regard to the Duke, but later it transpired that she had kept some letters back, but when her son George failed to get the commission in the Army she had expected him to get, she brought out a second edition of her pamphlet containing copies of letters from all and sundry and full of scurrilous material. This she followed up with a second pamphlet, addressed to the Right Honourable William Fitzgerald, Chancellor of the Irish Exchequer whom she had earlier approached unsuccessfully for help. It was libellous in the extreme about him, his family, his wife and his conduct, but this time she did not get away with it. He issued a writ for libel and when she came to trial on 7 February 1814, nothing could save her. She was sent to prison for nine months and bound over to keep the peace thereafter. She was just thirty-eight years old.

She was no longer a popular figure. 'Mary Anne, Mary Anne, Cook the slut in a frying pan,' shouted the street boys who burned her effigy instead of that of Guy Fawkes on 5 November. A lampoon of the time was even nastier:

7

And when I strove to chaunt my Mrs Clarke
With rhyme, confused. I knew not which
  was which,
But, as I went on fumbling in the dark,
I set down bitch for Clarke and Clarke
  for bitch.

Ironically, a few weeks later the Duke of York kept his word
and the young George Clarke was given his commission in
the British army.

When she came out of prison, Mary Anne left the country
with her two daughters and, after a while, settled in Paris. It
was here that her daughter Ellen was to meet Louis-Mathurin
Busson, a member of a family which had started to call itself
du Maurier.

Dr A.L. Rowse, the Cornish historian and writer who knew
Daphne longer and, to some extent better, than anyone else,
said of her that there was a great deal of Mary Anne in her,
coupled with 'the French peasant's instinct to be careful'.
He did not mean by this that she took after her notorious
ancestress in her life-style or flamboyance – rather the reverse
– but rather that she shared with Mary Anne 'the courage
and spirit of a basically lonely woman battling away on
her own'. Whatever she might have thought of that, she
is unlikely to have seen in herself any trace of French
peasantry, for the Bussons were not peasants but master
craftsmen glass-blowers.

Mary Anne seems to have shared something in common
with the women of the Busson family. She was wilfully independent, and fundamentally very strong. She was a survivor.
The women of the Busson family also seem to have been the
strong ones of the family. Just as Mary Anne was dogged by
weak men, her husband Joseph and her much-loved brother
Charlie (who, depressed and destitute finally drowned himself in the Pool of London), the Busson women seem to have
been the mainstays of the families into which they married.

8

Daphne traced the Bussons back to 1747 and then followed their fortunes in her book, *The Glass-blowers*, to the period immediately after the French Revolution. The family appears to have originated in Brittany, but she took up their story when they were living in north-west France in the area called la Sarthe, which had been part of the old provinces of Anjou and Maine before the Revolution. The master craftsmen in glass had a very real status. Skilled glass-blowers had remained as something akin to a medieval guild, the families keeping themselves apart with their own rules, customs and ways of life, marrying into the family whenever possible. Sometimes they operated on their own with their own independent foundries but, very often, they would be employed by one of the major landowners to live and work on his estate and provide glass for his needs, both in the country and in Paris.

Mathurin Busson was one such master craftsman. He had invented, among other things, a series of scientific instruments and his *instruments de chimie* were in great demand by all the main apothecaries of Paris. His brother, Michel, designed glass tableware. In 1749 the Marquis de Cherbon invited Mathurin Busson to leave his home in Plessis Dorin to work and live on his estate. Busson moved there with his pregnant wife, Magdaleine, and lived for a while in an estate farmhouse called le Maurier. It was here his eldest son Robert was born.

The family flourished and Mathurin and Magdaleine had a number of children. They did not stay long at le Maurier, but the fact that they lived there at all has an obvious significance. As the sons grew up, they moved away and worked as master craftsmen on their own account, and Magdaleine continued to run her husband's business after his relatively early death.

From the outset it seems as if Robert, the oldest son, was a problem. He was full of enthusiasm and ideas, but without either the talent or steadiness to follow them up. On numerous occasions he overreached himself and was continually having to be baled out of debt by his mother.

He had married against the wishes of his family and he soon tired of his wife who bore him one son. She died young, but the child survived and eventually became a soldier. The approach of the Revolution was greeted with a fair degree of enthusiasm by the Bussons, some of whom retained their belief in it until the end of their lives in spite of suffering great hardship during the period now known as The Terror. Robert, though, would have none of it. In 1789 he had remarried, a young girl straight out of a convent, and shortly afterwards he disappeared abroad. The family assumed he might well be dead until, true to type, the bad penny turned up again years later in 1802.

He had grown tired of his wife and family of six children and had decided to come back to France alone. Luck had played into his hands for, on the way over in the boat, a passenger had died and Robert had switched clothes and papers with him. His 'death' had been duly reported to his wife, Marie, and his children grew up assuming this to have been the case.

In the 1820s a female member of the Busson family was introduced to a young man who called himself Robert Mathurin-Busson du Maurier and she soon told the remaining members of the Busson family. Robert was truly dead by this time, but the younger Robert was amazed when he was told that his father had lived for years after his supposed death. That was not all. Robert senior, always something of a fantasist, had passed himself off in England as a minor member of the aristocracy fleeing the Revolution and had called himself du Maurier after the farmhouse in which he had been born. His children had grown up believing that the Bussons were descended from an aristocratic Breton family which dated back to the fourteenth century, from knights of Brittany with their own motto, *Abret ag Aroat*, First and Foremost. They also understood that their family had owned a Château Maurier which was burned down by peasants during the Revolution.

They were, finally, disabused of these ideas, but the name

had a good ring to it and so they adopted it. Robert senior's fourth son was called Louis-Mathurin and he seems, to some extent, to have taken after his father. He was an idealist, a dreamer, a man who was always on the brink of perfecting some remarkable invention, inventions which rarely came to anything. His sister, Louise, had become a teacher at an academy for young ladies in Paris, La Maison d'Education in the rue Neuve St Etiénne. Among the pupils she taught was an English girl called Ellen Clarke. Ellen and Louise became close friends, a friendship marred only slightly when poor Louise made a brief and disastrous marriage to a fortune hunter, Godfrey Wallace. Her brother, Louis-Mathurin, had been partly to blame for this as he had told the would-be husband the story of the Château Maurier, the exile of the 'du Mauriers' in England and their return to a grateful King and country and how Louis XVIII had granted the family a pension out of gratitude for their loyalty. Godfrey Wallace abandoned Louise within days once he discovered that it was all untrue.

The seeds of a friendship between Ellen and Louis-Mathurin were sown at Louise's wedding. Ellen had inherited from Mary Anne (who was still very much on the scene), independence and a strong character but she did not inherit her looks. She is described as having been very plain and of a sallow complexion. The courtship was a fairly leisurely one and the couple did not marry until 1831. They were married at the British Embassy and spent their honeymoon in Brittany. They were neither of them in the first flush of youth, both being thirty-four years old.

Ellen's life with Louis-Mathurin was never to be easy. They moved endlessly from place to place, as Louis-Mathurin was convinced that eventually one of his inventions would pay off. Another of Louise's pupils had married the Duke de Palmella and, for a while, the Busson du Mauriers lived in Portugal where the Duke had agreed to become Louis-Mathurin's patron, but he eventually tired of supporting an inventor who never actually came up with a practical invention. They lived

off the £200 annuity that Ellen had had from the settlement
reached with the Duke of York all those years previously and,
to some extent, on what Louis-Mathurin could borrow from
his older brother Robert. They had three children, George,
born in 1834, Eugene, born in 1836 and Isabella, born when
Ellen was forty-two years old in 1839.

Eugene, in personality, took after his father and grandfather and, indeed, his great-uncle Charlie, Mary Anne's
brother. He was charming and feckless like Robert senior and
Louis-Mathurin and, like Charlie, failed to make a successful
career for himself in the Army. Isabella was to marry the
drama critic, Clement Scott, a marriage which turned out
unhappily and they separated.

Eugene and Isabella (known by the family as Isobel) lie
in the same grave in the churchyard of St Stephen's Church,
Saltash, just over the Tamar on the Cornish side of the river.
The inscription reads:

'In Memoriam Isobel Scott, née Busson du Maurier, wife of
Clement Scott who died at Saltash, 26 November 1890,
aged 52.
'Awed by its lovely majesty I've seen,
God's star of purity above your eyes,
What sweeter faith than yours has ever been,
What greater gift, a love that never dies.'

CS

Presumably the verse was written by the estranged husband.
The inscription continues:

'Here rests also Eugene Alexandre Busson du Maurier,
brother of Isobel who died at Torquay, 25 December
1890, aged 54.'

Brother and sister had died within a month of each other.
Also buried in the grave are Eugene's wife, Marie Rosalie
who died on 21 November 1915, aged sixty-seven and the

daughter of Isabella (Isobel), Dora Footman who died in 1974 aged ninety-four.

I have mentioned this at some length because, fortuitously, these members of the du Maurier family went to their last rest in the churchyard of St Stephen's. Inside the church are plaques to the Rashleigh family who were then living at nearby Stoketon House. It was a strange quirk of fate which brought both families together in the same place, unknown to each other, for the Rashleigh family and Daphne du Maurier were to become inextricably bound together for most of her life.

The du Mauriers, Daphne was to write later, have traits in common. They are emotional, laugh and cry easily. 'The saving of money is not their strongest quality . . . they squander when and what they can . . . They are, generally speaking, easy to look at and easy to like. Their hearts are large, like their purses which contain so little and their sense of humour is apt to be warped and tinged with satire. They lie with grace and confidence as Gyggy (Eugenie) did before them and are forgiven just as easily. They die before middle age, often rather painfully.' And, she continues, they are soon forgotten. But this is, manifestly, not so. Kicky, she continues, was the wisest of them, the kindest and best. And who was Kicky?

The other child of Ellen and Louis-Mathurin Busson du Maurier is not buried with his brother and sister in Saltash churchyard, for his life took a very different course. This was George, the eldest son, known to his family as 'Kicky'. He became famous first as a brilliant *Punch* cartoonist and then as the author of a worldwide bestseller, *Trilby*. He was also Daphne's grandfather.

CHAPTER 2

George and Gerald

Again and again Daphne was to turn to her grandfather, George, and her father, Gerald, both of whom were to have far-reaching influences on her life. George was born in Paris and seems to have had a happy childhood but, by the time he reached adolescence, the family were endlessly on the move as Louis-Mathurin dreamed up more ways of making the family fortune. The nickname 'Kicky' was given to him as a small child by a Flemish nurse and was a corruption of 'mannikin'. He was called this for the rest of his life.

He had shown an early aptitude for drawing, but Louis-Mathurin had no wish for his son to study art. He wanted him to be a scientist and so the family moved to England and George studied, unwillingly, at University College, London. In 1852 Mary Anne Clarke died (at the age of seventy-six) and the annuity she had wrung out of the Duke of York passed to Ellen. On the strength of this (and some speculation on the side), Louis-Mathurin set up his own laboratory and George was duly expected to work in it helping his father with his 'inventions' but, hardly surprisingly, it was not successful and George's next job was as a superintendent of mines to the Victoria Gold and Copper Mine at Molton in South Devon, a post he had obtained because it was felt his scientific training would be useful.

This did not last either. In 1855 Louis-Mathurin returned

on his own to France to try and persuade either his brother, Robert, or his sister, Louise, to lend him money, but he was unsuccessful. Robert, already estranged from him, had sunk into what was then described as melancholia and now as clinical depression and eventually died in an asylum. Louis-Mathurin returned to the dreary lodgings in Pentonville where the family now lived and by the spring of 1856 he, too, was showing similar symptoms to those of his brother, eventually taking to his bed in a state of total misery. It was very hard on the family. The laboratory and its equipment had to be sold, Ellen took in lodgers. Money had to be sent to France to 'Gyggy' who was an officer cadet and the annuity just did not stretch that far. George was unable to get any kind of job, but there was no question of Louis-Mathurin being put into an asylum (which was suggested by a doctor). He was nursed at home and died in his own bed in June at the age of fifty-nine.

His death proved a release for George. He persuaded his mother to let him study art in Paris where he shared a studio with three friends who called themselves 'Ye Societie of Our Ladye in the Fields' as it was situated in the rue de Notre-Dame des Champs. One of his friends, Felix Moscheles, practised mesmerism and his experience in Paris was to form the basis of his novel, *Trilby*. All seemed to be going well until one day, while drawing a model, he found that he could not focus properly and then that he could not see at all. Specialists diagnosed a variety of things and he underwent much useless treatment, but it would seem to have been the result of a detached retina and a subsequent haemorrhage in his left eye.

Ellen came over from England to look after him and he convalesced at Malines. He was terrified that he would also lose the sight of his right eye. While at Malines he and Felix, who visited him there, both fell for a tobacconist's pretty daughter called Carrie and she appears to have been his model for the fascinating Trilby; Felix attempted to mesmerize her, but he was totally unsuccessful. He was no Svengali. Finally

Ellen and George were persuaded to visit an eye specialist in the village of Grafath, near Dusseldorf. There he was told that although the sight of his left eye was irrecoverable, his right eye was perfectly all right and, as long as he did not overstrain it, there was no reason why it should ever let him down. He could start painting again.

When he returned to London George was determined that he was not going to endure the poverty which had dogged his family or live on hope like Louis-Mathurin. He met a young woman, Emma Wightwick, with whom he fell in love but whom he would not marry until he established himself. Gradually he became known, not as an artist as he had hoped, but as an elegant and amusing cartoonist and finally, at the age of thirty-one, he was offered a full-time post on *Punch* magazine. It enabled him to marry Emma (he finally proposed to her outside the Oxford Street store, Peter Robinson) and they lived happily ever after, never spending even one night apart until his death.

He had established himself in London, ironically, on ten pounds borrowed from his mother from the money that she had inherited from Mary Anne Clarke. He mixed with the pre-Raphaelites and parodied the ballads of Swinburne and Rossetti. He envied the youthful Millais whom he described as 'beautiful as a young god', and he described the artist Watts sprawling on a sofa at his home in a velvet smoking jacket, surrounded and waited on by a bevy of beautiful, adoring ladies. He had a large circle of acquaintances, a busy social life and his weekly *Punch* cartoon was eagerly awaited.

A memoir of him, which appeared in *The Sunday Times* in 1937, written by J.M. Bulloch to mark the publication of a book of his writings and letters edited by his son-in-law, C. Hoyar Millar, gives a pen portrait of George. 'There was a contrast between George and the exquisites he drew, for his world was very simply pivoted, personally, on the thrifty ways of his French ancestors. There were few or no books in his house: politics had no interest for him. His philosophy of life was very simple: thus he saw only one sin in the world –

cruelty – and, though his *bête noire* was the average person, of whom he could say no good word, he was 'always careful to avoid anything unconventional'. The family in general had a rooted dislike of serious topics of any kind, taking their cue from du Maurier himself who was, essentially, of a humorous turn of mind from his earliest days in Paris, and never wished to be otherwise.

George and Emma had five children: Trixie, Guy, Sylvia, May and Gerald, not one of whom, like George himself, was to live to see old age. They moved from their first home in Great Russell Street to a large house in Hampstead, a place George loved as he could walk across the Heath whenever he felt like it. He became a wealthy man, but he was never robust and his sight did eventually deteriorate. Towards the end of his life he fulfilled a lifelong ambition and published his fist novel, *Peter Ibbetson*. It is a strange book which had a limited success. It is written in the first person by a convicted murderer who has gone insane and has been confined to an asylum. In his memoir the murderer details a love affair he had with a Duchess of Towers whom he meets only in dreams. He has murdered his rapacious uncle but even in the asylum he still 'meets' his Duchess who, like him, in the dream world never ages.

His second novel, however, written when he was nearly sixty was, as has already been noted, *Trilby*. It was the most enormous hit and Svengali, the evil genius who turned the artist's model, Trilby, into an opera star by the power of mesmerism, or hypnosis, has passed into that pantheon of villains which includes such luminaries as Professor Moriarty and Fagin. George sold the dramatic rights of the book to the actor William Terriss for seventy-five pounds, but then a dramatisation of it by Paul Potter was staged in New York so George brought the rights back again for £100 and agreed that it should be presented in London by Beerbohm Tree. *Trilby* brought in £52,000 at the box office of the Haymarket Theatre; George received only £1,694, while Tree built Her Majesty's Theatre out of his share of the profits.

However, the royalties from the play in the States amounted to £4,523, and George also received £4,741 from the US book rights in the first year. He had proved that he, a du Maurier, could become sensationally successful as a popular novelist although his last book, *The Martian*, never achieved the success of *Trilby*.

Emma proved a totally devoted wife and mother and her own children grew up unscathed by the early struggles of their father. Born on 26 March 1873, while the family were living in Church Row, Hampstead, Gerald was the last child. By the time he was one they had moved to New Grove House where they were to stay for twenty years. He was a spoilt child, particularly by his mother, leading his oldest sister, Trixie, to describe him as mother's 'ewe lamb', which she pronounced 'ewee'. He was considered delicate and he played on it and he also showed, from his earliest years, a gift for mimicry. The family lived comfortably and there were plenty of family holidays, mostly to English seaside resorts, more occasionally to France but, oddly, George did not seem to have had any real desire to introduce his children to the country of his birth. Both boys were sent to public school, the eldest, Guy, to Marlborough from where he went into the Army, and Gerald to Harrow.

George wanted Gerald to go into a solid profession, preferably the law, and embarked on a lecture tour to raise the large sum needed to set him up to train as a solicitor, but Gerald showed no interest in it. For a little while he worked as a clerk in a shipping office but eventually persuaded his father, not long after the publication of *Trilby*, to let him go into the theatre. George knew John Hare, the actor-manager who ran the Garrick Theatre which offered a programme of undemanding drama and comedy in which there was no hint of controversy. John Hare took Gerald on in a small part in a play called *The Old Jew* where he played Fritz, the waiter, making his début on 6 January 1894. The famous family name attracted the favourable attention of the critics and he never looked back.

George lived to see his *Trilby* performed on the London stage and his own son, Gerald, playing the part of the French dragoon Dodor, a character based on his now-dead brother Eugene, Gerald's Uncle Gyggy. But George's health was rapidly failing and by the autumn of 1896 he was a dying man. 'Si *c'est la mort, ce n'est pas gai*,' he said to Gerald the last time he saw him. He was sixty-two when he died on 8 October 1896. A daughter of William Powell Frith, the artist, writing her memoirs in 1908 described George as having had immense vitality and having been blessed with the most sunny and charming of natures. She also noted how fortunate he had been to have had such a devoted wife. 'There was not a load that Mrs du Maurier did not take from his shoulders when she could, not a thing she would not do to help him and see that no small worries stood between him and his work.' Emma, she said, was one of the loveliest creatures of her time with quantities of dark curly hair. She remembered George not only as an artist, but as a most moving singer, with a beautiful voice inherited from Louis-Mathurin, and she noted how he would sit down and accompany himself at the piano.

'I always think that those who knew and loved such a genius can never lose him, he may die, he himself may pass into the shadows, but how much he leaves behind.'

George would have appreciated that. He had his ashes buried in Hampstead Churchyard and on his gravestone are the last lines of *Trilby*:

> 'A little trust that when we die
> We reap the sowing! And so – goodbye'

By the time George died, Gerald's sisters had already married, and Trixie and Sylvia both had families of their own. Sylvia had married a rising young lawyer called Arthur Llewelyn-Davies by whom she had five sons. It was the two oldest Davies children who caught the eye of the playwright J.M. Barrie as they played in Kensington Gardens under the watchful eye of their nanny. Some time later Barrie found himself sitting next to Sylvia Davies at a dinner party and she told him she was George du Maurier's daughter and that she had called her youngest son, Peter, after her father's character, Peter Ibbetson.

The story of Barrie's involvement with the Davies boys has been told more than adequately elsewhere. How, when first their father died young of cancer of the jaw, he stepped in with financial help, and then when their mother tragically followed him within a short time, dying of cancer at the early age of forty-four, he undertook the responsibility of providing for the boys. The young Peter Davies became the character around which he built his classic play for children, *Peter Pan*. The role of the villain was created for the children's uncle, Gerald.

But that was in the future. Shortly after George's death, Gerald went off on a tour of America with Beerbohm Tree's company. In one of his first letters home he mentioned that a pretty French girl, Miss Sylvia, was a member of the company. Gerald could never have been considered handsome, his features were unremarkable except for his nose which was long and prominent, but he had the most enormous attraction for women, an attraction which was to last almost to the end of his life. Possibly because he felt somewhat isolated and homesick in the States, he became very friendly with Marguerite Sylvia and soon convinced himself he was in love with her. The first the family heard about it was in a newspaper report which described how the young Gerald du Maurier – the press had already picked him out as his father's son – had been invited to a reception at the White House along with his 'fiancée'. His brother Guy immediately despatched a cable asking if he could 'contradict the report', which produced the response from Gerald to his mother that he still put her before anyone but that if she could only speak to his beloved for five minutes her unhappiness would vanish. 'I love her and you must too.'

The engagement was broken off within a matter of weeks but in no time at all Gerald was in love again, this time with the sister of the famous Barrymore brothers John and Lionel. Ethel Daphne Barrymore was only nineteen at the time and she was to go on to be as famous as her brothers. It seems that this time Mrs du Maurier had finally nerved herself to accept that her ewe lamb would marry and began putting heavy pressure on the young actress to look after Gerald properly. Whether it was as a result of this or whether Ethel just fell out of love with Gerald is not clear, but whatever the reason might have been, she broke off the relationship and returned to the States. Her friends called Ethel 'Daphne' in private, and something of his feelings towards her must have remained as he eventually called his second child by that name.

It was becoming apparent that Gerald did not have to trade on the family name, he was developing into an extremely accomplished actor. It tends to be forgotten, as he became such a matinée idol, that he was inherently talented. He was innately gifted and brought to the English stage a style which was apparently natural and deceptively effortless but which was, in fact, based on endless rehearsals and an enormous amount of preparation; he often spent hours practising in front of a mirror. Sir Laurence Olivier was to say of him that he was the 'most disastrous influence on my generation because we really thought, looking at him, that it was easy; and for the first ten years of our lives in the theatre, nobody could hear a word we said. We thought he was being natural; of course, he was a genius of technicians giving that appearance, that's all'.

The final gloss was put on what might be termed his apprenticeship in 1900, when he left Tree and joined Mrs Patrick Campbell's company at the Royalty Theatre. According to James Harding in a recent biography of Gerald, the first time the lady clapped eyes on Gerald she said, 'How can I act with a dreadful, ugly face like that?' But she soon changed her mind, not only encouraging him as an actor but, as his daughter notes euphemistically, teaching him 'the facts of life. She was a mistress of stagecraft. She knew every trick of her trade, and her lessons were invaluable. She taught Gerald how to act and how to live, and he was eternally grateful. Under her tuition he became a man of certain depth, understanding and subtlety, instead of a spoilt, irresponsible boy.' The *affaire* lasted for about two years before it finally tailed off by which time Gerald was twenty-nine. He left her company but had no problem whatsoever in being offered other roles and soon he was at the Duke of York's Theatre rehearsing for the role of the Honourable Ernest Woolley in J.M. Barrie's new play, *The Admirable Crichton*. It was the beginning of his long association with Barrie who was later to give him what was probably his finest role as the father in *Dear Brutus*.

Playing opposite Gerald in *The Admirable Crichton* was a young actress by the name of Muriel Beaumont, one of the five children of a solicitor who had fallen on hard times. Like Gerald, she had had no formal theatrical training and had first appeared on stage in another Barrie play, *The Little Minister*. The attraction was mutual and immediate and on 11 April 1903, just six weeks after announcing their engagement, they were married.

Gerald was to remain true to Muriel, as the song from *Kiss Me Kate* says, in his fashion. There is no doubt that he was devoted to his wife, home and family, but he was continually attracted to women as they were to him, and he seems to have drifted in and out of a number of affairs. Daphne writes of her mother finding an item bought for a lady appearing on her own charge account at Fortnum & Mason and, on another occasion, of Gerald's car being seen in St John's Wood at different times parked outside the house of a young actress. James Harding speaks of a passionate affair with an actress called Audrey Carten whose talent Gerald admired as well as her physical charms. He spent hours tutoring her on the art of stagecraft as well as writing her long letters on the same subject. These letters were later destroyed which, as Harding says, 'is a pity for they would have given us the only permanent record ever compiled of his methods and techniques.' Women were to come and go in his life almost until the end; the last, apparently, was Gracie Fields to whom he was attracted, though the lady brushed him off.

Be that as it may, in the early days he certainly found all the excitement he needed in setting up home with Muriel. They had three daughters, Angela, born in 1904, Daphne, born in 1907 and Jeanne, born in 1910.

CHAPTER 3

The Silver Spoon

The Silver Spoon is the title of one of the books in John Galsworthy's *The Forsyte Saga*. It refers in part to Fleur Forsyte, born into the wealth of that 'man of property', Soames. It could as well be applied to the du Maurier girls and one is constantly reminded of Galsworthy's fictional family when looking at how the du Mauriers lived in the world of Edwardian England.

By the time his daughters were born, Gerald had become one of the most successful actors of his day. Almost all of the plays in which he appeared – apart from those of Barrie – have sunk without trace, but he was one of those actors who could persuade an audience, while he was on stage, that the piece was considerably better than it actually was. His apparently offhand and naturalistic manner was refreshing in an age of actor-manager declamatory acting. Nothing was pushed to extremes. According to Daphne if an actor approached a love scene with too much enthusiasm he would ask: 'Must you kiss her as though you were having steak and onions for lunch? It may be what you feel but it's damned unattractive from the front row of the stalls. Can't you just say "I love you", and yawn, and light a cigarette and walk away?' This is how he played it and gradually the casual but ubiquitous du Maurier cigarette became one of his trade marks and a brand was named after him.

Peter Pan was first performed in 1904, in which he was

a triumphant success in the dual roles of Mr Darling and Captain Hook – the play was revived every Christmas for years, with Gerald very often opting out of whatever else he was doing to play Hook – he later dropped Mr Darling.

For a little while following the birth of her first two children, Muriel continued her career as an actress, but after Jeanne arrived she gave up the stage and devoted herself to her family and to providing Gerald with the home and social background he demanded. In 1906, the year before Daphne's birth, he played one of his most famous roles, that of the gentleman cracksman, Raffles, in the play of that name. It is hard to imagine what a *frisson* it gave Edwardian audiences when they saw the portrayal of an ex-public-school gentleman who had become a successful jewel thief. The play made Gerald a substantial sum of money and so he moved his family out of their home in Chester Place to a very grand house, 24 Cumberland Terrace, near Regent's Park. It was an expensive household to maintain, but certainly not beyond his means; for the wealthy in that golden age before the First World War taxes were small, the cost of living low and servants cheap. The house was tall, with a basement, and stood in a courtyard behind an archway. The rent, for that period, was expensive – £150 a year – but Gerald was in a position to be able to afford it.

Angela du Maurier, remembering the move to Cumberland Terrace, notes that 'Mummie was still acting in those days and our lives were very much Nanny's. She never had a day off in all her eight years and I can only remember her taking two holidays, but I suppose I must be wrong.' She speaks of her own birth on 1 March 1904 which took place in an atmosphere of high drama, with Gerald upstairs in bed, suffering from diphtheria, 'for which a cat was blamed.' Angela remembers little of Daphne's birth except that her mother said she was a particularly beautiful baby. Daphne was born on 13 May 1907 and was christened at Christ Church, Albany Street by the Reverend Bernard Shaw, theatrically apposite but no relation. A large white pram was purchased for Daphne which 'matched the front door'.

1907 had proved a mixed year emotionally for Gerald. He had had a great success in his latest play, *Brewster's Millions*, but the birth of his daughter was marred by the death of his brother-in-law, Arthur Llewelyn-Davies shortly before. The early death of those close to him was to haunt him throughout his life.

Daphne started her life in luxury. A large nursery was specially prepared and as the children grew up they had what virtually amounted to their own suite of night and day nurseries. The household was also very well staffed. A nurse was hired for the birth of each child and the weeks afterwards. There was also Nanny, an under-nurse, parlourmaids, a cook and, presumably, a host of more lowly beings who cleaned and swept and carried the coal and hot water. Nanny, as Angela was to write later, played an enormously important part in the lives of the children, for the household had to revolve around Gerald and their mother, who led a busy social life. How many people owe the happiness of their childhood to the nurse who brought them up? asks Angela, writing about her childhood. 'I will only go as far as saying that *all* my happy early childhood can be laid at the door of my very dear Nanny.' Nanny stayed with the du Mauriers for eight years and Angela describes the sense of desolation when she left: 'It was like a child's first meeting with Death . . . I can see Nanny now, going down the top flight of stairs and carefully shutting the gate behind her, tears pouring down her face, and only then myself being told that she was gone forever. It was life's first misery for me. And all because with three children my parents had thought an under-nurse unnecessary! In those days under-nurses were symbols of *very* well-to-do people . . .'

1908 saw Gerald in an extremely successful Barrie play, *What Every Woman Knows*, although he did not find his role in it particularly sympathetic. After the first night he wrote to his mother: 'It's over and we're none of us sorry.

26

It was a highly strung, nervous business, and no good to one's internal arrangements. If Angela and Daphne look like following in their parents' footsteps, I shall put them in a convent. It was the biggest success Barrie has had, and you should have heard the applause. I'm told I played my bit well, and everyone was pleased all round, but what an effort it has been. There must be some happy medium in life between a rainy day in the country, with no immediate occupation, and the first night of a long and difficult part.'

Daphne's own first memories, as recalled in her autobiography of her formative years, *Growing Pains*, focus on the time shortly after the arrival of Jeanne, who was born in 1911. The years between Daphne's birth and these early memories had been full ones for the family. Guy du Maurier, the older brother and professional soldier, had tried his hand at play writing with a play called *An Englishman's Home* in 1909 and, after much work on the script by Gerald and J.M. Barrie, it was presented at the Wyndham's Theatre with the author's name given simply as 'A Patriot'. It dealt with a fictional invasion of Britain by a foreign power and, as originally written, had an unhappy ending with Britain falling to the conquering army; but for box office reasons Gerald changed this so that Britain won. The play was a success, the Secretary of State for War described it as splendid propaganda as it caught the mood of the country in the years immediately before the 1914–18 War.

Gerald had had another major personal success at about this time, as the French detective Arsene Lupin, in a play of that name and then, in 1910 he decided to set up his own company and become an actor-manager. He earned enough from his productions to hire Wyndham's Theatre, pay a company and still leave himself well off – although his attitude towards money was totally different to that of George; Gerald always lived well up to his income, if not beyond, but yet again, as increasingly was to be the case, professional success was marred by a family death, this time that of his sister, Sylvia.

But Cumberland Terrace was a serene and happy place and it was the only world the young Daphne had known. She recollects at the age of three returning from a walk in the park with Nurse who was pushing Jeanne in the pram. She came into the courtyard through the little archway and the parlourmaid was summoned to help Nurse up the steps with pram and baby. Once inside she climbed the stairs to the day nursery, where a fire burned brightly in the grate and the table was set for lunch. From the windows she could look down on the Royal Horse Artillery on their way down Albany Street and it was their bugle calls for reveille which would wake her from sleep in the morning now that she had moved out of the night nursery which had been given over to the new baby, Jeanne. After lunch the two elder children would be told to make themselves ready to go downstairs and, shepherded by Nurse carrying the baby, they would be introduced to the ladies being entertained by Muriel for lunch. In those days they all wore hats indoors, she writes, even 'M' (Mother).

According to Angela the children were dressed picturesquely 'in velvet in the winter (exquisitely embroidered by Mummie) and pastel linens in the summer *with knickers to match*' (her italics). Only common children wore drawers. They were expected to look pretty and behave well, and Gerald would see that they did. Angela describes how, at the age of six or seven, she shook hands with the stage manager of Wyndham's Theatre, Tommy Lovell, with the wrong hand, the left instead of the right, and how the heavens fell. 'I doubt if any child has ever had such a dressing-down for so small an offence.' She spent the rest of the day practising, shaking hands with legs of cupboards, handles of doors, curtains, fire-arms 'and the parlourmaid who was waiting at table (the "lesson" took place whilst my father was having his early dinner before returning to the theatre).' When he discovered Angela and Daphne fighting over whom baby Jeanne loved best, Gerald made the nursery into an impromptu court, became Judge and 'tried us and doubtless punished us in a way to give satisfaction all round.

Punishment, qua punishment, and corporal punishment of any sort was never meted out to us by anyone.' Yet Daphne recalls being smacked by Gerald for putting her tongue out at Nanny. There was, however, one thing on which Gerald insisted and that was that the children behaved quietly. He could not bear noise of any kind whether it was the sound of traffic, barking dogs or children at play. He and Muriel kept late hours, often going on to supper or a party after the play was over and were rarely in bed before two in the morning, so it was instilled in the children that they made no noise when they got up in the mornings. Daphne writes of them, after they had been dressed and had their breakfast, being allowed to go in and see their parents as they breakfasted in bed, Gerald wearing a green flannel coat over his pyjamas. He was, she says, never in a bad mood.

He would get up in leisurely fashion, choose his suit for the day and select a pair of shoes from the gleaming rack of about two dozen pairs always neatly arranged for him. If he was rehearsing then he would leave home in time to arrive punctually at Wyndham's for rehearsals at eleven. If there was no matinée then he would, more often than not, go off to play golf after lunching at his club. He would return home to prepare for the theatre but would always visit the nursery and entertain the little girls with stories and mimicry. Then came his siesta and an early supper before setting off for the theatre and the night's performance. It was a routine which hardly ever changed.

Gerald figures heavily in the early reminiscences of both Angela and Daphne, Muriel less so. It soon becomes apparent that, from the earliest days, there was a barrier between Daphne and her mother, and that Muriel recognized this. Angela remembers her mother as being blessed with natural beauty and a great dress sense. She was 'so chic'. She writes: 'Mummy was so pretty. When I was very small, four-ish, I used to love to powder her back for her when she was dressing to go out for a party. It was a great treat for me to see her in full evening dress. I loved to see her with her hair hanging down too, looking like a princess, I thought. I was very different to Daphne who could not bear to see my mother with her hair down. I can remember that she would let it down to tease Daphne, and Daph would go crimson in the face and pick grass or, if indoors, keep her eyes on the rug as if she were being made witness to something obscene.'

Why the sight of her mother's hair hanging loose had such an effect on Daphne, she does not say. Perhaps she never did understand it even when she came to write about it years later. She herself describes how she once came upon her mother and her Aunt Billy skipping in the garden. They suddenly took the pins out of their hair and let it loose on their shoulders while they jumped over the skipping ropes like small children. It should be a charming vignette, but the effect on Daphne was remarkable. 'I felt myself go scarlet. I bent down to the ground, not to see them, and began to search for pebbles on the gravel path. The lower I bent, the more they skipped and laughed. Were they doing it on purpose? It was terrible to think of that loose hair and the jumping feet. They had changed from safe people into strangers. Hide me, hide me . . .'

She also describes how, sometimes for a treat, she and Angela would be allowed down to the drawing room after tea, where Muriel would read to them. One book which made a particular impression on Daphne was *The Snow Queen*, where the wicked Queen steals the little boy, Kay, for herself and to turn his blood to ice, and how he was rescued by his little friend, Gerda. Afterwards Muriel pretended to chase the children, but this upset Daphne, for 'it was not funny at all, I saw her as the Snow Queen and I was frightened. If I could turn into Kay, and M could become the Snow Queen, then who was I really, where did I belong? The Snow Queen was an enemy, like that other queen, the stepmother who looked into a mirror . . .' This is, admittedly, written with hindsight over seventy years later, but it throws a fascinating insight into Daphne's earliest memories of her mother.

But whatever the feelings aroused by the parents in their

three daughters, it was a privileged childhood. Angela recalls how, at six years old, she had her first portrait painted by Wolfram Onslow Ford. At the height of the summer, Gerald would take a country house and in 1911, which broke all existing records for the heat, the family went to Croxley Green, commuting when necessary in their Rolls-Royce. Gerald and Muriel were invited to a Coronation Garden Party at Windsor Castle and the young Angela has some vague memory of strikes – 'coal, railway?' Other summers in other country places followed. Daphne remembers a large house at Slyfield where the River Mole ran through the garden. The children were allowed to run outside whenever they wanted, the nurses did not scold them as much, and 'the maids were jollier'. She overheard someone saying she was a different child in the country and her love of it was to stay with her for the rest of her life. Slyfield was old with a dark panelled hall and corridors, and a room where Elizabeth I had slept.

The children played imaginative games, David and Goliath, Joshua bringing down the walls of Jericho, knights and ladies, with Daphne choosing to play the boy's part. It is interesting to note that when she was young, Daphne continually wished she had been a boy.

She also recalls a summer holiday spent at Llanbedr in Wales when she was seven, when Gerald took a rare holiday from the theatre and filled the house with his family. Because of the numbers the children had to live in a cottage in the grounds of the main house. They enjoyed it enormously, seeing the cottage as 'ours', and the house, 'theirs'; parents and children seemed to be on different sides, them and us, although Daphne notes that Angela did not feel this anything like as strongly. 'You could never be sure of them, even relations. Although I liked D better than M (which must never be said even to myself), M's mother, our Little Granny was, so I thought, more lovable than Big Granny, mother of D.' Although Mrs du Maurier senior was, she says, kind and generous, she never felt at ease when visiting her in her flat in Portman Mansions. But in spite of the crowd gathered at Llanbedr, the ranks of Gerald's generation of du Mauriers continued to dwindle, his sister Trixie now having died as well as Sylvia.

Picking over the accounts of these early years as seen through the eyes of various members of the family, that sense of privilege is very strong. As Gerald went from success to success, not only as an actor but as a gifted director, the girls grew up totally cut off from the problems that beset ordinary families. Their world consisted of their home, the theatre and their parents' friends, most of whom worked either in the theatre or other branches of the arts. Their main playmates were their cousins, the 'Lost Boys', the children of Arthur and Sylvia, and the daughters of Muriel's brother, Billie. Even their education isolated them for, although Angela and Daphne were to attend a private school for a short time, most of their teaching was to come from governesses.

Gradually it becomes apparent that the shadow of the coming war was encroaching on this golden age. It was during the hot summer holiday at Llanbedr that such an eventuality began to impinge even on the children. The full house included, among the cousins, Trixie's children who were now grown up and Daphne mentions in particular Trixie's son, Geoffrey, his wife, Dorothy (who cried a lot), and their baby, Derek. The adults were continually talking about war, writes Daphne. First came the news that Germany had invaded Belgium and then one day, while the children were lunching with the adults, the telephone rang and the cousin who went to answer it rushed back to say that the Germans were now also fighting the Russians. Everyone talked at once, she says, and she wondered why they were so concerned.

Why, Daphne wondered, did everyone so loathe the Germans? Obviously someone needed to speak in their defence. Waiting for a pause in the conversation, she seized her chance and announced, 'I like the Germans. I would like to have a German to tea with me here today.' Everyone stared

32

and Muriel rounded on her, red in the face with rage, saying, 'You *stupid* little girl, how dare you talk about things you don't understand.'

There was a pause and then the adults continued with their conversation. The young Daphne knew instinctively that what she had said was probably foolish and ignorant and she was sorry to have upset her mother, but the independence of spirit which she never lost and was so much part of her was there even then. 'I felt ashamed and yet . . . there was a sense of secret satisfaction that I had somehow scored against the grown-up world.'

CHAPTER 4

Hampstead and the war

At the beginning of the war, Gerald had been invited to take his most recent production, *Diplomacy*, to Windsor Castle for a Command Performance. His leading lady was Gladys Cooper, who had come into the lives of the family some three years earlier when she was relatively unknown. Angela remembers being taken by her father one hot summer Sunday to meet her at the railway station as Gladys had been invited to visit them in their country home. Gerald asked the young Angela to go on to the railway station platform to meet Gladys and, when she asked how she would know her, was told, 'Just pick out the prettiest face you can see.' Among the crowd pouring off the train she saw a 'very lovely person in a blue hat which matched her eyes.' It was to be the start of one of Gerald's most successful stage relationships and certainly she played as large a part in the success of *Diplomacy* as he did. By the time of the Command Performance Gerald's ten per cent of the profits of the show was a substantial sum and Gladys earned the then large salary of forty pounds a week.

Recognition by the Royal Family had its effect on the du Mauriers for Gerald was offered a number of honorary posts including the Presidency of the Actors' Orphanage Fund. Much of the fund-raising for this organization took place at the Theatrical Garden Party, held annually in the Chelsea Botanical Gardens. Gerald turned it into one of the most fashionable events of the year, with visits from royalty, and stalls and events run by a host of famous stage names.

But 1915 was to be a grim year. First, just into the New Year, came the death of Gerald's mother, Emma. She was seventy-four and suffered from heart trouble and although she had been advised to have an operation she had refused to do so. Gerald was devastated. His mother had spoiled and indulged her 'ewee lamb' from birth and he could not imagine life without her. Throughout his life, whenever he did not see her for any length of time, he kept up a prolific correspondence with her. She had become saddened towards the end of her life by the deaths of Trixie and Sylvia and her son-in-law, Arthur, and had, therefore, turned more than ever towards the survivors, May, Guy and Gerald. When her papers were gone through after her death it was found she had kept everything her sons had ever written to her, even Gerald's and Guy's notes from their prep-school days. Both sons were with her when she died – on the anniversary of her wedding to George fifty-one years earlier – and she was buried beside him in the Hampstead Parish Church graveyard.

Deaths, they say, come in threes and Emma du Maurier's was the first. One February evening, just as Gerald was making up before the evening's show, he was handed a telegram informing him that his brother Guy had been killed in France by a shell, while evacuating his battalion from the front line. He lived only minutes. He was to have been promoted to Brigadier-General the next day. Afterwards Gerald was to wonder if his brother had had a premonition that he would not return for, on his last leave, Guy had given him his signet ring saying, 'Take this, one never knows and it was always meant for you.'

On 15 March came the third death, young George Davies, Sylvia's son and the oldest of the 'Lost Boys'. A Second Lieutenant in the Rifle Brigade he had been shot through the head and buried quickly in the mud of Flanders. The death shocked Gerald but almost destroyed Barrie who had loved him so devotedly for years. He was just twenty-one years old. According to James Harding, Barrie had written to George immediately before his death commiserating with him on the death of his Uncle Guy. Barrie wrote: 'He certainly had the du Maurier charm at its best – the light heart with the sad smile, and it might be the sad heart with the bright smile. There was something pathetic about him to me. He had lots of stern stuff about him, and yet always the mournful smile of one who could pretend that life was gay but knew it wasn't. One of the most attractive personalities I have ever known.'

Daphne recalls Angela coming out of their parents' room in tears and, in answer to her enquiry as to what was wrong, saying, 'Uncle Guy has been killed'. Guy had been Angela's godfather, but Daphne felt she had a special relationship with him too, as they shared the same birthday. A newspaper photograph of him carried the caption, 'A patriot, alike with sword and pen', and revealed that Guy was the 'Patriot' author of *An Englishman's Home*. Gerald now had only one sibling left, his sister May. For the first time Daphne realized that adults could be unhappy, even cry. The children wore black armbands when they went out for their walks in the park and, when asked, 'Who have you lost in the war?' could reply, 'Uncle Guy and Uncle George'. Daphne considered this made them feel more important and, therefore, better.

Gerald's major new play for 1915 was *The Ware Case* and here, for once, he made a break from his roles as light-hearted crooks or amusing detectives and played an outright villain. It was a melodramatic piece which was one of the first to use a major court case as the pivot of the action. Gerald's part was that of Hubert Ware depicted, as played by him, as selfish and callous, but appealling. Ware is accused of murdering his brother-in-law and the action of the play follows the progress of the case against him, at the end of which he is acquitted – only to tell the audience just before the final curtain that he was guilty after all. After his confession he takes poison and kills himself. It was a huge success.

It was about this time that the young Daphne became

aware, she says, that there really was something particularly special about her father. All three children were, by this time, used to visiting him in the theatre, meeting the theatre staff at Wyndham's and seeing Gerald in his dressing room. They were used to watching the change that came over him once he had taken off his stage make-up, of leaving with him and having to push through his admirers waiting at the stage door. But on one particular occasion, Gerald took the children to lunch at the Savoy Hotel and as they entered one woman said to her escort, excitedly, 'There's Gerald du Maurier!', and both of them stared hard. Then waiters hurriedly approached, bowing, pulling back the chairs from a table, while heads turned and people nudged each other . . . the matinée idol had arrived.

Later she was to speculate about Gerald's relationships with other women at this time, but noted that he always returned to his loving 'Mo', as the family called her. However exciting the chase, nothing was as important as his home life. In spite of the war the routine of Cumberland Terrace and the theatre continued for all the family. Gerald gave eight performances a week, returning home at the end of the afternoon even on matinée days, to his siesta and early dinner. There were no longer as many glittering, late-night social events, but Gerald and Muriel remained late birds; 'Mo' would wait up for him in her dressing-gown, cook him his favourite supper of bacon and eggs, and listen to his comments on his day and that night's performance.

The war did not stop the family retreating to the country in the summer either. In 1915 they rented a large cottage called Soulsbury, near Chorleywood in Hertfordshire. Gerald was at the theatre from Monday to Saturday and Muriel, too, spent much of her time at Cumberland Terrace, so the children had a good deal of freedom. Angela attended lessons in the morning with a neighbouring family, but Daphne was left free to do as she pleased and she spent her time exploring the local countryside, accompanied by the children's first dog, a highland terrier called Jock. Jeanne, aged four, became her companion and eagerly acted out with her scenes from the books she was avidly reading – such as *Treasure Island* and *The Wreck of the Grosvenor*. Daphne took the role of Edward, the second mate, in the latter and little Jeanne that of the Captain.

In 1916 Gerald moved his family from Cumberland Terrace up to Hampstead, the place which had held so many happy childhood memories for him – and where Mary Anne Clarke had also lived at one time. Daphne writes: 'Nostalgia belongs to the middle years of life, and at forty-three, D, with his mother, his two sisters and his beloved brother dead, believed that by moving to his birthplace, close to his boyhood home, he might, in some indefinable fashion, recapture them. As children we were, of course, unaware of any such sentiment. At twelve, nine and five, the future was all ours.'

Cannon Hall was enormous, a mansion, standing in its own grounds. The night nursery shared by Daphne and Jeanne had its own *en suite* bathroom and they no longer had a nurse or Nanny, but their own maid. There was also a huge day nursery which could be reached either by an imposing main staircase or that of the servants' backstairs. Gerald and Muriel each had their own grand bedrooms and there was a vast drawing room. The du Maurier children used to race each other through the house running up one staircase and down the other, a practice actively discouraged by their parents. Gerald spent lavishly on Cannon Hall, using the profits from *The Ware Case* and another crowd-puller, *London Pride*, in which he played a Cockney costermonger and was the only one of his plays which dealt in any way with the subject of the war, albeit in a light-hearted manner. The house had been built by George III for his physician, so Gerald decided to furnish it with antiques appropriate to this period. He covered the walls in pictures (Daphne remembers Charles I in profile and one of Elizabeth I) and dozens of theatrical prints, especially from Shakespeare.

The children would act out scenes from Shakespeare, often joined by Gerald who, apart from playing a minor role in

Henry IV, Part I, years before, had never played Shakespeare professionally although he could recite large passages from many of the plays by heart. He had a fund of stories about his own childhood in Hampstead and would take the children to see New Grove House and tell them about their grandfather, George, who had died before any of them were born. He showed them the pond where George used to take him to sail his boat and into which grandfather had once jumped to save a dog from drowning and had been tipped by the owner.

If he was free in the afternoon Gerald would play cricket with them, a game which was mandatory on Sunday afternoons for anybody who happened to be visiting. Daphne was aware of a growing closeness towards her father and perhaps it was this, she says, which made her so apprehensive if there was an air raid before he had returned from the theatre. She describes how they would be awakened by the wail of sirens, followed by the crash of nearby anti-aircraft guns. The maid would run from the room ('the coward'), and Muriel and Angela would appear to comfort them, Muriel carrying a thermos flask and some biscuits. She recalls how one day there was a raid in the early morning, which became known as the Zeppelin raid. When Gerald suggested he should go up on the roof to watch, she felt 'an agony of fear for him, never experienced before or since. I stretched out my arms and cried, "Don't go . . . don't go. Don't ever leave me." He stared at me, then looked at M. She said, "Gerald, *please*." Slowly he came downstairs and joined us in the hall. . .'

Angela and Daphne were sent to a local day-school for a little while which Daphne enjoyed but about which Angela had reservations. Angela would weep over her homework and when mathematics was involved, Gerald would ring up his business manager, Tom Vaughan, and ask him over the telephone how to do the sums she had been set. Daphne blithely forged her mother's signature on the weekly report they had to take home every Friday and cheerfully admitted to it when hauled up by the headmistress. 'Don't you realize, dear, that this is very dishonest, and is called forging? People can be put in prison for it.' It rolled off her, she says, like water off a duck's back.

It was at Oak Hill Park School, too, that she received her first literary criticism. The class had been given a short story competition. Daphne, said her teacher, a Miss Druce, 'has written the best story but with the worst handwriting and the worst spelling.' Someone called Olive, she said, was the winner.

In 1917 Gerald touched greatness in the role of Will Dearth in Barrie's play *Dear Brutus*. The title comes from Shakespeare's lines in *Julius Caesar*:

> 'The fault, dear Brutus, is not in our stars,
> But in ourselves, that we are underlings.'

The plot has a theme which was to be taken up later by J.B. Priestley in a whole series of plays, which revolves round time and whether we would live our lives differently if we had them all over again. In *Dear Brutus* a group of people meet in a mysterious house, owned by a man called Lob, on Midsummer's Eve. On that night a forest grows up around the house and all the guests become lost in it. While they are floundering among the trees, each one of them is given the chance to change their lives by adopting a different response to a crucial past decision, but even so the result turns out to be the same. Will Dearth is an unsuccessful, alcoholic artist with a failing marriage, who is sure he would have been different had they only had children. In the dreamtime in the forest he is given a daughter, spends the happiest night of his life in her company, only to find she disappears with the dawn.

It was to have a profound impression both on Gerald and Daphne. Daphne wondered later if the agonizing fear she had felt for her father during the Zeppelin raid was what haunted her when she saw him in *Dear Brutus*. 'It must have been the memory of that moment which made watching him act Will Dearth shortly afterwards – Will, who had lost his imaginary daughter in the wood – so unbearable to me, at ten years old.' She had to be taken out in floods of tears.

Sir John Gielgud, reviving the play years later with himself as Dearth, said that he kept remembering how marvellous du Maurier had been. 'I could not touch him.' Daphne saw traces of what she had been told about George in Gerald's playing of the part, his singing in French, the way he stood at the easel. James Harding, writing in his biography of Gerald, says: 'In no other role did he probe so deeply within himself to picture the desolation of failure . . . The supreme moment in Gerald's performance came when he realized that he had lost his dream daughter and broke into a sob. "Daughters are the thing," he had earlier exulted, "daughters are the thing," an opinion Gerald as father might have echoed.'

CHAPTER 5

Growing Up

In spite of the war, the du Maurier girls continued to grow up in a secure and comfortable environment. When she was ten Daphne spent two periods away from Cannon Hall, both of which were to have an influence on her writing. In 1917 she and her sisters were sent away to Cookham, on the Thames, as their parents were increasingly concerned about the air raids. Here she read two novels by Harrison Ainsworth, the Victorian author, whose popularity in his own time was considerable. His two best-known novels, *The Tower of London* and *Old St Paul's* would make heavy reading for an adult today with their stolid prose and simplistic religious message, but the strong storyline in both of them obviously appealed to Daphne in spite of the gruesome and detailed descriptions of the torture chamber in the first and of the rotting corpses in the plague pits in the latter.

'Bring down your dead!' Daphne would call up to little Jeanne, hanging out of the bedroom window at Cookham, and she would throw down all the teddy bears which were then collected by Daphne in a wheelbarrow to be put into a hastily dug hole in the flower-bed. They bought plasticine at the village shop and made it into plague pustules to stick on themselves as they cried out, staggered and 'died'. The adults involved drew the line at chalked crosses on the front door, however.

Scenes from the *The Tower of London* included the 'beheading' of Jeanne by Daphne (using a walking-stick), and sometimes Angela was also persuaded to take part, her particular favourite being Bloody Mary, although she was finding the children's games increasingly tedious.

In the autumn the girls were invited by a Mrs Fitzwilliam to visit her in her home, Milton, near Peterborough. Asked if it was even more magnificent than Slyfield, Gerald laughed 'contemptuously', and said there was no comparison. Milton was an enormous Tudor mansion in which the Fitzwilliams had lived for over four hundred years. Daphne, who had never enjoyed the social life of the du Mauriers and who found meeting strangers and visiting their homes something close to purgatory, recalls that she felt quite at home in the huge house. Echoes of the life-style there were to appear, much later, in *Rebecca*. The children would come down to breakfast to be waited on by a butler from a side table set with silver dishes of eggs and bacon, boiled eggs, kippers and cold ham. While Mr Fitzwilliam saw to his estate, his wife spent her days in the drawing room usually working on huge jigsaws. There were billiard rooms and a picture gallery. Much of the house was being used as a Red Cross Hospital, but Mrs Fitzwilliam did take Daphne into it and showed her the ancestors' portraits on the wall – Thomas Wentworth, Earl of Strafford, executed on Tower Hill in 1641, and early members of the Fitzwilliam family.

Researching for her last books, the biographies of Antony and Francis Bacon, Daphne was to discover that their grandmother had been Ann Fitzwilliam, daughter of Sir William who was a friend of Cardinal Wolsey and the first of the family to live there.

'Unforgettable, unforgotten, Milton remains a childhood experience that has never been surpassed in sixty years,' she was to write.

With the death of 'Big Granny', Emma du Maurier, the Beaumont grandparents played an increasing role in Daphne's life and staying with them on her own in Golders Green was a particular treat. Here, she says, she first read *Little Women*, lighter in weight indeed than Harrison Ainsworth, but she found it harder to understand. Here, to some extent, the real life of the world outside impinged on her, for Granny would take her shopping in Golders Green on a Saturday morning, actually bake her own bread and cakes and make Sunday lunch, which was eaten after attendance at the local church – Granny Beaumont was a devout Christian – where the Anglo-Catholic services with all their ritual reminded Daphne of a matinée at Wyndham's. Although she had no-one to play with she was happy there, it offered her a kind of security and often she felt reluctant to return home. Granny Beaumont was, her granddaughter was to write later, the only truly good person she was ever to meet.

In 1918 towards the end of the war, Gerald made a quixotic gesture. He decided to join up as a soldier although he was by now forty-five years old. Officer Cadet Gerald Hubert Edward Busson du Maurier joined the Irish Guards who were stationed at Bushey in Hertfordshire, where he was addressed variously as 'Demerara' or 'Demure'. He found the basic drill almost beyond him and could not even march in step. If he took a gun to pieces he could not reassemble it. When a mock battle was launched and he was detailed off to spy on the 'enemy', he arranged for Muriel to hire a car and meet him, bringing with her a false beard and spectacles. Not surprisingly he was picked up straight away. Unwilling to be separated from his family, he rented a house at Bushey and brought them out to be near him.

Angela had, for a brief period, been sent away to boarding-school and she notes how on the day she left – it was only to go to Wimbledon! – her cousin Gerald Millar came to tell them he was about to rejoin his regiment at the front and how no-one gave him a thought, 'as we were all weeping our eyes out for me and the front to which I was off.' She remained there only half a term and so returned to join Daphne and Jeanne for lessons with the governess in Bushey.

Gerald continued his army career managing, in spite of his

practical ineptitude, to keep his room clean and his uniform immaculate, creeping out of his bed before reveille to illicitly use the officers' bathrooms. He kept a stock of whisky and port concealed under the floor beneath his bunk, while Muriel sent him a continual stream of food parcels, extra clothing and medicines for his chest. Towards the end of his training he appeared in an amateur performance of Anstey's comedy, *Vice Versa*, in which, not surprisingly, he was a great success. The war ended before he had ever left the precincts of Bushey. To Muriel's unbounded relief he was never to see the mud of Flanders where his brother and nephew had died.

So the family settled once more into Cannon Hall and Gerald re-established himself as manager of Wyndham's. He made a tremendous hit in the title role of *Bulldog Drummond*, based on a series of violent and patriotic adventure stories rarely read today, but which were as popular in the 1920s as Ian Fleming's James Bond was to be forty years later. There are definite similarities between the two. Bulldog Drummond was also a man of action, there were usually scenes where he was captured by the enemy and underwent horrendous tortures without uttering a sound and, like Bond, he always won; unlike Bond, however, there was no string of glamorous girlfriends willing to leap into bed on every other page, as Bulldog Drummond remained ever faithful to the limp Phyllis.

The comfortable life-style of pre-war years was picked up immediately, although inflation meant that it was no longer so easy to make as much money in the theatre. Family holidays were taken in exotic locations such as Algiers, which required a small army of servants to accompany them to carry the enormous amount of luggage, golf clubs, Fortnum & Mason hampers, games, cards and magazines. They would travel (first class, of course,) across the Continent and Gerald would turn his sleeping compartment into as near an imitation of his own bedroom as possible, complete with the bath salts, hair creams and the patent medicines he always used, and with his suits arranged for him in the correct position to allow him to choose which he should wear in the morning. Train staff were encouraged by the lavish distribution of tips. But the holidays often proved wearing for everyone else for it was not uncommon for Gerald to become bored after a few days away and begin to pine for his social life in London and the theatre. The whole day, from breakfast to suppertime, was spent trying to keep him entertained and happy, to avoid the onset of boredom.

Angela was sent off to Paris to be 'finished' as Daphne reached early adolescence and this was an event for which there was, Angela recalls grimly, no preparation whatsoever in her youth. Angela had already been in trouble at the age of twelve for innocently retelling inaccurate versions of how babies were born passed on by other children. When she started menstruating she was forbidden to mention it to the other two girls. The way the subject was introduced to Daphne, the latter noted, should be a lesson in how not to go about it. She was called in to see her mother whose grave manner made her feel as if she had committed some terrible wrong. She was told that at some time in the near future she must not be surprised if 'something not very nice happens to you.' All girls, she was informed, bled every month and it was something which had to be endured until they were middle-aged. It could make one poorly and Muriel, as she pointed out, very often had to retire with sick headaches when it happened. This dreadful thing had already happened to Angela, but it must not be discussed and little Jeanne must certainly be kept in ignorance.

For a little while she forgot this portentous information, continuing to play imaginative games with Jeanne – by this time it was Cavaliers and Roundheads – and reading voraciously, especially Dickens. But one morning 'it' arrived and the maid Alice sent her off to be 'fitted up with something to wear.' She had backache and felt sick and considered the whole thing to be an appalling injustice. As promised, she never mentioned it to her sisters and 'so it began. The deceit, the subterfuges, of the grown-up world, destroying for ever more the age of innocence.'

It was then, and still is now, easier for boys Daphne was to say later. The onset of puberty in boys is marked by trials of strength and prowess and they are not made to feel ashamed (although she says nothing of the attitude towards masturbation prevalent at the same time). The whole business of growing up for girls was surrounded by taboos.

For a few years, until shortly before her marriage, Daphne was to keep a diary and she notes that its pages give no sign that she was really and truly growing up, filled as it was with notes of what she had been given to do by the governess during lessons or the books she had read. When she was four she had been asked by a governess if she could write and she had boasted that not only could she write, she had written a book. When asked its title, she rejoined *John in the Wood of the World*. It had never existed but in 1920, at the age of thirteen, she noted that she had begun to write a book entitled *The Alternative*; trying to remember what it was about though left only 'a total blank in the memory'. She remembers having a crush on the actor Basil Rathbone, who was later to star in a film made from her novel, *Frenchman's Creek*, and who was then playing the part of Peter Ibbetson in an adaptation of George du Maurier's first novel. But the passion did not survive his appearance at a Cannon Hall garden party dressed prosaically in a straw boater.

Once again death was to impinge on this comfortable scene. This time it was Michael Llewellyn-Davies, the second of the 'Lost Boys'. He was at Oxford, a clever and good-looking undergraduate just short of his twenty-first birthday. Mystery still surrounds his death. It seems that, although unable to swim, Michael had bathed in the Thames with a friend, that both had then got into difficulties and drowned, apparently without putting up a struggle. It has since been suggested that there was an intense homosexual relationship between the two of them that was unacceptable in the climate of the times and that they had drowned together in a mutual suicide pact; something about which the truth will never be known. For Barrie, still suffering from the effects of George's death in the trenches, that of Michael was something from which he was never to recover. He continually dreamed night after night of searching for him in the river where he had drowned. He became a virtual recluse in his flat in Adelphi Terrace where a portrait of Michael, at twelve, held pride of place on a wall.

In 1922 Gerald received the final accolade. In the New Year's Honours List he received a knighthood. Although Muriel professed not to know the reason for this, it was, quite obviously, that he was the leading theatrical personality of the day, coupled with which he had become almost equally well known for his connection with an ever-increasing number of good causes. He thoroughly enjoyed his investiture at Buckingham Palace and from then on, apparently, liked to pay his bills in gold sovereigns instructing the recipients to keep the change, and tipping ever more lavishly wherever he went.

His daughters adored him, most especially Daphne. The early feeling of estrangement from her mother had not improved with the passage of time. 'Poor darling M,' she was to write. 'Was I a trial to her? Never ill-mannered, never rude, of that I'm sure, but perhaps I made some remark that caught her in an off mood. She was not an easy person to understand and both as a child and as a growing adolescent I could never feel quite sure of her, sensing her disapproval in her attitude towards me. Could it be that, totally unconscious of the fact, she resented the ever-growing bond of affection between D and myself? He was her whole life and next to D came Jeanne, petted and adored, while Angela and I – until we were both adult and life adjusted itself – came off second best.'

She continued: 'A possessive mother, demanding, searching, possibly does more damage to daughter or son than an indifferent one, her thoughts elsewhere: nevertheless, in both cases seeds are sown of doubt, insecurity and the child who cannot rush to his/her mother in times of stress, telling all, will look elsewhere for comfort or become a loner.'

But it was not Gerald's knighthood or her relationship with her mother which she was to recall most vividly from the year 1922, but memories of a character she invented, a lad called Eric Avon, captain of cricket at School House, Rugby. She was absorbed by the game at that time and Eric Avon developed into a brilliant hero who shone at sport in general and cricket in particular. She invented admirers for him, the 'Dampier brothers', and imagined him bowing from a balcony after captaining the winning team in a Rugby-v-Marlborough match. His final triumph came when he played his last match in July 1922, two and a half months after Daphne's fifteenth birthday which proved his last, and most exciting victory, before he was laden with prizes and despatched to Cambridge – but not before he had given his definitive performance as Hamlet in the school play.

She was to wonder later how her creation would get on at university and afterwards, whether he became terribly successful or died young. He owed much, she admits, to her having recently read *Tom Brown's Schooldays* and watching the Eton-v-Harrow match at Lord's, as she did every year with the family. She never considered inventing such a heroine even though she also read Angela Brazil's boarding-school novels for girls.

Eric Avon, whom she describes as her alter ego, haunted her unconscious for years, laying the basis for the narrators of the five novels she was to write which are narrated in the first person by a man – *I'll Never Be Young Again*, *My Cousin Rachel*, *The Scapegoat*, *The Flight of the Falcon* and *The House on the Strand*. Yet none of these fictional characters in any way resemble the successful and supremely self-confident Eric, each being subordinate to a stronger male character and each being somehow flawed. Perhaps, after all, she, too, seeing something of herself in her male narrators, enjoyed playing a role, acting being in her blood.

With Angela in Paris and the faithful governess 'Tod'

employed elsewhere, there were no more lessons although she continued to read avidly – Dickens still, Thackeray, Scott and the contemporary Galsworthy and Maugham.

But side by side with Eric Avon there had come, a little earlier that summer, the first real-life 'emotional involvement. It was with her cousin Geoffrey Millar.

CHAPTER 6

First Love and Paris

I t was the same cousin Geoffrey who had been visiting the du Mauriers in the summer holiday home in Llanbedr when the war broke out, along with his wife, Dorothy – who cried a lot – and their baby son, Derek. The weeping Dorothy had been divorced, a still relatively uncommon step at that time, and Geoffrey had married again. He and his new wife were visiting the du Mauriers during another summer holiday, this time at Thurlestone in Devon, in August 1920. He was thirty-six years old.

One day, when they were all on the beach, he caught Daphne's eye and smiled and she felt an extraordinary sympathy pass between them along with a feeling she could not understand. She had known him since babyhood. He was a close friend of Gerald's as well as a relative, and there was only twelve years between them in age. Like Gerald he, too, seems to have fallen in and out of love with a succession of women. The smiles and the understanding grew and Geoffrey was careful that Gerald should not see it. When they all lay in the garden to catch the sun, with rugs over their knees, Geoffrey would lie beside Daphne and hold her hand under the rug. At seventy she was to write that nothing that came later in her life ever surpassed 'that first awakening of instinct within myself', brought about by physical contact coupled with the knowledge that nobody must know about it.

He persuaded Gerald to let her go to dances and they

danced together. On the last day of the holiday he took her to look at the sea and told her how much he would miss her. Looking behind them they saw Gerald staring down at them and Geoffrey laughed and said he must be spying on them. Years later that particular pattern was to repeat itself and not only with Geoffrey.

Daphne noted his departure in her diary and said she felt depressed. She had learned that, without volition, a strange, emotional understanding could develop between two people which was unspoken. Geoffrey never overstepped the proprieties, there were no kisses, no 'fumblings in the dark', no hint, she says, of the sexual impulse he undoubtedly felt and which he admitted to years later. Just what possessed him to awaken such feelings in a very young girl less than half his age, she does not surmise, but the effect on them both – and on an increasingly jealous Gerald – was to be an enduring one. However, Daphne's relationship with Gerald is so crucial to her make-up that it requires a separate chapter.

Coincidentally or not, Geoffrey – who was also an actor – was offered a part in Gerald's revival of *Bulldog Drummond* at Wyndham's, a production which was about to go on tour across the States; she never knew whether or not this had been a deliberate move on Gerald's part. Although this first mysterious awakening had such a profound effect on her, it never found its way into her novels so far as she was aware.

Life returned to normal, galloping over Hampstead Heath with Jeanne on hired horses, going to the theatre, cricket at Cannon Hall the following summer, and all the time reading – Samuel Johnson, Emily Brontë, even Ethel M. Dell. There were still selected lessons, this time from a governess called Dora Vigo. Angela, who had returned from being 'finished' in Paris, officially 'came out', something hardly imaginable now, when the young women were paraded at a series of balls and dances, culminating with being presented to royalty. Gerald's theatrical involvement meant that Angela did not follow exactly the same pattern as her contemporaries, but she did live a hectic social life and her clothes allowance was looked on with envy by her sisters who still only had pocket money. Gerald spent extravagantly and his family had centre court seats at Wimbledon, boxes at the opera and ballet, and days at Ascot.

There was never any question that the girls should go on to higher education, let alone earn a living. They never had to struggle for anything and could, once they were grown up, do exactly as they wished and go anywhere they wanted to. Angela's own account of her youthful years given in her book, *It's only the Sister* (taken from a quotation from one of Daphne's fans who thought Angela was the famous novelist), reads like a mammoth 'Jennifer's Diary' of the twenties. There is no hint that there was any other kind of life – the post-war turmoil and coming Depression cast no shadows on the round of parties and happy weekends at Cannon Hall. The attitude is well summed up by Angela in her book: 'They say that every generation looks back with nostalgic yearning. That every cry from the heart of the elderly man and woman is "Ah – when I was young . . ." Those dear dead BAD OLD TIMES as the Labour government and their supporters insist on calling them. Well, maybe they were bad for some people, but for those with childlike enthusiasm for enjoyment, who grasped gratefully the pleasures that leisure gave, they were GOOD OLD DAYS . . .' – which indeed they were for those who were fortunate enough to enjoy leisure which was not enforced by unemployment and which was assisted by the ability to pay for other people to do all the usual boring household chores.

Meanwhile Daphne had begun to write short stories, a pursuit in which she was encouraged by Dora Vigo who suggested she might work at them instead of continuing conventional English lessons. Eventually she showed them to Gerald who thought they were very promising and asked his secretary to type them up. She also embarked on a novel about a boy called Maurice, a project soon abandoned. The only plot from those early stories which remained in her memory years later was about a man and a woman who

53

meet in a thick fog on the Thames Embankment and, when it suddenly lifts, discover they had once been in love.

Writing in her diary in 1923, Daphne notes that she had acquired jaundiced views on marriage, thinking suddenly one day, 'how awful just being married would be. I should be so afraid, so terribly afraid, but of what? I don't know . . .' Possibly she had picked up resonances from her parents' marriage, for this was the year of Gerald's serious involvement with Audrey Carten. She also noted that, while on holiday in the New Forest that Easter, she had seen a married couple who were so obviously happy with each other that it made her feel lonely; it was a kind of happiness she felt she would never achieve.

The following year, 1924, was chiefly memorable for Angela, because, although she had had no theatrical experience whatsoever, Gerald decided to cast her as Wendy in that year's production of *Peter Pan*. Reading between the lines of her account of the experience it is fairly clear that the rest of the cast, and the staff of Wyndham's, were less than enchanted with the idea and her début was something they put up with out of affection for Gerald. Luckily, Angela received good notices and she obviously enjoyed it all thoroughly, especially being visited in her dressing room by theatrical stars, including Tallulah Bankhead who had been brought over from the States to play one of the two female leads in Gerald's production of a play called *Dancers* – Audrey Carten played the other.

December 1924 also saw the end of Daphne's lessons with Dora, who had now become Mrs Meade and was expecting a baby. So, like Angela, it was decided she should be sent to be 'finished' in Paris. Angela had not found the experience all that enjoyable, so a different finishing school was chosen for Daphne. It was just outside Paris, near Meudon. It was arranged that she could go there with another Millar cousin, 'Doodie', so that she would not be lonely. She found the experience of a school, after years of special tuition in her own home, a difficult, indeed a galling one, because there were four classes organized as to ability, an early form of streaming in fact. She was mortified to find she only just scraped into the second class. The girls in the first class were allowed all kind of privileges, from choosing their own places for meals, to soirées with the directrice, Mlle Yvon, in her salon.

Daphne decided that, somehow or other, she had to become part of that special élite band. Doodie had no such ambition and was happy enough to chat and dance with the other girls as a recreation and so, one evening, Daphne took the bull by the horns and just walked into the soirée uninvited. Mlle Yvon was so amazed at her temerity, that she was allowed to stay and to become part of the privileged few throughout her time at the school; Daphne repaid this generosity by becoming totally devoted to Mlle Yvon. She developed what she herself recognized as a 'crush' on her, hanging on her every frown and 'the smile from her green eyes. Less harmful, maybe, but as insidious as a drug to an adolescent of the 1970s, the approval of my idol became a necessity. I was well and truly hooked.'

Her involvement with Mlle Yvon, Fernande, was intense and it lasted for years as they became close and intimate friends. Much later she was to say that possibly what she sought in Fernande was the mother/daughter relationship missing in her own life and that so far as she was aware there were no other overtones. She had never disapproved of physical relationships between women but saw them only as a feeble substitute for something else, a sign of immaturity. Looking back on that relationship a strangely cool note creeps into her writing as she wonders why Fernande returned her affection, wondering if perhaps her motives had been mixed when she made Daphne one of her favourites, mixed because of her knowledge that Gerald was so famous and 'knew everyone'. It seems an ungenerous response to someone who, she says herself, became a devoted friend, wise counsellor and an unfailing correspondent until her death from leukaemia in middle-age.

Whatever the reason for their friendship, Daphne became so devoted to Fernande that she stayed at the finishing school for three terms not one as originally planned, and between the second and third decided, instead of joining the family on a holiday in Italy, to accompany Fernande to La Burboule, to 'take the waters'. Fernande regaled her with anecdotes from her own life which sounded highly romantic to Daphne, from the fiancée killed in the 1914–18 War to the cousin who wanted to marry her, and her friendship with a film star who had died in a motor car accident. She never did marry. Daphne returned to Paris for her final term full of enthusiasm, after a brief trip to Hampstead to visit her family. She was now writing stories in every spare minute and Gerald's secretary had brought her one of the theatre typewriters so that she could type them out.

She returned to be finally allowed into the première class but almost immediately went down with influenza. A doctor diagnosed a spot on one of her lungs and her parents became increasingly concerned because she was rapidly losing weight. An American friend of the family, who was living at the Crillon Hotel in Paris, insisted on removing her from the school and subjecting her to a bizarre treatment of injections of sal volatile, exposure to ultra-violet rays and electric pads to the stomach which, needless to say, did no good at all. In fact the weight loss accelerated until she was down to seven stone. Muriel then wrote suggesting that possibly Daphne might have a holiday in Switzerland after Christmas to see if that would improve her health and agreed that Fernande should accompany her, but the doctor insisted it was necessary that his treatment should continue.

At the beginning of December, Muriel took matters into her own hands and arrived in Paris accompanied by Jeanne. Daphne was apprehensive that she might not warm to Fernande but, fortunately, the two women got on very well. She took Daphne home for Christmas, promising to send her back to finish her 'treatment', before any further decisions were made. She returned to Paris early in the New

Year, crossing over on the ferry where she was spotted by a friend of Lord Beaverbrook's who at once offered her his private cabin so that she could lie down during the rough crossing. Fernande was waiting for her at the Gare du Nord and saw her safely installed in a small hotel. They decided that the 'treatment' was a waste of money and Fernande was asked by Gerald and Muriel to deal with the doctor and see him paid off, which she did.

Eating out in Paris soon put back the lost weight and, for the first time, Daphne began to experience the joys of the city, that city which George du Maurier, whom she had never known, had loved so much and which is the setting for all three of his novels. The sights, sounds and smells of the streets of Paris proved intoxicating, not least because it was so very different from London. For a month she retraced George's steps, discovering his city, taking trams to Montparnasse, looking for his old studio in Montmartre, walking along the river banks, eating out in Left Bank restaurants and cafés. Now completely bilingual, she read French literature with enthusiasm – Maupassant, Paul Bourget and Pierre Louis. She was to return to Paris again and again until her marriage.

At the end of that happy month, Fernande returned to her teaching at the finishing school and Daphne went back to London, accompanied by Angela who had joined her for the last few days. She was loath to go. It poured with rain during the last day and the rain was followed by thick fog. She woke up, wailing in her sleep, after a night of bad dreams.

CHAPTER 7

Du Maurier Country

All the du Maurier girls were blessed with good looks, but Daphne's most noticeable feature all her life were her eyes – 'an extraordinary shade,' A.L. Rowse recalls, 'lavender, not blue.' It was certainly the colour of her eyes which struck me. Gerald had their portraits painted at regular intervals and they were also photographed – a photograph of Daphne at thirteen shows a wistful-looking girl who could truly have portrayed the dream child of *Dear Brutus* except, possibly, for a determined chin. It is worth noting the chin, for Daphne was never the gentle romantic which mythology was to create, she was a very determined woman.

1926 was the year of the General Strike, when the feelings of those who had imagined they had fought a war in order to make a land fit for heroes, discovered that the country had no shortage of heroes but a distinct shortage of homes, jobs and a great unwillingness to properly remunerate those who had spent years of their youth in the Flanders mud. Daphne recalled the Strike only in terms of its inconvenience – there were no buses and you had to walk a good deal or take a taxi – but it did not affect her because Muriel had allowed the chauffeur to give her a few driving lessons in her own car: there were no such things as driving instructors, examiners or tests then, just a matter of learning the controls and setting off.

Angela refers to the Strike in passing, saying that it did not affect the success of Gerald's new play, *The Ringer*, the first of his fruitful associations with the thriller writer, Edgar Wallace. (In many ways the two men were quite unalike – although they shared a proclivity for extravagant spending – but their working relationship was a good one and they became great friends.) Referring to the politics of the day, Angela writes: 'There was none of this ghastly so-called Class Hatred which politicians ladle one out with nowadays like spoonfuls of soup from an inexhaustible tureen.' It existed, of course, but it was just that they never came into contact with it. Gerald had little interest in politics, apart from a general feeling that it was best to keep the established order of things going, which meant voting Conservative if you voted at all. For Angela 1926 was a 'year of enchanting visits', of a glorious trip to the Riviera, a summer in rural France, visits to friends in Devon, first nights at the Russian ballet and the opera and parties all the time. The youngest sister, Jeanne, had been sent to a private day-school in Hampstead to complete her education.

Daphne was not as happy for she was becoming aware of a growing sense of isolation from the social scene around her, even though there were aspects of it she enjoyed. As soon as she returned from France she began writing short stories again although, as her own standards rose, she was finding it more difficult to write with ease. She was much influenced by the short stories of Katherine Mansfield whom she revered, but felt that they were of a standard beyond her capabilities. She became moody and disconsolate, refusing to join in the trips to the theatre, the first-night parties. She began to pine for the countryside and that Easter Jeanne suggested they might take a holiday in the Lake District. Muriel agreed and booked rooms in a farmhouse saying that she would stay with the two girls for ten days (Gerald would not spare her for longer), but agreed to Daphne inviting Fernande over from France for the final week. Daphne found the Lake District both beautiful and stimulating, and she and Jeanne walked for miles, coming home in the evenings to hearty suppers before a blazing log fire.

Fernande did come over for the final week, but the weather changed, it poured with rain and she, Daphne and Jeanne were confined indoors – possibly to the relief of Fernande who had shown little inclination for fell walking and hill climbing. She was to spend her time telling the Clarke family, who owned the farm, about the incredibly talented du Mauriers, the grandfather who was a bestselling novelist, the father the best-known actor on the English stage. At the end of the week, the small party returned to London where Fernande found a letter waiting for her from the headmistress of her finishing school: she had been sacked. No explanation was given but as Miss Wicksteed, the headmistress, was actually staying in London, Fernande went to see her to find out why her services were no longer required. Daphne found there was very little interest at home in Fernande's plight. The first night of *The Ringer* was only two days away and the main concerns of Gerald and Muriel were that and the Royal Academy Private View to which they had been invited.

Fernande was unable to extract from Miss Wicksteed any explanation for her decision. There had been no disagreement between the two women, no criticism of her work and it was nothing to do with the holiday in Cumberland – what she did in her holidays was up to her. But one is left feeling that the headmistress of such a school might well have found such an overwhelming preference for one girl, albeit now an ex-pupil, an embarrassment. What the real reasons were for her dismissal were never to be known, but Fernande was devastated and, in an awkward scene with Daphne, she asked her if she could persuade her father to consider her as an actress and find a role for her on the stage; she saw herself as a second Yvonne Arnaud. Daphne was appalled, knowing that Gerald would never countenance such a bizarre idea and eventually persuaded Fernande to drop it. Finally Fernande left again for France to see if she could raise the funds and backing to start a small finishing school of her own, leaving

Daphne to attend the first night of *The Ringer*. 'The General Strike was about to begin, but I was more concerned over the future of a Frenchwoman out of a job than with the English miners.'

She returned to her short-story writing and began to dream of emigrating, of living in a far-flung colony, possibly South Africa. She also started to think seriously of earning money for her own needs and becoming independent of the generous allowance given to her by Gerald. She recognized that Angela did not see things her way at all, as she was perfectly happy living at home with her busy social life. But writing was rapidly becoming ever-more difficult and she was overwhelmed by a sense of failure, feeling strongly that she was actually writing worse at nearly nineteen years of age than she had as a young adolescent. J. B. Priestley once described the effort of beginning to write anything as one of the most daunting tasks in the world – 'the first thing you have to face is heaving the elephant off the typewriter.' Daphne did not write directly on to a typewriter, but the pile of chewed pencils grew and, in despair, she turned back to the entertainments offered by the family, going to films, plays, operas, ballet and dances, at one of which she danced with the Prince of Wales.

In the summer she returned to Paris and then took a holiday in Brittany with Fernande – one is constantly struck by the number of holidays the girls took each year, the series beginning with winter sports in Switzerland and continuing through the spring, summer and autumn, with prolonged visits both at home and abroad. Fernande was far from well, exhausted with trying to set up a school of her own, and suffering from heart trouble. But Daphne found Brittany enchanting and decided that perhaps, after all, South Africa was too far away, and that what she wanted was a seaside home either on the Brittany coast or on one of the small islands off it. Her happiness was marred only by the news from home that her pet dog had been found drowned in a rain-water tank. Muriel broke it to her in a letter which also enclosed some money and a suggestion that she may like to remain in Brittany for a further three weeks.

She returned home in August to find that Gerald had developed a new enthusiasm; what the family needed, he felt, was their own country home where they could go for holidays whenever they wanted without either the bother of renting a house in the country or the effort of travelling abroad. *The Ringer* had been a tremendous financial success and money was therefore no problem. If Daphne liked living by the sea then there was no reason why a suitable seaside house could not be found and so the du Mauriers started looking for a house in Cornwall. Twice, when Daphne was a child, a remarkable caravanserai made up of Muriel, the du Maurier children, nurses, a nursemaid and a holiday governess had crossed the Tamar for a family holiday in Cornwall. The first time, when Daphne was only five years old, they stayed at Mullion Cove; on the second occasion they went to Kennack Sands. Daphne had pleasant memories of both, particularly Mullion, but in spite of that she wondered if it was a plot, devised by her parents, to prevent her from going to live abroad. She decided, however, to give them the benefit of the doubt. In the meantime, she returned to her writing.

It had become a habit when she was at home to spend time on a Sunday evening on her own with Gerald, as he sat in the dining room after family dinner with his brandy and his cigarettes; one of the things his contemporaries always recalled was his excessive need to smoke. For the first time in a long while she showed him some of her short stories and some poetry; Gerald was delighted. He told her that he had always hoped that she might one day write novels like George, the grandfather she physically resembled. Her father's enthusiasm encouraged her to continue.

In September Daphne heard from Fernande that she had, finally, found a property suitable for a small school; she had received backing from a bank and was looking for pupils. But any plans Daphne might have had to go over and see how it was progressing were quashed by Muriel. On 13 September she took the three girls down to Looe, in Cornwall, to start the search for a suitable summer home. They found the small town and fishing port disappointing, but someone suggested that they might have a look around Fowey further down the coast. They decided to hire a car and drove down the coast to Bodinnick, the little village on the opposite side of the Fowey River where they had a choice of either crossing straight over to Fowey itself, or lunching at the Ferry Inn in Bodinnick. They chose the latter, a decision which was to change Daphne's life irreparably.

The Fowey estuary is extraordinarily beautiful still, although there are brash and expensive houses in the woods behind the Ferry Inn. Fowey Town has retained a great deal of the charm which enchanted the du Mauriers even though it has become far more heavily dependent on the tourist trade. Nothing can ever take away the beauty of the wide stretch of water between the small fort above Readymoney Cove and the village of Polruan tumbling down the steep slope on the opposite side, or the breathtaking sweep of the river which can be seen along the length of the coastal path from Polruan to Boddinick. A memorial has subsequently been built here to Sir Arthur Quiller-Couch, the writer who first made Fowey famous, in a spot which would do honour to a Celtic chieftain. Whatever the time of year, whatever the weather, Fowey grips the heart. For Daphne it was to wipe everywhere else from her mind, even Brittany.

On their way to the Ferry Inn for lunch, the family noticed a For Sale sign on a gate by the ferry, behind which was a strange, rambling old house looking, Daphne was to recall, rather like a tumbledown Swiss chalet. It was, in fact, called Swiss Cottage, a name redolent now with one of London's most appallingly congested traffic blackspots, a name the du Mauriers were to change to the more appropriate 'Ferryside'. It was built on three floors, the ground floor having been used for boat building, the second as storage and net lofts and the top as living quarters. Over lunch they discussed the potential of Swiss Cottage and Muriel chatted with the proprietor of the inn about it and other possible properties, but by this time Daphne was driven by a daemon which could brook no delay. She raced down to the house leaving her mother still chatting in the inn, walked round Swiss Cottage and then stood beneath it looking out towards the estuary, watching the boats of all sizes bobbing in Fowey Harbour. A large cargo ship was on its way up river to find a mooring.

'It was astonishing the effect it had on her,' says Rowse. 'Perhaps it was some kind of strange throwback to her Breton ancestors, but whatever it was, it was all-consuming.'

Years later, after her death, Rowse was to say how jealous he had been of her, of the so-obviously wealthy family background where nobody ever had to struggle and how easy it was for them to come down to that part of Cornwall and see only its physical beauty. Almost exact contemporaries, at the time she was having gentle lessons with a governess, he was clawing his way out of a background of bone-breaking poverty in the china-clay country between Fowey and St Austell, his family struggling against the financial odds so that he could go to the grammar school in St Austell. He then went on to become a local phenomenon – the working-class boy from the clay country who made it to Oxford. It is a story he has told most movingly in his well-loved memoir, A *Cornish Childhood*, and even today he remembers with pride Daphne's solicitor and friend picking up a copy of his book and saying, 'Of course, this is the real thing.'

For Daphne, gazing down the river that sunny September day, 'there was a smell in the air of tar and rope and rusted chain, a smell of tidal water. Down harbour, round the point, was the open sea. Here was the freedom I desired, long sought-for, not yet known. Freedom to write, to walk, to wander, freedom to climb hills, to pull a boat, to be alone. It could not be mere chance that brought us to the ferry, and the bottom of Boddinick Hill, and so to the board upon the gate beyond that said For Sale. I remembered a line from a forgotten book, where a lover looks for the first time upon his chosen one – "I for this, and this for me".'

This love affair was to last all her life and although she was to write a host of novels and dozens of short stories, it was those set in Cornwall which were to make her a household name across the world. Again and again she was to return in her writing to that dream Cornwall in which she was to wander both physically and in the spirit, the magic land which was to give so many of her novels such a sense of place.

Later they were to call it 'du Maurier country'.

CHAPTER 8

Gerald

The purchase of Ferryside changed Daphne's life for ever as Cornwall became increasingly more important than either London or France. She spent more and more of her time there, wrenching herself away only with an increasing effort until, apart from the early years of her marriage, she returned to live in the county for good. Her feeling of estrangement from the social round of the du Mauriers had not diminished, but it was in the winter of 1926 that she finally decided that she needed a study of her own if she were to write seriously.

On her return to London, she took over the room above the garage at Cannon Hall which had hitherto been used only by guests changing for tennis parties. There she wrestled with a play in blank verse, some poetry and more short stories. Du Maurier connections brought about an interview with the publishers, Heinemann, to whom she took her poetry, but nothing came of it. During a trip to Cambridge, she was invited to tea to meet Sir Arthur Quiller-Couch for the first time, because he had heard that her family had purchased the house on the opposite river bank to his own. Meanwhile a small army of builders and decorators had been organized to gut Ferryside and prepare for the first family holiday in the summer of 1927. Other holidays, of course, continued; Daphne stayed with Fernande again, went skiing in Switzerland with Angela (where she found herself much pursued by young men), and followed that up with a week in Berlin. Her writing, though seriously pursued when she was in England, must have taken place only sporadically, because of the time she spent away. Gerald had encouraged the trips to Switzerland and Germany, uneasily aware that his daughter was now something of a 'loner'. He also encouraged a friendship with the actress Viola Beerbohm-Tree, possibly, Daphne felt, because he saw she needed an older woman in whom she could confide, someone who might help fill the place which should have been taken by Muriel. A photograph of Daphne with Gerald, taken at that time, makes them look more like guilty lovers than father and daughter – he gazes at her in obvious adoration, she looks into the distance, the unflattering cloche hat of the era and the fur coat making her look much older than she was.

Gerald also pushed her into taking a film test for the part of Tessa in a film adaptation of the highly popular stage play *The Constant Nymph*, an ordeal which she went through in order to please him, feeling deeply relieved when nothing came of it.

At the beginning of May, Muriel went down to Fowey taking Angela with her to oversee the laying of carpets, fitting of curtains and installation of the furniture purchased especially for Ferryside. Daphne joined them on 9 May, accompanied by Daisy, the housemaid. Inside, the place was no longer recognizable; the dilapidated but functional old ferry house had been transformed into a luxury holiday home suitable for Gerald's exacting tastes. On 13 May Daphne celebrated her twentieth birthday there and the following day Muriel and Angela returned to London leaving her behind in Fowey, alone except for 'a Mrs Coombs who came into cook, but this didn't count.' Day followed day as she explored the countryside on foot and crossed and recrossed the Fowey River by ferry. Gerald was having a motor cruiser built for use on the river, but Daphne began to pine for a sailing-boat of her own. After her initial explorations she also began to set aside time each day to write short stories.

On one of her afternoon walks she cut through the woods and walked up to the head of Pont Creek. The tide was out and only a thin trickle of water ran through the mud flats. In those days the creek was still full of the relics of the days of sail and rotting hulks of old schooners could be seen lying in the mud at low water. She clambered down and waded out across the mud to look at the old boats and was intrigued to see that one still had its figurehead attached, that of a young woman. It was called *Jane Slade*.

Day followed idyllic day, in a pattern of writing, now with increasing ease, walking and boating. Then came a voice from the past. Cousin Geoffrey, he who had aroused in her the first stirrings of sexual attraction, wrote to say he was not only back in England, but staying nearby in Plymouth and could he come and see her? She found him much the same (he was forty-two by this time); he found her changed and grown up, but they spent a happy day together. Remarkably, somehow or another, Gerald had got wind of this and after Geoffrey had returned to Plymouth that evening, she had a telephone call from Gerald wanting to know why Geoffrey had visited her, what they had talked about and what they had done. Geoffrey paid several more visits until sufficient parental pressure was put on Daphne to return to Hampstead which she did, with great reluctance, only to escape back to Fowey in July, this time chaperoned by Jeanne.

She remained haunted by the abandoned schooner, *Jane Slade*, and so set about trying to discover its history. Here she was in luck for Gerald had employed a local man, Adams, as a skipper for his motor cruiser, *Cora Anne*, which finally had been delivered to Fowey. Adams was a naval veteran of the war, a local man who knew the river and coast like the back of his hand, and was only too happy to teach a willing pupil how to handle a boat; but he also revealed that his wife had herself been a Slade, actually the granddaughter of Jane Slade after whom the schooner had been named. He offered to let Daphne look through a box of letters he kept at home which not only covered a great deal of family history but also detailed how the boat was built and why, but before she could start properly on her research the rest of the family arrived for their summer holiday. It was Gerald's first visit to Fowey and he was greeted by torrential rain, causing much trepidation in the family fearful that he might dislike it and, even worse, be bored by it. The rain was the least of their problems for the holiday was dogged with mishaps, from Muriel spraining both ankles to Viola Beerbohm-Tree, who had come along as well, falling off the slipway into the harbour. Gerald, determined to use his motor cruiser at all costs, persuaded Adams to take him out in rough weather where his own efforts to steer the craft nearly ended in disaster on the rocks off Polperro. Daphne longed for them to go back to London as the peaceful atmosphere had been totally destroyed. Fear of Gerald's boredom meant a continual stream of guests arriving from London while Muriel insisted on the house being kept neat and tidy, and frowned on a daughter who had taken to dressing in seaboots and sweaters. It is amusing in these informal times to note that one of the very first mentions of Daphne in the press was a note in the *Daily Telegraph* that she had set a fashion as 'the starter of the hatless movement which young people have taken up so enthusiastically.' A photograph of her taken in 1928 shows a person of apparently indeterminate sex, peering from under the brim of an enormous sou'wester, wearing trousers and seaboots and holding an ugly-looking conger eel hook.

Finally the du Mauriers returned home to Cannon Hall and Daphne was left to continue with her round of mackerel fishing with Adams, improving her handling of *Cora Ann*, walking and, of course, writing. Angela had remained at Ferryside with her, but in October they both returned to London, Angela eagerly, Daphne with very real distress. She wrote in her diary: 'I think Fowey means more to me than anything now. The river, the harbour, the sea. It's much more than love for a person. I don't know how I am going to exist back in London', dreary, bloody London as she was to call it. Entertainments laid on by her parents paled into insignificance beside the pleasures of the river and Fowey; worst of all, the creative spark which had led to a continual flow of short stories, vanished as, day after day, she sat in the room over the garage completely unable to write. Thoroughly depressed, in November she fled again, this time to Fernande and Paris, where she spent a month. While she was there she received an affectionate letter from Geoffrey informing her that the du Mauriers had decided to spend Christmas at Ferryside and that he had managed to get himself invited to join them. It seems that Fernande did not approve of a relationship with 'a married man twice your age', but whatever she or anyone else might think about its suitability, Geoffrey did indeed spend Christmas in Fowey, despite his current wife being seriously ill in a nursing home in London.

It was a good Christmas as, most unusually, even Gerald enjoyed being out of London. They ate and drank well, played all kinds of games, while Geoffrey fondled Daphne's knees under the table. Eventually his conscience pricked him sufficiently to drive him back to London and his sick wife, leaving Daphne in a thoughtful mood. New Year's Eve dawned with a bitter cold unusual for Cornwall (it even snowed), and as the New Year came in to the sound of ships' sirens and the explosion of rockets, an enormous black cloud covered the moon and Daphne wondered if it was a bad omen and what the coming year would hold for her. She was troubled by her relationship with Geoffrey. Within a short while, she was to become involved again, this time in a far more serious affair with a young actor called Carol Reed, later to become better known as a film director. She found them both attractive in their different ways, but they were neither of them to have a lasting effect on her. It was Gerald who would ensure that, Gerald whose emotional influence she would never be able to shake off. Their relationship was crucial to what she was and what she was to become, and its impact would affect her, indeed haunt her, for the rest of her life.

* * *

'What happened to Daphne was that she was deeply in love with her father, her emotional life was really entirely tied up with him even though before her marriage she was not happy in his world. She was very much the odd girl out, the one who hated the social scene. In those days she did not even enjoy the theatre particularly,' says A.L. Rowse. Years later, when she came to write her slender autobiography, Daphne would discuss with him her relationship with her father. 'He was a man of extreme charm,' says Rowse, 'and he was fond, not to say possessive, of all three daughters but he had an absolute fixation on Daphne which she reciprocated.'

The emotional bond with Gerald scarcely diminished with time, surviving her involvements with Geoffrey and Carol, and even her marriage. To the end of her days she could never get away from Gerald. There is no doubt that he had a charismatic personality, coupled, as Rowse notes, with that enormous charm, and that he had a powerful effect on young women. At close quarters his personality must have been overwhelming, especially to a shy and introverted girl such as Daphne. He cannot have been unaware of her feelings for him, that it was him to whom she always turned, and he must have noticed how cool the relationship was between Daphne and Muriel. There is no doubt that he fostered it. By the time she was in her early teens, if Daphne did not want to attend church with the rest of the family, then she need not go; Gerald preferred to spend his Sunday mornings walking on Hampstead Heath, so why shouldn't Daphne join him? She readily agreed and so, weekend after weekend, they would walk the Heath together, while he poured out to her his feelings about his family, the new play and, when she was older, his early emotional entanglements.

It was Gerald who, with heightened instincts, immediately felt the attraction between Geoffrey and Daphne that first summer when she was not quite fifteen, although no responsible parent would have encouraged an emotional and physical involvement between a fourteen-year-old girl and a cousin twice her age. That being said, however, Gerald

71

was always to remain deeply suspicious of his nephew. The situation must have been incredibly confusing for Daphne, as she struggled with her adolescence and the first stirrings of sexuality. Although the du Maurier household was unconventional by the middle-class standards of the day, sex was not a subject that could possibly have been discussed even if Gerald and Muriel had been very different parents. Wrestling with those early strong emotions, she was unable to understand why what she was beginning to feel towards Geoffrey so closely mirrored her feelings for Gerald. After that Christmas at Fowey, when it must have become apparent to Gerald that Geoffrey had never lost his interest in Daphne, he tackled him about it, asking him outright if he were in love with her.

Geoffrey admitted that he was, in spite of his second marriage, but also told Gerald that he fully realized nothing could ever come of it; by that time Daphne had told him so herself. Trying to come to terms with such strong feelings engendered by members of her own family she looked to medieval Italy and the Borgias. If she were Lucretia then Geoffrey must be Cesare, her Borgia brother, and Gerald Alexander, the Borgia father; a reference to the supposition that Lucretia had enjoyed incestuous relationships with both. Shortly after Gerald had set off abroad once more on a theatrical tour she had to have a tooth extracted under gas. She emerged from the anaesthetic calling out for Gerald. 'So it was not the Borgia brother but the Borgia father that the unconscious self demanded.'

She always maintained that she had never been much of a 'signal sender' to either sex. She saw the sexual relationship between men and women in the most matter-of-fact way. It was all to do with chemistry, a fusion brought about by the need to perpetuate the human race. She was and never had been, she said, 'a very sexy person'. Her later relationship with Frederick 'Boy' Browning, who was to become her husband, meant a great deal to her; she only realized how much after his death, but it fitted into a separate compartment in her life and its physical side was not what was important to her. Emotionally, too, it was on a different plane to her feelings for Gerald. A.L. Rowse believes that because of her relationship with Gerald there would always be a part of her she could never give either to her husband or her children. 'I think that is why she shut her eyes to Browning's infidelities, even to the affair that went on for years.'

Intense father/daughter relationships are a recurring theme in her books and stories, the oddest incarnation occurring in *The Progress of Julius*, completed just before her marriage. As a novel it will be dealt with later, but its theme is relevant now – that of a man who, having treated all the previous women in his life badly, becomes totally obsessed with his daughter, an emotional fixation of such intensity that, rather than see her leave him for a husband, he murders her on the eve of her wedding. This is the most melodramatic handling of the theme, but in a later novel, *The Scapegoat*, it is the surrogate father's relationship with his precocious supposed daughter that provides the emotional pivot of the book, not the adult women who are involved to a greater or lesser extent with the man the Scapegoat impersonates.

In the short story 'A Border Line Case', the young actress heroine causes her father to have a heart attack after seeing her playing Viola in *Twelfth Night*. He dies as a result and, heartbroken, she goes to Ireland to seek out his dearest friend, a man who had meant so much to him years before but with whom he had lost touch. She tracks him down on an island in a lake, from which he runs an IRA active service unit, and immediately falls in love with him. Only after they have made love does she realize that it is he who is her real father, not the man with whom she had grown up, the man who had married her mother in all good faith, believing that the child she was carrying was his. His seeing her dressed as a boy and looking like his friend had caused his death. In another strange story, 'The Archduchess', a Utopian society falls apart when, following a Marxist-style revolution, the reigning family are no longer allowed to marry incestuously, the luck of the principality having depended on brother/sister, father/daughter marriages.

'There is no such thing as romantic love,' Daphne wrote towards the end of her life, in an essay written shortly before the death of her husband entitled 'This I Believe'. She ponders if in future all children might be conceived in test-tubes and if this might well be a less wasteful and time-consuming way of reproduction, although she recognizes that for most people there is an emotional necessity to conceive and rear children within a family; for even in the sexual act what we are seeking, she says, is long-lost comfort as we look for basic peace and reunion within ourselves. It is our misfortune that so many marriages fail. Then she sums up her philosophy. 'Incest being denied us, we must make do with second best.' Amplifying this later, in conversation, she explained that in part what she meant was that incest, not necessarily the physical act, but the emotional quest for the father, brother, sister – the perfect 'other' – ruled the world; at least the emotional world. Gerald would always be the perfect other.

When Gerald learned she was to marry Frederick Browning, after a very brief courtship, his reaction was to cry, 'It's not fair'. Marriage must have come as a relief after such an intensity of mutual attraction and by marrying as she did she had made a statement, an attempt to break the suffocating tie. But if she really thought she could rid herself of Gerald, even write him out of her emotional consciousness after his death, then she did not succeed. Her biography, *Gerald*, written shortly after he died, brings him to life with a painful honesty she was never able to reveal when writing about herself.

In the introduction to the last book on which she worked, *The Rebecca Notebooks*, compiled when she was seventy-three, she writes yet again about George, and then turns to Gerald, apologizing for the fact that, 'I have not, as yet, written about my own children and my seven grandchildren.' Except indirectly, she never had and she never would.

Her essay on Gerald, entitled *The Matinée Idol*, written in 1973 when she was sixty-six, retraces his life once again although this time in brief. It also deals rather more directly with his emotional entanglements than the biography, where no doubt she felt she had to spare Muriel's feelings, although it affirms his deep and abiding affection for Muriel which was so totally reciprocated. She recollects yet again the moment in *Dear Brutus* when, acting as the failed artist Will Dearth, Gerald realizes he has lost his 'dream daughter'. Daphne recalls that the lost, bewildered, anguished expression in his eyes at that moment was something she had never forgotten and would take with her to the grave.

As she grew older, his almost ghostly presence became ever stronger so that scarcely a day passed when she was not reminded of him, whether it was by photographs, his many small possessions which were all around her or by his signet ring which she always wore. She recalls him dressed in his beautiful silk pyjamas ('from Beale & Inman of Bond Street'), cigarette in mouth and, unaware of her standing watching him, waltzing with an imaginary partner to the music of a gramophone playing the 'sensuous' waltz song, 'Charmaine'.

'Unseen by friends or fans, and unobserved, so he imagines by any member of his family, Gerald obeys the instinct of a lifetime and is acting to himself.' As an image it is potent stuff, so potent that nothing was ever able to match it.

CHAPTER 9

Menabilly

After Christmas the family returned again to London leaving Daphne behind. Gerald was immediately swallowed up in the world of theatre. As popular as ever, 1927 had seen a whole string of successes, starting with *Interference*, a play in which he gave a *tour de force* of a performance – a scene in dumbshow when he faked an alibi for his wife's death. This was followed by his direction of Gladys Cooper in a play by Somerset Maugham, *The Letter*. Also, Sir Squire Bancroft, the old Shakespearean actor, had died at the age of eighty-four leaving him the rights to the cast-iron melodrama, *Diplomacy*, and future plans included staging this and also directing Gracie Fields in a play called *SOS*.

The du Mauriers had not been particularly happy about letting Daphne stay on in Fowey; they thought that she was both silly and selfish but, as she set off for a walk with her dog Bingo after waving them off all she could feel was a sense of profound relief. Once again she began working on her short stories although she was also becoming increasingly fascinated by the history of the Slades and their schooner. She considered writing a poem about it, and as she was heavily involved in reading the works of Emily Brontë at the time, even debated beginning it with the line, 'No battered hulk am I' – in memory of her. She had plenty of spare time. Although Muriel had not left her with a cook this time, arrangements had been made for her to eat at the Ferry Boat Inn. One marvels at the luxury in which provision was always made so that Daphne would be spared any household chores and her time be entirely her own.

Daphne soon settled back into a routine of writing, followed by walking, sailing, rabbiting or fishing. She was invited to tea at The Haven by the Quiller-Couches, an excursion which was to have long-lasting results. 'Q', Sir Arthur Quiller-Couch, was the son of a Cornish doctor who, as well as being editor of the first *Oxford Book of English Verse* and holding the chair of English at Cambridge, was also one of the best-loved writers of his time. It is, perhaps, somewhat ironic in view of the way matters evolved that it was he, and not Daphne, who first put what was to become known as 'du Maurier' country on the literary map. His most popular novels and short stories were set in and around Troy Town, his beloved Fowey, and he even went so far as to christen his daughter Foy, which is the way local Cornish people pronounce 'Fowey'. Daphne's first visit to The Haven was to result in a long and affectionate friendship with Foy.

The helpful Adams had also found a large sailing-boat which he thought might be just the thing for Daphne and the two of them went off to Falmouth together to have a look at her; Gerald had offered to pay half the cost of it if Daphne decided it was what she wanted. Full of enthusiasm at the prospect of soon owning the boat, she agreed to return to London again only to discover, soon after she was back at Cannon Hall, that the owner of the boat had changed his mind. Nor could she use the room over the garage to write in any more because the ubiquitous Cousin Geoffrey had installed himself there prior to going off on another tour of Australia.

The affair progressed a little from the hand-holding and knee-stroking of Christmas to kisses in the drawing room after everyone else had gone to bed. In some respects Geoffrey and Gerald seem to have been very alike; both enjoyed recounting tales of past conquests, Geoffrey raking over the embers with Daphne while they sat in their dressing-gowns in the drawing room, Gerald holding forth on his during the strange tête-à-têtes he continued to hold with Daphne in the dining room after Sunday supper. In February 1928 Geoffrey finally left on his foreign tour (after the conversation with Gerald already recounted in the last chapter) and Daphne went over to visit Fernande in Paris where she received a constant stream of letters from him. Before leaving she had submitted several of her short stories to the literary agent, A.P. Watt, and this time she had a far more positive response than she had had to the poetry she had earlier taken to Heinemann. Gerald still had dreams of Daphne making a career in the cinema and had persuaded Ivor Novello to give her a small part in a film he was planning to make, but this time Daphne was adamant, she would not then – or ever – work either in the cinema or the theatre, no matter how hard Gerald might pressurize her.

In April she returned from Paris for her parents' silver wedding celebration on the 11th and found it all rather sad and touching, not least because neither was pleased with the presents they gave each other. Muriel had had her portrait painted especially for Gerald, but it was obvious, Daphne recounts, that he did not like it at all. He, on the other hand, had brought her an extremely expensive bracelet which turned out to be too small for her.

Then it was back to Fowey and this time nothing was to prise her away until October. Adams suggested to her that instead of trying to find a suitable sailing-boat she should get Slade's boat-yard to build one to her own specifications. The idea instantly appealed, especially because the boat would be built by the family who had actually built *Jane Slade*. So the boat was ordered and, at the same time, she began seriously researching Jane's history, learning what she could about her family from the current boat-builder, Ernie Slade; finding Jane's grave in Lanteglos churchyard and, to her delight, being given the figurehead of Jane when the old schooner was finally broken up. As more and more material about the Slades came to hand, she realized that there was far too much to be fitted into a short story and, for the first time, began seriously to consider the possibility of writing a full-length book. The Slade's family bible contained a family tree going back to the birth of Jane's husband and gradually Daphne began to see the possibility of a book spanning the generations, starting with Jane and ending in the present day.

For her twenty-first birthday in May, Muriel gave her a thirteen-foot rowing boat of her own so that she could play around on the river while waiting for her sailing-boat to be finished. It was taking considerably longer than anticipated, because it was luxuriously fitted out, even down to cooking facilities and a lavatory. *Marie Louise* as she was to call it, was finally launched in August, with Gerald and Daphne on board, Daphne having broken a bottle of champagne on the bow for luck, but it was September before she was finally able to take it out on the river accompanied by Angela, who was seasick. It was a large and substantial craft, ketch-rigged, with two masts and five sails. Sails in those days were made of heavy, closely-woven cotton sailcloth, no man-made fibres or terylene, and it is obvious that *Marie Louise* was a very heavy craft for a woman to handle. It says something for Daphne's talent for seamanship that she was able to manoeuvre her in the tricky waters of the South Cornish coast.

She agreed to return to London in October with Angela, but this time Muriel, sensing defeat, told her that there was no reason why Ferryside should not become her base, particularly if she could earn money from her writing to help pay for its upkeep. But before she left Ferryside she was to discover the house besides which almost everything else in her life was to pale.

From her walks above Sandy Cove she could just see a roof showing through the trees across the river and, after making some enquiries about it, she was told it was that of an old house called Menabilly whose owner, a Dr Rashleigh, rarely lived in it. The Rashleighs are a very old west-country family – in fact they can trace their ancestry directly back to the thirteenth century. In early Tudor times they had had a town house on the quay in Fowey – it is now the Ship Inn – but later, as their fortunes improved towards the end of the sixteenth century, they had built themselves a manor house a few miles outside the town. Menabilly today looks very different than it did when Daphne first saw it, for then it was not only neglected and covered in creeper, but was almost swamped by a huge wing built in Victorian times which the late Philip Rashleigh and his wife, Veronica, have now had removed.

Daphne, however, was so intrigued by that glimpse of the house that she asked the Quiller-Couches if they knew anything of its history. They told her how the Rashleighs had held out there during the Civil War and had suffered severely for it when the house was sacked by the forces of Parliament. She was also told that there was supposed to be a ghost – a lady in blue – and that there had been talk, when the new wing was built in Victorian times, of a Cavalier's skeleton being discovered bricked up in a wall. According to her informants, the present owner disliked the place, as it held unhappy memories for him of when he had lived there with his guardian as a small boy, following the early deaths of both his parents. Encouraged by this, she set off one afternoon to see if she could find the house, accompanied by a reluctant Angela with her Pekinese. They started walking along the overgrown drive, but soon began to think they must have taken the wrong turning, as it twisted and turned for a good three miles while the weak afternoon sun faded and there was still no sign of any house.

Recounting her own feelings about the expedition later, Angela notes that she found the whole experience distinctly eerie as they clambered with difficulty over fallen tree trunks and pushed their way through thickets of rhododendrons in the failing light, to the accompaniment of hooting owls and the distant barking of foxes. Even the dogs, her peke and

Daphne's Bingo, seemed uneasy. Finally they stumbled into a cove which they recognized, but knew to be a good long walk from home; as by this time the moon was rising, they called it a day and trudged back home along the coast to Fowey and so to Bodinnick. Daphne, however, was all the more determined to get to the house and the following day dragged Angela out yet again to look for it. This time they made their way along another drive and eventually reached it. The immediate reactions of the two sisters are interesting.

To Angela, Menabilly was a distinct let down, a disappointment after all the effort they had made – more than that even, she actually found it a lonely, gloomy, indeed a frightening place. She could well believe that it really was haunted as they pressed their faces to the windows and saw the furniture inside covered in dust, stacks of old pictures and a child's rocking-horse.

To Daphne it was love at first sight, in spite of its air of neglect, the gloomy creeper and the Victorian windows which spoiled the façade. For her Menabilly was bathed in grace and charm, a place holding secrets that would be divulged only to those 'who loved her well'. She determined there and then that one day she would live there. The now-returned Rashleighs guard Menabilly with love and care, only too well aware that Daphne's association with it has made it world famous; casual visitors and tourists are not encouraged. But it is easy to see, even at the end of this brash twentieth century, that Menabilly has a genuine magic, and a sense of a past continuum which is becoming increasingly rare. To a visitor it has something of the fairy-tale air of the strange château described in Alain Fournier's novel, *Le Grand Meaulnes*.

Strangely enough Daphne was not the only writer to be haunted by the neglected, but beautiful old house. Several years after Daphne first saw it, while it was still derelict, May Sarton, the American writer, was paying a visit to another old house, Kilmarth, which later would become closely associated with Daphne. Kilmarth was another Rashleigh property, a dower house, and it had been leased to Professor Charles

Singer, who was writing his *History of Medicine* at the time, and also carrying out scientific experiments in the basement. It was the remains of these, discovered later, that helped trigger off the idea for Daphne's penultimate novel, *The House on the Strand*. May Sarton was twenty-four at the time; recovering from a serious illness she had been sent to Kilmarth to convalesce.

In an article published first in *The New Yorker* and later in her book, *I Knew A Phoenix*, she tells of the chaotic Singer household at Kilmarth and how Julian Huxley, a fellow guest, was researching the possibility of growing eucalyptus as a crop to feed koala bears. He was also interested in varieties of bamboo and it was suggested that it might be an idea to explore a nearby overgrown estate, where bamboo was running riot after twenty years of neglect; and so, May Sarton set off, 'encased in mackintoshes, armed with rubbers and canes', to find Menabilly.

'We got out and began to penetrate into what looked like jungle, and in an hour moved from Himalayan brooks where rhododendrons towered, to forests of bamboo which might have been Malaya. We gazed up through a roof of flowering laurel to immense jungle-growth of English beeches, found ourselves in an avenue of camellias walking on carpets of white snow, and came out into glades of classic English spring where bluebells grew so thick they made blue pools. We went up and down and around while Julian Huxley, a long-legged stork, darted here and there whooping with delight or, silent as an Indian and as concentrated, tracked a bird, naming off and calling back to us the individual songs he could distinguish from what sounded to me like an indistinguishable chorus. When we stopped for a moment in a misty grove of bamboo, someone remarked that it would not be too surprising to meet an elephant . . .'

Eventually they reached the end of the drive. 'At last we climbed out of the jungle part of the estate to the ghostly house itself, a Victorian pile, surrounded by lakes of grass, by grazing sheep, by ancient English oaks, and covered with flowering japonica. We climbed up onto the terrace and peered through the windows, and there, intact, was a complete Victorian world, untouched by fifty years, sending us back our own reflected faces, as if we ourselves were ghosts being summoned from a distant past. I did have the sensation all through that weekend that I was dreaming: What was real? What was unreal?'

Daphne left Fowey that October determined to return within weeks but, as fate would have it, it was to be six months before she saw either Ferryside or Menabilly again. The secure and comfortable life of Cannon Hall encompassed her once more, leaving her wondering why she should be discontented with her lot and why in spite of everything she felt so estranged from the way of life that both her sisters enjoyed so much. A.P. Watt had had no success to date in placing any of her stories, so the notion of instant earnings from writing looked even more remote. However, 'Uncle Willie' Beaumont, who was editor of the magazine *The Bystander*, offered to publish one, *And Now God the Father*, for a fee of ten guineas if she were prepared to work on it and then cut it down to length, but this she refused point blank to do. Eventually, amused by her stand, he agreed to consider some of her other stories, saying that if he thought they were any good he would try and publish one or two, if and when space became available. Bored and disconsolate once more, she went off to spend Christmas in Switzerland with Edgar Wallace and his family where for the first time she actually seems to have enjoyed the round of parties and dances which followed winter sports, the late nights spent chatting over drinks, and even went so far as to flirt with a number of the young men who obviously found her attractive, one of whom was Carol Reed.

Carol Reed's background was almost as exotic as Daphne's. He was the son of the great actor-manager (and friend of Gerald), Sir Herbert Beerbohm-Tree, his mother Beatrice May Pinney, Tree's most permanent mistress. Tree was as attractive to women, in his own way, as Gerald. He had three daughters by his wife, Maud (herself an actress), one of whom was the Viola who became such a close friend of the du Maurier family. Maud was a flamboyant and strong-minded woman from whom Tree sought relief with a series of passing fancies, some of which developed into long-term relationships. Among these was May.

May Pinney, the daughter of a clergyman, who had had a most conventional upbringing, was an unlikely person to become the mistress of an actor. That she did so was almost fortuitous. Ten years after Tree's marriage to Maud, the seventeen-year-old May Pinney went to the Haymarket Theatre one day to see Tree in *The Dancing Girl* by Arthur Jones, then one of London's most successful dramatists. May developed such a crush on Tree that she wrote to him saying she had fallen in love with him and could she meet him? He wrote back with words to the effect that this happened to him all the time, he was married, a meeting was out of the question, but he thanked her all the same.

Nothing daunted May who wrote again, pleading with him to meet her. Her letter was forwarded to Tree while he was away in Austria and, having decided enough was enough, he threw it into the fireplace of his hotel room with other waste paper and set light to it. When he returned later that night, the only piece of paper which had not been burned was the corner of May's letter with her address on it. He decided that Fate must have taken a hand and so replied to her.

They met and within no time became lovers. May was soon pregnant with their eldest child, Claude, so Tree took a house for her on Putney Hill where she was to bear him a further four children, in all four sons and a daughter, changing hers and their names to 'Reed', saying it was 'because I was but a broken reed at the foot of the mighty Tree'. Commenting on the situation years later, Maud Tree remarked drily that her husband's affairs generally 'started with a compliment and ended with a confinement'. Later the two households would be joined by a third, that of the ex-Gaiety-Girl-turned-actress,

Constance Collier, but even that was insufficient, it seems, for Tree who continued having affairs with young actresses right up until his death in 1917. But whatever his attitude might be towards the women in his life, he seems to have had equal affection for all three households of children, and indeed, the odd children fathered elsewhere as well.

Carol was born on 30 December 1906, five months before Daphne, and he seems to have had a similar temperament as he was considered bookish and introvert. Like her he appears to have had a preference for the world of the imagination but, unlike Daphne, he was drawn towards the theatre and does not seem to have enjoyed his robust schooling at King's School, Canterbury. Carol was only ten when his father died, but he remained very proud of him and deeply protective towards his mother, causing eyebrows to raise at a time when boasting about being an illegitimate child, albeit of a famous father, was unheard of. When the time came for him to leave school his mother tried to persuade him at least to consider another occupation and suggested he joined his brother Guy who was working as a farmer in America. He did so, hated it, and returned to London where he seriously set about getting himself work as an actor. Among the people he approached was Sybil Thorndike who, in turn, put him in touch with Bruce Winston who took him on in his first acting part. He was just eighteen.

Later he was befriended by Edgar Wallace, who gave him work in his own film studio, and it was through him that he became involved with Gerald du Maurier's theatre company. Carol seems to have enjoyed his early years as an actor, but then found himself becoming more and more interested in directing. It was while he was working in Wallace's film studio that he and Daphne first met. He was twenty-two years old, slim and handsome. He pursued Daphne once they had both returned to England in the New Year and it appears she quickly returned his interest, even admitting to herself that she must be in love with him, 'at least a bit'. The affair progressed rapidly as they went out together several times a week for intimate dinners, followed by a film or show and often supper at the Kit-Kat or Café Anglais. Carol owned a battered old Morris and sometimes they would put on their old clothes and drive out to the suburbs or to the country, returning home in the small hours. Daphne had moved into the garage room, using it as a study/bedroom and when Carol had brought her home she would lean out of the skylight window talking to him for hours; she had dissuaded him from climbing in with her for fear of his being seen by the family.

Gerald, closely watching the progress of the affair, quickly became deeply jealous and the continuing sessions between Daphne and he, still held after Sunday supper, became a desperate ordeal. Gerald questioned her on whether or not she was in love with Carol, how deep her feelings were, what she did when they were out together late at night, after the restaurants and theatres had closed, exploding into raging disbelief when she told him they went driving out into the country or along the Thames to the East End. She tried to explain to him that apart from anything else the excursions to the country or down river to Limehouse Reach and Wapping gave her good ideas for plots for stories, but he would have none of it. He told her that coming home in the early hours must stop and, finding he was getting nowhere, enlisted Muriel's aid. Muriel's cold disapproval only brought out the obstinacy in Daphne who was determined she would continue to see Carol as and when she chose, a situation which became more and more intolerable. It meant that after a passionate good-night, Carol would have to drop her somewhere along Cannon Hall, leaving her to creep home only too well aware as she did so that Gerald was lurking behind a twitching bedroom curtain.

It was all too much for her to cope with and in April 1929 she returned to Fowey, leaving an unhappy Carol behind. Two days later she got up at five o'clock in the morning and rowed herself in her dinghy across to Pridmouth Cove below Menabilly. This time she had no trouble finding her way to the house which soon lay in front of her, bathed in the early morning light. She prowled around the outbuildings, pressed her face to the windows again, imagining the generations of Rashleighs who had lived and died there. It was midday before she was able to bring herself to leave, by which time she was light-headed from lack of breakfast.

This time, however, she was unable to walk away from her emotional pressures. Geoffrey had separated from his second wife and had returned to London where he was living alone without a job or any money, writing miserable letters to her full of self-pity about his wasted life, while an increasingly impatient Carol wrote and telephoned, daily begging her to come back to London. Her moods swung widely (she was to note on one occasion that she had suddenly understood Christianity for the first time!), but the story of Jane Slade was finally beginning to take shape at the back of her mind. She was haunted by a picture of herself as Jane, standing on the cliffs below Castle Point deep in an emotional conversation with a grown-up son. As an image it recurred constantly, and she knew she should really try to get something down on paper. Gloomily she decided that in her present state of mind she was likely to reach forty before she organized herself sufficiently well to actually write it.

Just after her twenty-second birthday *And Now God The Father* was finally published in *The Bystander*, but only after she had given in and agreed that it should be cut. Thus, feeling very self-conscious, she walked into the local branch of W.H. Smith's in Fowey and bought a copy of the magazine so that she could actually see herself in print for the first time. The next obvious step would have been to start working hard on a first draft of the story of Jane Slade, but she was emotionally unsettled, torn between remaining in Fowey to write and returning to Carol in London, with all that would mean in terms of family problems.

The haunting Menabilly had bitten deep into her soul, even deeper than Ferryside and certainly deeper than the still shadowy world of Jane Slade. She could hardly have foreseen that eventually her mixture of determination and obstinacy was to overcome every difficulty put in her way, and that Menabilly was to become not only her home but the inspiration behind a whole string of bestsellers of which the story of Jane Slade, *The Loving Spirit*, was but the forerunner.

CHAPTER 10

The Loving Spirit

929 marked something of a turning point in the lives of both Gerald and Daphne. His smooth career in the theatre and extravagant life-style were to become ever more difficult to maintain, while she was to take a major step, that of sitting down and writing her first full-length novel. Within two years she was also to marry although that was something neither of them could have foreseen.

As has already been mentioned, the current events of the day seem to have affected the family little, neither Angela nor Daphne finding them worthy of much note in their diaries or memoirs. We learn that 'the King died', or that a Labour government had been elected, but nothing of the desperate problems facing most of the population, the Depression and growing unemployment. Obviously, the increasingly serious economic situation could hardly fail to affect Gerald's income, not least because shortage of money meant hard times for theatres. He was also being hotly pursued by the Inland Revenue. He had never paid much attention to his income tax and now, after years of ignoring the situation, the demands were getting ever more pressing. He began casting around frantically for ways of making extra money, one of which was to lend his name to 'du Maurier' cigarettes. According to his biographer, James Harding, he did not actually smoke them himself, preferring those without cork tips as he enjoyed the feeling of the 'raw smoke curling right down into his lungs.'

Not surprisingly in view of this, his health began to decline. He had a persistent cough, which he put down to catching chills, but which failed to respond to the wide range of medicaments, both conventional and otherwise, with which he dosed himself; it seems likely that it marked the onset of the cancer that would finally kill him, a cancer almost certainly of the lungs. He also became subject to a depression which Hardy puts down to his financial worries along with his being unable to reconcile himself to growing older; but it is significant that in this he showed symptoms of a family trait, both Robert and Louis-Mathurin and his own father, George, having fallen victim to it.

Gerald had also lost his guide, friend and mentor, Frank Curzon, who had died suddenly at the age of fifty-nine. This meant that Gerald himself had to take on far more responsibility for the financial side of management, something for which he was not suited and which he had always happily left to Frank. As if this was not enough, his lease on the Wyndham's Theatre expired and he had to move to the St James's Theatre. Gerald's problems are not mentioned in the memoirs of either of his daughters, but it is impossible to imagine that they were not aware of them.

Be that as it may, Daphne went into 1929 still living what would seem nowadays to have been a highly privileged lifestyle. There was London and the continuing relationship with Carol and, to a lesser extent, with Geoffrey; there was Fowey, where she sailed *Marie Louise* on the river and also explored further afield in Cornwall, accompanied by the friendly Foy Quiller-Couch; and Paris and Fernande who still continued to play an important role in her life, while she also accepted invitations to join holiday parties elsewhere in Europe.

Back in Hampstead after her short visit to Fowey, Daphne was once again plunged into emotional turmoil. It seems she still could not entirely shake off her attachment for Geoffrey, who had wanted to pick up the threads of their relationship where they had left off, but now there was also Carol. She notes how thin and pale Carol looked when they had dinner together on her first night back (before she had to dash home so as not to upset Gerald and Muriel), whereas Geoffrey, whom she had met the same day for lunch, seemed well and fit despite his miserable letters. Possibly, she thought, she did love Carol but was certainly not swept off her feet by him. Geoffrey was still the Borgia brother, perhaps Carol was the Borgia son?

Following the success of her story being published in *The Bystander*, 'Uncle Willie' introduced her to Nancy Pearn of the literary agency Curtis Brown, who took some more stories from her, promising to try and place them. Carol was acting in a play at the Shaftesbury Theatre and she saw him nearly every day, often waiting in his dressing room during matinées, when he would dash down and kiss her every time he was off stage. They would spend hours together driving in the car either talking exhaustively or sitting in companionable silence. He was indeed lovable, she thought, but immature, even childish. Daphne was now twenty-three and quite capable of knowing her own mind; but her parents' reaction to the relationship continued to be hostile and eventually when she did not get back from a supper party until one o'clock in the morning, Muriel told her that both she and Gerald had had quite enough and had written to Carol to tell him so! Carol apologized to the du Mauriers, promising it would not happen again but neither he nor Daphne could see how that could be, as the curtain did not come down on his play until well after ten, which meant that by the time they had had supper, she was bound to be late. He pondered on whether he could scrape up enough money to enable them to marry, she was not so sure about it, foreseeing that if she did marry him the independence she enjoyed so much in Fowey would be gone forever.

In June she had a strange interlude when she was invited by a millionaire Otto Kahn, whom she had met in Berlin in 1927, to join him and his party on a steam yacht in the Norwegian fjords. Gerald and Muriel enthusiastically encouraged her to accept (although she wondered why they could be so happy about sending her off to spend weeks in a confined space on a boat with a host of young people neither of them knew) and so she finally accepted. It was not the young men, however, who turned out to be a problem, but her host Otto Kahn who was in his sixties and had a definite penchant for young women. The yacht was luxurious, the life-style lazy, the country beautiful if a trifle forbidding and it reminded Daphne of an idea she had had for a story once about a young man running away to sea. Perhaps, she thought, he could also go to Norway.

The attentions of Otto Kahn became embarrassing leaving her wondering what to do about them without actually offending him. The course she took was certainly unusual and might well have been totally misconstrued. Finding herself manoeuvred into a lonely situation with him on the banks of a fjord she announced she could not wait to have a swim and, there and then, stripped and dived naked into the water. Apparently the ploy worked and later he offered to buy her a fur coat which she declined, choosing a dagger instead . . . Meanwhile the sexual activities of the rest of the party (apart from a hearty fellow who spent the trip reading a book called *The Sexual Life of Savages*), made the *après-ski* goings-on during her holiday in Caux seem like 'a kindergarten'.

She returned to find Carol about to go off on tour in his play, *The Calendar* by Edgar Wallace, and so almost immediately she went to see Fernande in France. Perhaps it was these continual journeyings when she was young that left her wanting to remain mostly in the one place once she was older. She read Katherine Mansfield with avidity during her trip to France and visited her grave at Montparnasse. Ideas for stories flooded her mind as she walked the streets or sat in cafés and she wrote constantly, carried away and unable to stop, so that by the time she returned to England she had a sheaf of them to give to Curtis Brown, where Michael

Joseph had been asked to act for her. Joseph was to play an enormously important part in her professional life and, after they had discussed her work and he had made a number of constructive suggestions as to how it could be improved, she told him about her idea for the story of Jane Slade, which had continued to brew at the back of her mind. Carol was still away on tour, so it seemed the ideal time – finally – to go down to Fowey and write a book.

Unfortunately the family chose this moment to go down as well, so that the house was always full, with friends coming down in relays, a hectic scene which drove Daphne out of the house and, once again, to explore the Menabilly estate. This time she took three friends to see the house with her and to their surprise they found they could open one of the windows. Gingerly they tiptoed round the house where everything seemed to be just as the last occupant had left it – even to a corkscrew lying by a bottle on the sideboard – but all covered in dust like a scene out of *Great Expectations*. They peered into the library, pushed the rocking-horse which creaked on its hinges . . . In the end the atmosphere drove all of them out into the sunlight and away, but Daphne felt herself becoming ever more haunted by the past, the past of the Rashleighs in the strange, empty old house, and that of the Slades and their schooners. She found the constant laughter and chat of the family holiday at Ferryside hard to take, but had no wish to leave it although she was receiving pressing letters from Carol nearly every day.

Finally, at the end of September, the last of the family left, even Muriel and Angela. This time Muriel decided that to economize the house must be shut up and arranged for Daphne to stay with a Miss Roberts in a cottage opposite, though she allowed her to keep one room at Ferryside open to use as a study. Miss Roberts cosseted her and cleaned for her, filling a hip-bath with hot water for her every morning, putting her hot meals down in front of her at regular intervals. Still deeply involved with Emily Brontë's poetry she took the title of her book from a line in one of her poems and finally, on the morning of 3 October 1929 laid out a clean piece of paper and wrote in capital letters 'THE LOVING SPIRIT'. Jane Slade, she decided, should become Janet Coombe; Polruan, along the coast from Boddinick and opposite the entrance to Fowey Harbour, Plyn; and so she started.

She disciplined herself into a set pattern of writing all morning, then either going for a row in the afternoon or a walk in the woods with the dog, Bingo. The book, she decided, would be divided into four parts, each one dealing with a different generation. She must have worked at a tremendous rate because she had finished the first part in two weeks; by which time she could hardly tear herself away from it, and exercise, the boat, and everything else went by the board. By 3 November, a month after starting, she had finished Part Two. Part Three was more difficult, as it brought the story nearer to her in time and she felt she needed to research the London of the 1880s, though it appears that all she had to do was express a wish and someone would grant it, for within days of her telling her landlady that she needed the information, a man appeared with an armful of detailed, well-illustrated source-books.

By the end of November she was still writing away, by this time with a lump on her finger from holding the pen, breaking off only for Sunday suppers at the Quiller-Couches. Daphne always stressed that from the earliest days she had noted down events or situations which might one day make a story, and she also seems to have had a remarkable facility for committing them to memory until they were needed. She might well have done this with a story originating from Foy Quiller-Couch.

Oenone Fisher (née Rashleigh) used to spend holidays with the Quiller-Couches at this time, coming down to Fowey from Stoketon every year for the Fowey Regatta. She did not meet Daphne until later – 'although they used to tell me about their young friend who lived over the river and was a writer' – but Foy Quiller-Couch, she says, was a splendid raconteur who should have written her stories down. One of them was of a strange man called Crawford who turned up at The Haven one day claiming to be the lawyer who had defended the notorious Madeleine Smith.

Madeleine Smith was the daughter of a wealthy Glasgow architect who, in 1855, embarked on a love affair with thirty-four-year-old Pierre Emile L'Angelier from Jersey. In 1856 they secretly became lovers, but Madeleine's father began to suspect something was going on and forbade his daughter to continue to have any further contact with L'Angelier and, more than that, told her he had already found a suitable husband for her. L'Angelier became difficult and jealous and Madeleine felt it was better to break the relationship off, demanding the return of all the indiscreet love letters she had written to him. Not only did he refuse to do this, he threatened to send them to her father to inform him of the exact nature of their relationship. In February 1857 L'Angelier became ill. The bouts of illness became more and more severe and on 23 March after returning to his lodgings following a meeting with Madeleine, he died. An autopsy showed his body to contain eighty-two grains of arsenic.

Madeleine admitted that she had bought arsenic, to kill rats and in June 1857 she was tried for murder, the prosecution case being that she had poisoned L'Angelier by putting arsenic in a chocolate drink that she had given him. But it turned out that L'Angelier had taken arsenic himself as a medicine (it was a popular remedy at that time in small doses). The result was that the jury were unable to make up their minds as to whether Madeleine was guilty or not, and so brought in the Scottish verdict of 'Not Proven'.

Crawford, so Foy Quiller-Couch told Oenone, fell deeply in love with Madeleine himself and the couple went first to Italy and then to America. Gradually, Crawford became convinced that Madeleine was also trying to poison him and became so frightened that he left the States without telling her, for fear she might follow him. (In fact Madeleine finally married a man called Sheehy, stayed in America and lived to the ripe old age of ninety-three.) Crawford left a box of papers with the Quiller-Couches to be opened only on his death and it remained untouched until after both he and Sir Arthur himself had died. Foy finally opened it, hoping it would contain revelations about Madeleine Smith, only to discover that it was full of rambling documents about the provenance of the Holy Grail!

If Foy told Oenone Rashleigh the story, she is equally likely to have told it to Daphne and its similarity to the plot of *My Cousin Rachel*, which Daphne was to use years later, is striking. Rachel, too, might or might not have poisoned both the men who had been in love with her.

To return, however, to *The Loving Spirit*; by 17 November she had finished Part Three by which time Muriel was pressing her to come back to London for Christmas. She agreed although she was somewhat offended by the letter from her mother which informed her curtly that she trusted she would cease her practice of staying out late every evening 'which made me', writes Daphne, 'feel like a maid receiving a reproof from the mistress of the house.'

Carol greeted her with delight but the couple were restricted as to the amount of time they could see each other; he was in another play, Gerald was playing Captain Hook for the last time and so was always up and around late at night at Cannon Hall, while an increasingly depressed and now irritable Geoffrey continued to haunt her. She would like to have been able to confide in Muriel but found it impossible. Aware that Muriel was putting the finishing touches to the decoration of the house for Christmas, she felt unable even to offer to help her. 'Why did I not offer to help M with the flowers? Fear of a rebuff? A lack of interest? A chance, surely, for companionship, ignored by both of us. A mutual shyness between mother and daughter which would endure until after D died five years later . . .'

She bought Carol a gramophone and some records for Christmas, creeping up to his room in the Park Lane Hotel while he was in the theatre, to leave it as a surprise, and noting how badly his clothes needed repairing, the lack of buttons on his shirts. He was delighted when he found it and gave her his own gift, a cigarette lighter with a fountain pen to match. Michael Joseph's present carried a heavy hint, a copy of his own book called *Short Story Writing for Profit*, but she put it to one side, determined to return to Fowey and finish Jane Slade. She saw the Old Year out with a skating party and finished reading *Goodbye to All That* by Robert Graves, before returning to Miss Roberts at The Nook and to rain, hail, sleet and snow.

So she tackled the last and hardest section of the book, Part Four, breaking off only to go and see the remains of a wreck off Pridmouth Cove below Menabilly – a sight which remained in her memory and was to be recalled when she came to write *Rebecca*. The Quiller-Couches found her a typist to whom she entrusted the first three parts of the book, handing it over fully aware of its faults, her poor spelling, clumsy punctuation and tired handwriting. On 30 January 1930 she finished *The Loving Spirit*, all 200,000 words of it – a remarkable achievement in just over three months including several weeks' break for Christmas, and all written by hand as well. She was so excited after she had delivered the final pages of the manuscript to the typist that she was quite unable to eat, and so walked up to Lanteglos churchyard to pay her respects and give thanks at the grave of Jane Slade.

The Loving Spirit has many of the faults of an early work. The style is uneven (the dialogue in the first few pages reads more like stage Irish than indigenous Cornish), Joseph, Jane's son, is portrayed almost as a character in melodrama and all but he and Jane come over as two-dimensional people, but the novel carries within it the seeds of what was to make her such a popular writer, seeds which are not there in the two novels which followed, *I'll Never Be Young Again* and *The Progress of Julius*. They are the seeds of a strong and compelling storyline and a sense of place.

CHAPTER 11

Apprenticeship

It was with a sense of achievement and a feeling of relief that Daphne finally sent her typescript of *The Loving Spirit* off to Michael Joseph before returning to Hampstead. Her mind was already seething with ideas for two more full-length books as well as some short stories. She would continue to write short stories throughout most of her working life; she enjoyed the different techniques the two forms demanded, the first needing the ability to sustain the storyline of a full-length novel, the second the discipline of brevity. The short stories also allowed her to realize a darker side of herself. In those early days it is apparent that the creative spring bubbled up from an apparently inexhaustible well.

She returned to London to find Carol busy in rehearsals, the family on holiday in Capri. Rooting around at Cannon Hall she found an old notebook which had belonged to George and which he had used partly as a diary. She read it with increasing fascination as it mirrored with uncanny accuracy her own wild swings of mood. Later she was to use the little black book to write down her own plot ideas – for luck. After a few weeks nosing around on her own, she took off again for Paris, as Fernande had moved into a larger house in the suburb of Neuilly where she was running her own finishing school for girls from all over Europe.

The Bystander published another of Daphne's stories

entitled *Our Elders and Betters* and she notes that friends and family found it 'shocking'. Just as the shadowy Jane Slade had been in her mind until she could no longer be ignored, so too the young male narrator of her second book was increasingly taking shape.

On 30 March, two months after she had finished *The Loving Spirit*, Michael Joseph wrote to her to tell her that it had been accepted by Heinemann for publication both in Britain and the States where it would appear under the Doubleday imprint. There is no doubt that the du Maurier name helped Daphne in those early days. As the daughter of an actor who was a household name, the granddaughter of the famous *Punch* cartoonist and author of *Trilby*, she was an attractive proposition. *The Loving Spirit* is pleasant enough and it is academic now to consider what might have been the fate of a similar manuscript submitted to a major publisher by a completely unknown twenty-three-year-old girl; if it would ever have reached the bookshops. It did show promise, but a promise which was not realized by the two subsequent novels. Quite possibly, if she had not been a du Maurier, her career as an author might have ended with *The Progress of Julius*. Happily she was and it did not.

The news that the book had been accepted brought the holiday in Paris to an end, as Michael Joseph demanded she return to make cuts, because the book was far too long. This time she did not argue although she told him she was disappointed that Heinemann did not plan to bring it out until the following year. Joseph showed her what needed to be done, how she needed to cut ruthlessly and she took it home steeling herself to edit out whole pages which she had worked so hard to get right.

Almost immediately she started work on *I'll Never Be Young Again*, after making a brief trip to Cornwall where she went on a riding trip to the Lizard peninsula with Foy. This book, however, was written in London as her godmother offered her the use of a room in her office in Orange Street, off Leicester Square. Once again she wrote at a furious pace, this time finishing the book in only two months, on 18 July. She was obviously enthralled by her idea of a young man, about the age of Carol, running away from a stuffy family and having a host of adventures, but the narrator never comes to life and most of what happens to him is entirely unreal. It also suffers from the fault which dogged the next book as well, a strange kind of prurience about sex.

In this, the first of the five books which she narrates in the first person as a young man, the man in question is estranged from his poet father, after showing him some pornographic verse that he has written. We then meet the young man on Waterloo Bridge, possibly about to throw himself off, where he is discovered by the mysterious, but manly, Jake (who has killed a man). Together they take ship and go off on a series of adventures including a trip to the Norwegian fjords where the narrator, Dick, loses his virginity. On their way back to England the ship is wrecked off the coast of Brittany in the Baie des Trépassés, and Jake is drowned. Dick makes his way to Paris, lives off the streets, and by working in brothels, finally sets up home with a music student called Hesta, whom he has seduced and who finally leaves him, whereupon he returns home, finds his father has died and becomes respectable.

Angela was to describe it as, a 'charming piece in the style of Hemingway' (which it certainly is not), while the anonymous *Punch* reviewer, quoted on the back of the current paperback edition, says: 'Daphne du Maurier's descriptions of riding in Norwegian mountains, of life before the mast and in foreign capitals ring as true as her transportation of a young man's thoughts and talk', which might well be taken two ways. When she showed the book to Quiller-Couch he told her he did not like it and that people just did not talk in such a way. It is assumed he meant that he was shocked by the things her characters said to each other, but it seems more likely that he meant exactly what he said. People do not talk to each other as do the characters in *I'll Never Be Young Again*, certainly not young men. The best thing in the book are the descriptions of Paris.

Having written two books in well under a year, she went off to Brittany and spent a holiday there with Fernande, where she went to the Baie des Trépassés, which she had described in her book, but had never seen. She found it an eerie experience.

The Baie lies immediately to the north of the Pointe de Raz, the Land's End of France, and has changed little since Daphne first visited it, apart from the addition of a brash new hotel. It is also uncanny, in view of her setting her shipwreck at that spot, that the Baie des Trépassés ('Trépassés' means 'The Dead'), has its own legend of shipwrecked sailors. The local mythology claims that on certain moonlit nights, all the mariners who have recently perished at sea wait silently on the beach for the arrival of the Ship of the Dead. If a fisherman passes by at that moment, a voice calls to him which he is unable to resist and he is drawn, inexorably, towards the shore to wait for the ship. When it appears he goes aboard, with the souls of the sailors, and takes the tiller. Very rapidly, in spite of there being no wind, the ship sails away to the Fortunate Isles which are where the sun sets. The invisible passengers then disembark and the boat returns to the Baie des Trépassés with the fisherman, who goes ashore – but remembers nothing; a suitable tale for a Daphne du Maurier short story.

After her visit to Brittany, Daphne returned, refreshed, to London, but as Carol Reed was touring America in his current play, she went down to Fowey.

Menabilly still haunted her, so much so that the Quiller-Couches suggested she wrote to the owner, Dr Rashleigh, and ask for his permission to walk in the grounds. They also introduced her to a member of the family, Alice Rashleigh, who had lived there as a young girl. Somewhat to her surprise Dr Rashleigh allowed her to walk in the grounds, if she wanted to, and so she spent the long days of summer exploring to her heart's content. The book that was rapidly forming in her mind had nothing whatsoever to do with Cornwall or ghosts of the past, but she was storing away the experiences of that summer for future use.

She also made excursions into other parts of Cornwall with Foy Quiller-Couch, who introduced her to Cecilie Rogers, Lady Vyvyan, at Trelowarren, the family's beautiful sixteenth-century stone house on the Lizard peninsula. Cecilie was, like Daphne, an 'incomer' to Cornwall, but the Vyvyans prided themselves on being one of the oldest surviving families in the county. Indeed, legend has it the Vyvyans once lived in the lost land of Lyonesse and that on the night of the great inundation, when the whole land disappeared forever under the sea, the single survivor was a young member of the family who escaped on his white horse, an event commemorated by a white horse appearing on their coat of arms. Lady Vyvyan was very much an outdoor person, whose passions were her garden and the preservation of the countryside. She loved holding picnic parties in the grounds of her estate and on the sea shore, where guests were expected to tuck up their skirts or roll up their trousers and join her in one of her enthusiatic shrimping expeditions along the mud flats of the Helford River.

Later she, too, was to write about the west country, notably in her books, *The Helford River* and *The Isles of Scilly*. She would never write as well as Daphne, but her books are evocative all the same. On the south side of Trelowarren lies the creek whose proper name is 'Frenchman's Pill', later to become immortalized by Daphne as Frenchman's Creek. It is now one of the very few beauty spots in Cornwall which remain unspoiled and for that we have to thank Lady Vyvyan, who refused to allow on her land any of the development which scars the rest of the Helford River. When she died she left Frenchman's Pill and the land along the south bank to the National Trust and because of this it is still possible to see it much as Daphne had on that first visit. The only access is by boat or on foot and it retains its mystery as a secret place, come upon suddenly from the path in the woods. It is truly magical whether flooded with bluebells in the spring or hot and still with the scents of summer.

Another expedition with Foy would also lead eventually to a book, but this was to have a less happy outcome in aesthetic terms, for the place in question. Daphne had remained in Cornwall into November and as there was an unusually mild spell of weather, she and Foy decided to explore the high bleak landscape of Bodmin Moor which runs between the main road through Cornwall and the north coast. It is not as grand or as massive as Dartmoor, but it is a wild and bleak place, an area regarded in the past by Cornish people living elsewhere as a strange and dangerous place peopled almost by another race. The two young women were staying at a temperance-house called Jamaica Inn, which had once been a coaching inn on the high moors almost exactly halfway between Bodmin and Launceston. Even today the hamlet of Bolventor, which consists of little apart from the inn and a few cottages, remains a lonely windswept spot.

On this particular day the girls decided to ride over and visit a friend at nearby Trebartha Hall on North Hill, assuming that it would only take them some forty minutes or so to get there. That might well have been the case had it been possible to do the journey as the crow flies, but they had not taken into account the rough terrain, the streams and gullies which seamed the land or the hills in between. Although they set off at two o'clock, they were still no nearer North Hill an hour later and had run into a boulder-strewn landscape almost impassable for horses and, within no time, not even passable on foot. Like all such upland areas Bodmin Moor is prone to sudden changes in the weather and as they were wondering what to do and where to go, the heavens opened and it poured with rain. Desperately they sought shelter and, after frantic searching, discovered a ruined cottage only marginally better than nothing as it had no windows and most of the roof had fallen in. The rain fell steadily for an hour, by which time the light had almost gone, while to make matters even worse the nasty fog common to the moor began drifting in to thicken in front of their eyes.

Foy's suggestion was that they should walk with their horses and trust them to bring them home; but where, pondered Daphne, was home? Thirty miles away in Fowey? Jamaica Inn? Neither of them felt happy in the ruined house and Daphne began to fantasize about a morose and violent owner who had drowned himself in the brook which ran outside it. So they let their horses lead them, and for a while it seemed they might well take them home until suddenly they found themselves on what appeared to be some kind of railway track. Foy thought it must be for trolleys, leading either to china clay pits or a quarry. Whether or not some of the legends of Bodmin Moor passed through their minds – such as the ride of the Wild Hunt, or the doings of wicked Black John Tregeagle – Daphne does not recount. (John Tregeagle is supposed to have been a real person, either steward to a medieval Earl of Radnor or an evil lawyer who murdered his wife and children, who sold his soul to the devil. Either way he has become mixed up in various myths, from having to empty Dozmary Pool as penance, using a limpet shell with a hole in it, to being overcome by a variety of Cornish saints.) What Daphne does say is that she kept thinking of a book she had read in her youth, where a young knight, lost in a wilderness, is 'rescued' by a character called the Little Master who turns out to be the devil. The book was vividly illustrated with a picture of the knight's horse rearing up above a precipice.

Hours passed and still they struggled on until, just as they had given up hope, the horses led them on to a properly made-up road. It was indeed the Launceston – Bodmin road and they were literally within a hundred yards of Jamaica Inn. The horses had led them home, and there, coming towards them, were the landlord and other searchers holding lanterns. Thankfully they collapsed before a turf fire where they were served with piping hot eggs and bacon and a pot of tea.

As Daphne herself was to write later in *Vanishing Cornwall*, all is changed, 'changed utterly' and she writes about how she felt embarrassed as she passed Jamaica Inn and saw the coaches parked outside, how it was her own novel, *Jamaica Inn*, which helped bring about such drastic change. It has changed even more since then, sprouting annexes, a souvenir shop, restaurants, a folk museum, a 'Joss Merlyn Bar' (with a brass plate in the floor purporting to show where he met his end), and now boasts 'the Dame Daphne du Maurier' room, complete with Daphne memorabilia. Even the vast open fire place, the only unchanged feature, which burned whole tree tunks, has recently been cut down in size to more modest proportions and, worst of all, a new by-pass will isolate Jamaica Inn on to an island in the middle of the busy A30. However, those who want to discover a whiff of what attracted Daphne to the area can still find it in the little moorland village of Altarnun. The beautiful church remains unspoiled with its magnificent roof and one of the finest collections of carved pew-ends in the country, depicting a galaxy of saints and demons, jesters and local worthies, even a flock of sheep. The vicarage, in which she was to place her sinister vicar, Francis Davey, still stands near by, but now serves teas. No vicar of that name appears on the register in the church although there are Daveys remembered on the 1914–18 War Memorial outside.

Shortly after this adventure, she received the advance from Heinemann for *The Loving Spirit* – £67. It was the largest sum of money she had ever earned. Her family also wanted her to return home. Again she was living not at Ferryside, but in The Nook with Miss Roberts, and a story she tells throws an odd light on how she and the family regarded those who looked after them. She notes that on one occasion Miss Roberts, 'who was so brave', spilt a kettle of boiling water on her legs, scalding them 'terribly', and how she, Daphne, would have known nothing of it had she not been called into the kitchen where Miss Roberts apologized for her supper being a little late. 'I went to her and she was sitting there with long strips of skin falling from her knees.'

So the round continued, family Christmas at Cannon Hall (Carol gave her a cigarette case she kept for the rest of her life), then a trip to see Fernande in Paris, and the burgeoning plot of *The Progress of Julius*. Julius, she had decided, would be a French Jew called Levy, born into humble surroundings, and as his life would span the Franco-Prussian War, she made use of her time there in research, assisted greatly by the fact that she was bilingual.

Michael Joseph wrote to say that *The Loving Spirit* would be published on 23 February, and that Heinemann had accepted *I'll Never Be Young Again*. When she received her first author's copies she immediately sent one to Gerald who told her he liked it very much.

The reviews of *The Loving Spirit* are brief. *The Times* of 10 March 1931 covers it along with a book by the daughter of another theatrical family, Helen Granville-Barker, in the 'among the new novels' section. It is a favourable review, describing it as a, 'fine, widely sweeping romance of family life over three generations, of strong sentiment with lively episodes.' It concludes: 'Miss du Maurier's power of depicting the life of the little Cornish port and her sympathetic touch upon the emotional stops give promise that with the gaining of firmer outline and greater experience, she will tread very worthily in her grandfather's footsteps.' The *Observer* reviewer recounts that she writes 'on the grand scale . . . a rich vein of humour, satire, observation, sympathy, courage and a sense of the romantic are here.' 'The narrative flows smoothly and easily,' notes *The Times Literary Supplement*, and there are episodes 'and descriptions of considerable power.' Within weeks it had gone into a second impression.

She returned to Fowey to work on the third book, picking up her life again with Miss Roberts (who had presumably recovered from her appalling accident), writing, sailing and visiting the Quiller-Couches. Sir Arthur, she says, was very nice about *The Loving Spirit*. A.L. Rowse again looks back down the years to the jealousy he felt about her then, because not only did she live such a comfortable life, but she was published with equal ease. 'Yes, I was jealous . . . there was so much money, so little struggle. We were all part of that group which revolved around "Q", he was guide and mentor to us all. I remember being so pleased when I discovered he never really rated Daphne as a serious writer, although she had admired him so greatly. But in later years I realised I had under-estimated her.'

The Progress of Julius progressed rapidly as she worked hard in the mornings and devoted most of her afternoons to trying to arrange the Ferryside garden into some kind of order, sawing the branches of fallen trees for logs, digging and turning over the hard ground. It was then, quite unexpectedly, that the man came into her life who was to resolve once and for all her feelings about Carol and Geoffrey and who was to prise her away, so far as anyone would ever be able to, from Gerald.

Frederick Arthur Montague Browning, known to his friends either as 'Tommy' or 'Boy', was thirty-five years old when they met, handsome, extrovert and extremely attractive. It was an unlikely match. He was born into an army family, had been educated at Eton and Sandhurst and, as a very young officer in the Grenadier Guards, had served with distinction in the 1914–18 War. When he was only twenty, he had won the DSO and the French Croix du Guerre, hence the sobriquet 'Boy'. He was utterly unlike Gerald, a real athlete and mad on all kinds of outdoor sport, including bobsleighing, running and, significantly, sailing. He had represented England in the high hurdles at the Olympic Games and won the English title for three years in succession. At the time they met he was a regimental officer, a major in the Guards who had just acquired his pilot's licence. Unknowingly, Daphne had called him to her. In September 1931 he and a friend sailed into Fowey Harbour in his boat, *Ygdrasil* called after the tree of Norse legend. They were drawn to Cornwall by *The Loving Spirit*, which he had read and thoroughly enjoyed.

Angela noticed him first, and told Daphne she could see a 'most attractive man' going up and down the river in a white motor boat. Although Browning wanted to meet her, he appears to have been shy of presenting himself to the du Mauriers unintroduced, and so spent most of his time either in his boat or hanging around the harbour. Although Daphne noticed his presence and agreed he was very handsome, on first acquaintance he does not seem to have made much of an impression. She was more interested in completing *The Progress of Julius* and she was also not feeling well, having brought on what she describes as 'a mild attack of appendicitis', through all the energetic hard work she had undertaken in the Ferryside garden.

She finished *The Progress of Julius* on 25 November. It had taken her much longer than the other two novels – nine months in all. She notes that as she drank to its completion in sloe gin, she could not possibly have known that just a year later she would be married and pregnant with her first child.

If *I'll Never Be Young Again* was a disappointment after the promise of *The Loving Spirit*, then *The Progress of Julius* now seems, quite frankly, dreadful. The sexual prurience which had been present in the second book takes over in the third. While it is unlikely that Daphne was herself at all anti-semitic, Julius is a stereotypical grasping Jew, with an overwhelming greed for money and power, and with perverted sexual tastes. His first involvement is with a twelve-year-old Egyptian prostitute he first sees dancing naked and lasciviously in a North African brothel, and it is clear that her sexual attraction for him lies in her extreme youth. With today's growing awareness of child sexual abuse, these chapters can only be read now with a kind of appalled fascination. One is left wondering just why she wrote them, whether it was out of a deliberate desire to shock, or to show she was capable of tackling any theme. Julius lives with the girl into her teens (as she becomes progressively consumptive) and, after turning down medical treatment for her which he could well have afforded, she dies leaving him free to pursue a rich Jewish heiress, Rachel, whom he marries.

There follows a horrifying childbirth scene where Julius wrenches the emergent child from Rachel to ensure it survives (he is not very concerned about the mother) only to find it is a daughter, not the long-hoped-for son and, even worse, his wife will never be able to have any other children. In no time at all, he has become obsessed with his daughter Gabriel, on whom he lavishes everything she wishes for materially along with all his affection. The pair spend an increasing amount of time together as Gabriel reaches her teens, until Rachel is virtually discarded. Both father and daughter are relieved when Rachel conveniently dies of cancer, her death hastened by Julius. The passionate relationship continues until, eventually, on one of the few occasions Gabriel is away from Julius, she meets a young man with whom she falls in love and whom she wants to marry. Beside himself with jealousy, Julius first tries to dissuade her and then, when he sees he has failed, spends the last evening before her marriage with her. They go to the seashore together and, as Daphne did with Otto Kahn, Gabriel strips off and goes for a swim. Julius lets her strike out from the shore and then follows her out and drowns her. Nobody ever knows.

The Progress of Julius might well be dismissed as an aberration, except that it has a subtext which may not be interesting from the literary point of view, but which is psychologically fascinating. It is not the fact that Julius is a callous, ambitious over-reacher, greedy for wealth and political power that makes him interesting, but his sexual desire for very young girls, his incestuous love for his daughter, and their joint rejection of Rachel, whose death is deliberately accelerated by Julius with the connivance of the girl; not to mention the consuming emotional and physical jealousy which drives him to kill her the night before her marriage. It is all grossly overstated and badly written; one can only conjecture just what it was that Daphne was desperately trying to exorcize – the feelings Geoffrey had stirred in her when she was fourteen? The overwhelmingly possessive emotional ties between her and Gerald? Her rejection of her mother?

In the New Year of 1932 Daphne's appendix which had been grumbling away finally flared up and she had to have it removed, after which she returned to Fowey to recuperate. Nothing daunted, Tommy Browning returned once more to the chase and this time persuaded a neighbouring boat-builder, George Hunkin, to mention to Daphne that he would like to meet her. Tommy followed this up with a note saying he was sorry to hear that she had been ill and could not sail her own boat. Would she like to join him on the river in his? For good measure he threw in the fact that his own father had met Gerald as they were both members of the Garrick Club.

On 8 April 1932 she joined Tommy on board *Ygdrasil* for the first time and he put the boat through her paces, obviously showing off. Daphne found him one of the most easy-going people she had ever met and they spent the evening at Ferryside talking for hours over a roaring fire. Her relationships with Geoffrey and Carol had been emotionally and physically limited. Browning had no such limitations. He had not wasted his thirty-five years and had plenty of experience of women, knowing exactly how best to set about his pursuit. They spent the next two days together before he had to rejoin his battalion, promising her that he would return as soon as he could. Just a week later she came downstairs to find him in the garden sawing logs for the fire, after having driven down through the night. He was dressed in old clothes and seaboots and as he saw her, he looked at her, opened his green eyes wide and smiled . . . she was hooked.

CHAPTER 12

Deaths and Entrances

I t is ironic that Daphne and Browning should meet when they did for she had finally realized her ambition: at last she could be financially independent. Michael Joseph had assured her that with the royalties she was now owed by Heinemann in this country and Doubleday in the United States, coupled with the fact that Heinemann were going to publish the two succeeding books, it meant that for the foreseeable future she would be self-supporting. She could live wherever she chose, go wherever she liked as she had always done, but now without having to rely on Gerald. It would bring her complete freedom, a freedom she was about to relinquish.

I'll Never Be Young Again was published in May 1932 to a rather more mixed reception than *The Loving Spirit*. It was clear that the reviewers had been expecting another historical novel and did not quite know what to make of it. *The Times* critic commented only that it was 'worth reading', and then went on to give a brief summary of the plot without further comment.

Browning's courtship of Daphne was a swift one. For the next two months he spent every spare minute that he could in Fowey, shamelessly using the fact that his colonel was one of his closest friends in order to get leave. The couple became inseparable, she showed him her favourite walks, they sailed the river in both of their boats and

Daphne introduced 'Tommy', as he had become known, to all her friends and neighbours. By the end of June they had decided they would marry and both were faced with the prospect of informing their families. Browning had already been engaged at least once before and did not anticipate anything but encouragement from his mother (his father was dead), but Daphne had to face breaking the news to Muriel and Gerald – and to poor Carol who still felt the same about her, and to whom she had hardly given a thought for weeks. And so she gave them all advance warning by letter.

On 2 July the couple visited the Browning family at Pirbright and they proved very welcoming, so much so that she was to write in her diary that she felt as if she had become a ghost and was living in some kind of dream. On 6 July they drove to Cannon Hall which, she noted with understatement, was a 'bit of a strain'. There would be no more independent summers spent in Fowey, they would have to live near to where Tommy's battalion was stationed; so Muriel and Gerald offered the young couple a cottage at the bottom of the garden at Cannon Hall.

Nobody knows what Geoffrey or Carol were to make of it. Asked many years later what happened to Geoffrey she said she did not really know. He continued acting off and on, separated from Meg, became a chicken farmer, lived with someone and died; she did not know when. She had stopped keeping a diary once she married, otherwise she might well have noted that, 'poor dear Geoffrey died today . . .'

Carol Reed went on, of course, to fame and fortune as a very fine film director. Some years after the end of the relationship with Daphne, he became romantically involved with the actress, Diana Wynyard, and the couple lived together, intending to marry. During that time, however, he fell deeply in love with another actress, Penelope ('Pempe') Dudley-Ward, but went through with his marriage to Diana as he felt it was the decent thing to do. Not surprisingly the marriage was a disaster. He was unable to give up Pempe, had a child by her, Max, and, finally divorced Diana to marry her.

But it seems he was never entirely able to shake off the effect Daphne had had on him and, according to his biographer, Nicholas Wapshott, would visit her in Cornwall for the rest of his life, when Tommy was away, repeatedly referring back to their early love affair and on two occasions, actually going so far as to ask her to marry him.

Asked once which subject he would most like to direct, he responded with Daphne's second book, *I'll Never Be Young Again*, which Wapshott describes as Daphne's 'autobiographical description' of their relationship. This, however, is very hard to understand as neither the male protagonist with his pornographic leanings and amoral Parisian life-style, nor the young woman with whom he becomes involved, seem to have anything in common with either Daphne or Carol. Possibly the link is that, because she was writing it during the time they were seeing each other, she discussed it with him. Certainly one of the ideas for the book came to her when they were down in the London docks one night watching a ship put out to sea.

However, the director Bryan Forbes is probably nearer the mark when he suggests that it was Daphne's long-lasting influence on Reed that enabled him to 'conduct love affairs through the lens' with many of his young actresses. Throughout their lives, Daphne and Carol never lost touch and when, in 1976, he died suddenly of a heart attack, Daphne was one of the first people Pempe rang with the news.

On 8 July the *Daily Telegraph* ran a news story under the heading: 'Miss du Maurier's Romance – To Wed Guardsman.' It noted her engagement, giving her age as twenty-five, and went on to say that she had already written two novels with a third to be published shortly, a good record for someone who only 'began her career as an author two years ago.' Miss du Maurier, it continued, spends ten months of the year in the little Cornish village of Bodinnick, near Fowey, 'where she is a familiar figure in her grey flannel trousers and blue jersey.

It was at Bodinnick that she first met Major Browning who was sailing a boat past her home.

'Miss du Maurier, who is very slim with curly fair hair and bright blue eyes, was the unconscious starter of the "hatless movement" which the younger set have taken up so enthusiastically. She speaks French without an accent and usually spends the remaining two months of the year in Paris. Major Browning, who is thirty-five, is one of the youngest majors in the British army and an all-round athlete. He is known to his friends as "Boy" Browning and is the son of the late Col F.H. Browning of Rousham, near Oxford.'

When, years later, she wrote *Growing Pains*, Daphne devoted only two or three pages to the last years before her marriage after which the story stops dead. There was to be no long engagement: the wedding was set for 19 July, eleven days after the engagement notice appeared in the *Daily Telegraph*. No doubt Muriel yearned to see Daphne married in a designer wedding dress in the Guards' Chapel, walking out of it under an arch of swords; but Daphne would have none of it. She was determined to be married like Jane Slade in Lanteglos Church and the ceremony was fixed for the unusually early hour of 8.15 a.m., to enable the wedding party to sail up Pont Pill on the tide to reach the church. Muriel had to wait until her granddaughters were married to realize her ambition of a smart family wedding, as neither Angela nor Jeanne ever married.

Not only was Daphne not married in white (in 'wreath and veil' as the Cornish used to say), unlike Janet Coombe, the heroine of *The Loving Spirit*, she was determined to wear an old blue serge suit which Muriel had to brush down and iron the night before. The days before the wedding were nervous ones; Daphne felt much as she had done just before she had her appendix out, and Tommy, despite his wartime heroism and medals for gallantry, became 'white about the gills' at the thought. He complained of chronic indigestion. Gerald was completely silent on the subject, but the ubiquitous Cousin Geoffrey, determined not to be left out, had talked Tommy into letting him be best man.

So, early on a fine summer morning, they set off for the wedding, Gerald, Muriel, Geoffrey and Daphne in the family boat, *Cora Anna*, Tommy and the neighbouring boat-builders, the Hunkins (who had formally introduced the couple), following in *Ygdrasil*. Then they all walked up the steep hill to the isolated church of St Willow, Lanteglos-by-Fowey, a church with one of the most beautiful interiors in the west country, from its magnificent wooden ceiling to the medieval pew-ends, carved with owls, dolphins and lively faces. It would be hard to imagine a more appropriate setting for the wedding of a budding novelist with a strong sense of history.

After the ceremony the wedding party returned on foot to the two boats and sailed back to Ferryside. Here, Daphne's dislike of ceremony went even further. There was to be no wedding breakfast or reception, no speeches, nothing at all. The family assisted the young couple to load stores on to *Yggy*, and watched them sail off down the Fowey River on their way to the open sea and the voyage south to a honeymoon on Frenchman's Creek. On their way to the river mouth they were hailed by the Quiller-Couches from their rowing boat, who handed them a bottle of their own sloe gin for luck.

There is a brief note of the wedding in *The Times* of 20 July:

Major F.A.M. Browning and Miss D. du Maurier

The marriage took place at Lanteglos-by-Fowey yesterday of Major F.A.M. Browning, Grenadier Guards, and Miss Daphne du Maurier, daughter of Sir Gerald and Lady du Maurier. The service was conducted by the Rev. R. de Courcy O'G. Murley, rector of Lanreath. The bride was given away by her father. Those present at the ceremony included Lady du Maurier, Mr Jeffery (*sic*) Millar, and Mr and Mrs George Hunkin. Major and Mrs Browning left for their honeymoon in their small motor yacht, in which they will cruise along the south Cornish coast.

In one of her last jottings before her marriage Daphne noted that she would come to know what it was to love a man as her husband, not a son, not a brother. She did not mention a father. And so they headed 'down-channel for the Helford River and Frenchman's Creek. We couldn't have chosen anything more beautiful.'

So they sailed away into a land of legend and lived happily ever after . . .

Writing in the 1960s, not long before Tommy's death, in an essay entitled 'Romantic Love', Daphne was to aver that there was no such thing, and she chose to illustrate her point with a somewhat random selection of examples from fiction to show that so-called romantic love only takes place within its pages and always requires tragedy and/or disaster. She cites Lancelot and Guinevere, Tristan and Iseult, Paolo and Francesca, Antony and Cleopatra, Romeo and Juliet, and so on. But the great novelists, she writes, do not in fact write about romantic love; there is nothing romantic about Madame Bovary, or Angel Clare and Tess, or Catherine and Heathcliff. Romantic love ends all too often in jealousy, treachery, deceit, passion and death. 'It is not, alas, the gods who make men and women mad, but the chemistry in the blood. "Men have died . . . and worms have eaten them",' she says, quoting Rosalind, '"but not for love . . ."'

However, in spite of what she wrote many years later, it is obvious that Tommy Browning really did sweep her off her feet. The beautiful setting definitely played its part, assisted by the fine weather, the highly romantic way in which they met and their mutual love of boats. She was to return to that first meeting again and again. Both her previous involvements had been with actors whose lives, inevitably, were bound up in rehearsals and performances, the atmosphere in which she had always lived. Browning brought a dramatic breath of fresh air into her life and, although she was to say so often that she had always felt cool towards physical lovemaking, it seems reasonable to assume that in those early days she was deeply stirred. The very speed of the courtship must have come as something of a shock.

The marriage was a major change of circumstance. All her adult life she had been able to do as she pleased, unhampered by the usual confining ties of lack of money or need for employment. She could live in Fowey, sailing and writing, or in London with its comfortable, theatrical social life. She could take off for France, to Paris or to Brittany, whenever she chose to spend time with the still ever-sympathetic Fernande, and she had finally achieved financial independence. Now that was all changed.

It must have been difficult for both of them. Tommy had also been a free agent and was ten years older than Daphne. Now he had not only acquired a wife, he had acquired a deeply possessive and famous family. He would also be living on their doorstep in a house at the bottom of their garden, so near that there was no possibility that Daphne could break completely free from the suffocating family ties. She, on the other hand, not only lost her precious freedom, but had been catapulted into a way of life of which she had no experience. The wife of a serving officer at that time was expected to follow a standard code of behaviour, take a full part in the social life of the regiment and provide a suitable background for a career soldier, especially a high-flyer like Tommy Browning. On top of which, within a few weeks, she was pregnant and although she never had any problems with either pregnancy or childbirth, it was, of necessity, a further restriction. It is not surprising therefore that those early months of marriage seem to have been stormy ones with the biggest rows arising out of Tommy's exasperation over her relationship with her family, or when he teased her about her French blood.

Neither was all well at Cannon Hall. Gerald increasingly had had to turn to films to make money, and after a lifetime of late rising, leisurely days and long lunches at the Garrick Club, he found himself faced with having to be at the studio or on location at the crack of dawn, only to spend much of his time afterwards hanging around waiting to play his scene. Although he was well paid for what he did, his earnings went into his theatrical ventures and little went to help Muriel, who was fighting a grim battle with the upkeep of Cannon Hall. Any money left over went into paying back taxes.

Early in 1932, Gerald was rehearsing another Edgar Wallace play, *The Green Pack*, when Wallace died suddenly on a visit to Hollywood from a combination of his diabetes (said to have been caused by his addiction to sweet tea) and pneumonia. He had no assets and left debts of £140,000, much of it owed to the Inland Revenue. As always, his play was an enormous success and it did enable Gerald to return to the stage in a final line of roles of which his best known is Bulldog Drummond; however, he still could not shake off his persistent cough.

The Progress of Julius was published in the spring of 1933 and seems to have made little impression, the best reviews merely damning it with faint praise. Whether or not it was because the last two novels had proved somewhat disappointing is not clear, but whatever the reason, *The Progress of Julius* was the last book she wrote for Heinemann, apart from a strange and uncharacteristic publication which will be dealt with later. The new publisher found for her by Michael Joseph was Victor Gollancz, and she was to remain faithful to the firm for the rest of her life. Gollancz was the shrewdest of operators, known later for his famous Left Book Club but initially, where authors were concerned, for his unerring skill in picking real winners. Daphne joined a stable which already contained another female bestseller, Dorothy L. Sayers, author of the Peter Wimsey books.

Presumably it was during her pregnancy that Daphne discussed with Gerald the idea of writing his biography. According to Angela he was agreeable in principle. He had enjoyed *The Loving Spirit*, but had been less enthusiastic about the latter two novels. It is not known what he made of *The*

Progress of Julius. In July Daphne gave birth to her first child, Tessa, in the cottage at Cannon Hall. It was an easy confinement; she had spent the previous afternoon watching the first day of the Eton-v-Harrow match with Gerald and Tommy. The two men both returned the next day to watch its outcome while Daphne literally laboured away at home. The *Daily Telegraph* of 18 July noted the birth, ending its report with the words: 'Mrs Browning, under her maiden name, wrote a novel, *I'll Never Be Young Again*, which was banned in the Irish Free State . . .' As soon as Daphne was up and able to travel, Tommy took her down to Fowey and the baby was christened at Lanteglos Church.

During 1933 Gerald's health began to deteriorate rapidly and by the spring of 1934 it was obvious to everybody that he was a sick man. Just before his sixty-first birthday on 26 March he made his will, leaving everything to Muriel including the residuary interest on his share in George's estate. In the event that she died before him, then his assets were to be equally divided between his three daughters, after a legacy for his sister-in-law, 'Billy Beaumont', who had acted as his secretary for so many years. Increasingly frightened at the possible outcome of his illness, Gerald saw specialist after specialist, as well as continuing to take his array of patent medicines. Shortly after his birthday he finally accepted that the only hope was surgery.

Newspaper reports of the time merely say it was for 'an internal condition', cancer being the word that could never then be mentioned, but Daphne confirmed later that that is what it was and there is little doubt that it was cancer of the lung.

No-one in the family had been prepared to face the truth about the gravity of Gerald's condition. 'Nobody seemed to imagine there was anything really wrong,' says Angela, 'nobody told us how serious the operation was going to be.' Gerald faced his death with great gallantry. Angela writes movingly of the aftermath of the operation: 'And when it was over and they said it was successful one wondered – as one looked at his pale haggard face – what an unsuccessful operation led one to look for in a patient's face.' Gerald died on 11 April, the thirty-first anniversary of his wedding.

The newspapers for the next few days were full of his obituaries. The one in *The Times* was printed by an odd coincidence alongside those of two artists, George Spencer Watson and the Hon. John Collier. The paper notes that two months previously John Collier 'presented to the Hampstead Public Libraries Committee his portrait of his friend, Sir Gerald du Maurier, which was exhibited at the Royal Academy in 1922, and now they have died on the same day.' Gerald was widely praised for his achievements, the only regrets expressed were that he had never had the artistic courage to widen his field as it was felt that his talent would certainly have enabled him to do so successfully. Much emphasis was given to his great personal charm, as well as the amount of work he had undertaken for charity, especially the theatrical charities. It was noted that the King had taken a personal interest in the progress of his illness and that his was among the many messages of sympathy delivered to the grieving family at Cannon Hall. Like all too many of his family, Gerald died before he reached old age.

His career had been a remarkable one and he was, as James Harding writes, one of the most naturally gifted performers ever to appear on the English stage.

Both *The Times* and the *Daily Telegraph* report that the funeral was to be strictly private by the express wish of Lady du Maurier. 'Neither the date nor the place will be made public and only close relatives will be present.'

Muriel went to the most extraordinary – not to say bizarre – lengths to ensure that this was indeed the case. Gerald's body was taken at dead of night to the Lady Chapel of Hampstead Parish Church in what must have looked like a medieval procession. The bearers carried him in, lit only by the light of candles, their feet echoing on the stone floor. They left him embowered in hothouse flowers whose heavy scent filled the building. 'He would have appreciated the rather theatrical and macabre entry to the church itself late at night', writes Angela, 'when his bier was taken in, in utter darkness except for the candles which preceded it, with only Billy, my cousin Geoffrey and myself there. He had been born in Church Row, he had returned, and was ready to sleep eternally with his beloved ones in the place he knew so well.' The following day he was buried in the du Maurier grave alongside his mother, George, his brother Guy's wife, and his sister May and her husband. Later Muriel was to lie beside him.

The entry into the church at midnight and the quick and quiet funeral the following morning achieved what Muriel desired, that Gerald should go to his grave surrounded only by his relatives. On this last occasion, at least, Muriel would ensure that the family had him to themselves.

A week later she put Cannon Hall on the market and it was duly advertised for sale by Goddard and Smith of King Street, St James's, London, who stressed both the history of the house and the lavish way it had been maintained. Gerald left the modest sum of £17,996. 4s.3d., a small amount indeed for someone who had earned so much money all his life. The sale of Cannon Hall was, however, to ensure that Muriel would be able to live in comparative comfort for the rest of her life. It was the end of an era.

CHAPTER 13

A Different Life

Within six months of his death, Daphne had
published her biography of Gerald. She had
employed a nanny for Tessa and, with help in
the house as well, she was left free to give her
attention to the book before she had to become involved in a
series of moves, resulting from Tommy's army service.

Daphne was to write a number of non-fiction books
including three more about her family, but this is completely
different from the rest. Her early non-fiction, however
interesting the subject matter, is curiously lifeless as if as
a novelist she was unable to reconcile the world of the
imagination with that of research and reality. The first few
such books are a mixture of detailed, but often ill-digested,
factual information, lying uneasily beside excursions into
imaginary events and dialogue, a technique which rarely
succeeds and one the reader finds frustrating. But this does
not apply to the biography of Gerald. He comes straight off
the pages as a real person because she writes about him with
such moving honesty, an honesty which caused a great deal
of offence when the book was published. Many of his friends
and admirers hated it.

She traces his life from his birth to George and Emma,
the much-spoiled youngest son, the 'ewee lamb', through his
career, marriage and family life. She shows that behind the
apparently effortless performances lay a perfectionist who,

in spite of his *dégagé* air, would spend hours ensuring that any stage trick with which he was involved worked, or in researching the reality behind a character even to the point of visiting a condemned cell in a prison, when he was about to play the part of a murderer. He was, she says, baffling to his friends and often a problem to himself. 'He was so easily moved to laughter and to tears, careless one moment and emotional the next, with sudden inexplicable silences and equally sudden indiscretions.'

She touches only briefly on his relationship with herself and her sisters, her style becoming strange when she talks about herself, using the third person 'Daphne', as if she were someone else. She writes about how Gerald found it hard to come to terms with his daughters' adolescence, how he worked himself up into emotional and distressed states over them, 'creating an atmosphere of suspicion and unrest, asking sudden and embarrassing questions.' He longed for them to tell him everything, share their troubles, but the very quality of his emotion made the girls shy. 'It was not only Gerald's tragedy. It is the tragedy of every father and every daughter since time began,' she writes, 'but he took it harder than most.' Their protection was, she says, to walk away from him emotionally, but as she showed years later this was something she was never able to achieve.

'He was a creature of contradictions, so old in experience, so young in wisdom; a faun one moment and alderman the next; a child in the morning, a blasphemer at night; citizen of the Empire with great ideas of justice, a beachcomber with his face in his hands; an unfrocked priest shaking his hand at heaven; a laughing cockney alone in a wild wood. There was never a moment, decisive and clear for all time, when you could point a finger and say of his mood, 'There, that is Gerald. That is the man. That is his portrait.' For he would be away, and changed, and lost in the shadows and the man who stood in his stead had other eyes.' She never again wrote in such a way about a man.

Gerald's personality, in spite of his great talent, was flawed.

The spoiling and indulgence that he had received from his parents were continued by Muriel and the rest of his family. He was shamelessly egocentric, the life of theatre and the life of the home circled around him and his needs, he was unable to stand outside himself. He needed a constant diet of admiration and he could not cope with growing older.

She does not flinch from describing the fits of depression which were to descend on him increasingly in his later years, even before his terminal illness, and how in those last months he had had few illusions as to its outcome. He had tried in vain to prepare Muriel, his 'darling Mo', for what was to come. As one of a family in which so many members had died young, he did not think he could survive once he had been told he had to face major surgery. As death came closer, he felt nearer to the sisters and brother who had died before, especially Guy. It is a deeply loving memoir of a real human being. Years earlier, when discussing the biography of another actor with Daphne, he had said that it did not tell the truth and that if ever he decided to write his own, he hoped he would have the guts to do so. To the best of her ability Daphne carried out his wishes.

Gerald: A Portrait was considered to be deeply shocking, because for so many of his admirers he had been an idol without flaws. They did not really want to know the reality behind the image, preferring a work of hagiography. It thoroughly unsettled the reviewers who described it variously as being 'staggeringly candid', 'a merciless tribute', the biography of a man who was 'spoiled and indulged'. The *Morning Post* of 1 November 1934 gives the book a major review, carefully picking out Daphne's most candid sentences. It also criticizes her for that fault which was to become so trying in the succeeding non-fiction books, of making no division between memory and fantasy or, indeed, fact and fantasy; although it is nothing like as apparent in *Gerald*. It was considered remarkable that she wrote about her 'father's love affairs with strangely little reserve', but this, too, is not what it seems as she writes only of the affairs he had before his marriage. She

124

did not even mention his extra-marital affairs until years later and then only in passing. On balance the *Morning Post* gave *Gerald* favourable, but shocked, approval.

The Times reviewer had more sympathy with what she was trying to achieve, saying that while the biography 'by no means leaves out the wart on Cromwell's nose, it has been written without a trace of malice. The portrait leaves out no spark of his brilliance, his lovableness, his courage in adversity and disappointment, his honourable adherence to his own code of behaviour and duty to his profession and its members. And seeing deeply into his nature, and seeing it also clearly in its relation to its setting from childhood to close, the author is able to reveal, without asking for sympathy, the want of any abiding purpose or ideal that could steady or satisfy that restless, moody, hungry, spirit.' It could hardly have been expressed better.

Before the publication of *Gerald*, the Brownings had to leave the cottage in the grounds of Cannon Hall as Tommy had received another posting. During the early years of marriage Daphne was continually having to uproot herself; she moved five times in six years. She had hitherto been a person who liked to have a familiar base – Ferryside, Cannon Hall or Fernande's house at Neuilly but, as she said, they were both young and life was still an adventure. Tommy would make it as easy for her as he could. He organized every aspect of each removal down to the written labels attached to every piece of furniture, telling the removal men where it should be placed in the new house. He would try and recreate the old house as much as possible; he was, she said, a stickler for routine, both in his professional and personal life. He would then oversee the arrival of the furniture van, check that everything had been put where he wanted it and arrange familiar small objects in the right order, leaving Daphne 'to wander around in a daze', imagining the lives of those who had just moved out. She always felt the house they had just left would be a melancholy place without them.

After Tommy and Daphne moved out, the second of the

Cannon Hall cottages also became vacant so Muriel decided that she would have the two knocked into one and made into a house suitable for her, Angela and Jeanne to live in, once they had had to move out of the main house. Their new home became known as 'Providence Corner'. Angela, writing twenty-five years later, notes that Muriel became most annoyed when it was suggested that the move had been necessary because the du Mauriers had fallen on hard times, and Daphne remembers how Sir Malcolm Sergeant, whom she had met shortly afterwards at a supper party, had asked her if she was all right for money! Certainly the amount made from the sale of Cannon Hall allowed Angela to continue on her apparently endless round of foreign holidays, long weekends in the country, trips to Fowey, tickets for the opera and ballet and lengthy visits to friends in Scotland.

Far more trying to Daphne than moving house was the social round that went with army life, the invitations to dinner that had to be reciprocated, the cocktail parties and regimental balls. Holidays in Cornwall were now snatched affairs, dependent on Tommy's leaves. On one occasion, in September 1938, Tommy took down 130 guardsmen to celebrate the Silver Jubilee of Fowey's restored Charter. It was most likely on this occasion that, fired by Daphne's descriptions of the Rashleighs' involvement in the Civil War, Tommy attempted to reconstruct one of the sorties fought in the area, an attempt which failed dismally when his 'troops' became hopelessly lost.

Being away from Cornwall so much fed Daphne's need to forge some kind of continuing link with it. She was to find it in her next novel, *Jamaica Inn*.

'"Oh, it's you, is it?" he said. "So you've come to us after all? I'm your Uncle, Joss Merlyn, and I bid you welcome to Jamaica Inn."' With these words introducing 'a great husk of a man nearly seven feet tall, with skin the colour of a gypsy,' Daphne cleared the hurdle into the popular novel stakes at a single bound. She never looked back.

The adventure on Bodmin Moor when she and Foy

Quiller-Couch were lost in the fog proved the starting point, the isolated inn the focus. Throw in a gang of ruthless smugglers and Cornish legends of wreckers and you have a heady brew – not to mention a sparky young heroine, her far-from-respectable admirer and a sinister vicar. There is still controversy, even today, about 'wreckers'. Certainly the Cornish availed themselves with enthusiasm of anything the sea might wash up on their inhospitable coast – a trait that can still be witnessed today – and for people who were bone poor and living on the breadline a wreck could, quite literally, be a godsend. A prayer attributed to a seventeenth-century vicar of St Just prays not that God should cause wrecks, but that if he should ordain they occur then that 'they might be sent into the shore near St Just for the benefit of the poor inhabitants'. The more sinister version is that in the days before lighthouses, ships were deliberately enticed on to the rocks by those who saw profit in it and that survivors were killed without mercy.

The only documented record of harsh treatment meted out to a survivor is that concerning Sir Cloudesly Shovel whose ship, *The Association*, was wrecked in a storm off the Isles of Scilly in 1704. It is said that he was washed ashore alive, but left to die by a woman who had wrenched a valuable emerald ring off his finger, something she confessed to her priest on her deathbed. Whatever the real truth about wreckers, Daphne's version has now passed into local mythology, becoming inextricably entangled with the genuine history of the bleak Cornish coast and its people.

There is no doubt that *Jamaica Inn* is a rattling good yarn with a strong and compelling storyline which sweeps the reader along, right from page one when we first meet Mary Yellan to the denouement, high on Bodmin Moor when she is rescued from the clutches of the villain; in this too, Daphne kept up the suspense introducing a red herring, which makes the reader believe it is Uncle Joss who is the villain of the piece, only revealing at the end that it is the wicked vicar of Altarnun. In him she foreshadowed some of the characters that would appear in her more macabre short stories. He had, she writes, 'strange eyes, transparent like glass and so pale in colour they seemed near to white; a freak of nature she had never known before ... his face was white too under his black shovel hat, and Mary stared back at him in some perplexity, for his face was unlined, and his voice not that of an elderly man. Then, with a little rush of embarrassment, she understood the reason for his abnormality and she turned away her eyes. He was an albino.'

She also made good use of sinister imagery: 'A last little ray of moonlight made a white circle on the floor, and into the circle moved a dark blot like a finger. It was the reflection of a shadow. Mary looked up at the ceiling and saw that a rope had been slung through a hook in the beam. It was the rope's end that made the blob in the white circle; it kept moving backwards and forwards blown by the draught from the open door.'

It was the first of her novels to be turned into a film, one of only three made by Charles Laughton's own independent film company. It starred Laughton himself and was directed by the young Alfred Hitchcock, who had had a run of successes from *The Lady Vanishes* to *The Thirty-Nine Steps*. In spite of all the talent that went into its making, Daphne disliked the result and, to quote her, nearly 'fell out' with Hitchcock over it. Since then it has been adapted for the stage, radio and television many times and is now, according to Christine Alexander who runs a bookshop specializing in du Maurier books, the single most frequently requested novel of all by visitors, and correspondents, from all over the world.

In those early married days Daphne never stopped writing whatever the circumstances. Between *Jamaica Inn* and her going overseas with Tommy, she turned her attention again to family history. It had been one of Gerald's regular Sunday pastimes to turn out the contents of his bureau, sifting through the pile of family papers and photographs amassed over the years. His children had found his enthusiasm for this rather boring but now the archive would provide a rich well on which Daphne could draw.

She begins the family history *The Du Maurier* before the marriage of her great-grandfather, Louis-Mathurin, to Ellen Clarke and takes it to the point when George du Maurier, who has survived poverty and near blindness, marries and starts his successful career on *Punch*. It never comes to life however and is not assisted by the addition of that imaginary dialogue that had first begun to creep in with *Gerald*, and is more suitable to a novel. George is portrayed far more vividly in the biography written by his son-in-law, Hoyar Millar, entitled *George du Maurier and Others*, published the same year. Millar also sets the du Maurier family in the context of the times in which they lived, in particular during the passing of what was for the middle classes the golden age before the First World War.

In 1936 Tommy was posted to Egypt as Commanding Officer of the second battalion of the Grenadier Guards and Daphne went with him, taking with her Tessa and her nanny. The army headquarters were in Alexandria and the Brownings had a large and pleasant house close to Ramleh Beach. Daphne was soon caught up again in the round of dinners and parties expected of service wives abroad and the ex-patriate Britons living in and around the city.

It was a year of major political events both nationally and internationally. It saw the beginning of the Spanish Civil War which foreshadowed all too clearly what was to come in Europe, while at home people took to the streets in the Jarrow Hunger Marches. The war in Spain, which was to prove so deeply divisive politically, and provoked such strong feelings that nearly 3,000 Britons actually went there and fought for the Republic, is described by Angela as a war in which relatively 'too few people were involved, apart from the Spanish themselves, to bother about the horrors which to the Spanish must have been appalling.' She goes on to say that in Britain the ordinary people went on with life as usual. But it is clear that the possibility of conflict could not be ignored by those stationed abroad, for one of the tasks Browning and his battalion had to undertake was a survey of the area known as the Qattara Depression and it was he who reported to his superiors, back in England, that in his opinion in the event of trouble with Libya it would be necessary for British forces to hold El Alamein at all costs, not Mersa Matruh which was then preferred, a view in which he was proved to be absolutely correct.

During that first year in Egypt Daphne became pregnant again, and decided she wanted to have the child back home in England. So, early in 1937, she returned to London with Tessa (who was then nearly three and a half), to await the birth of her second child. Tessa had been called after the tragic heroine of the then popular novel, *The Constant Nymph*. It was decided that if the new baby was a girl it would be Flavia, after the princess in *The Prisoner of Zenda*. Daphne rented a flat in Queen Anne Mansions in central London and settled in with Tessa's nanny and Angela who had promised to stay until the arrival of the nurse who would be taking charge of the actual confinement. Bored with her pregnancy, Daphne sought diversion and on 1 and 2 April went out for excursions in Angela's small car, journeys which, apparently, were full of bumps and jolts. At teatime on 2 April, Muriel and a friend arrived to take the sisters out to the cinema, at which point Daphne went into labour two weeks before the baby was officially due. Angela blamed its early arrival on the bumpy car rides, but as everything went very well it seems more likely that the baby had chosen its own time as they usually do. Muriel sent for the doctor, the nurse was tracked down and, four hours later, Daphne gave birth to Flavia.

Once safely over the birth, Daphne returned to Egypt and the beach house at Ramleh. She decided, as Tommy's tour of duty was to be a short one, to leave both Tessa and the new baby behind in England, in the care of their nanny and supervised by both grandmothers.

Browning was much caught up in his work and Daphne

found herself once more on the unwanted wheel of Alexandria's social life. She says she put a brave face on it, while becoming more and more homesick for Cornwall, almost to the point of obsession – but an obsession which was to give her the idea for another Cornish novel, this time with a contemporary setting.

The seed began to grow in her mind and she started making notes as the ideas became firmer. Then any further development came to an abrupt halt as the battalion was recalled to England. Once back home, and ensconced in yet another house, she returned to her notes. So there came about one of the bestsellers of all time, a book which was to go into thirty-nine impressions in the next twenty years and was to be translated into over twenty languages.

It is called *Rebecca*.

CHAPTER 14

Rebecca

Every now and then a literary quiz in a magazine or on the radio will ask for the title of a book from which a famous opening phrase or sentence comes. Among those most often included are: 'It was the best of times, it was the worst of times . . .' (*A Tale of Two Cities*); 'Call me Ishmael . . .' (*Moby Dick*) and 'At a certain village in La Mancha . . .' (*Don Quixote*). Often, too, there is 'Last night I dreamt I went to Manderley again . . .', which continues, 'it seemed to me I stood by the iron gate leading to the drive, and for a while I could not enter, for the way was barred to me. There was a padlock and a chain upon the gate. I called in my dream to the lodge-keeper, and had no answer, and peering closer through the rusted spokes of the gate I saw that the lodge was uninhabited.'

An interviewer on a radio programme broadcast as a tribute to Daphne shortly after her death, claimed that *Rebecca* is as good as *Jane Eyre*; however, this type of comparison is unnecessary, *Rebecca*'s success can be measured in its own terms. Daphne never made such a claim and always made clear her own debt to Charlotte Brontë's original, a book which she had loved from childhood. (The same interviewer said her stories were as good as anything written by Maupassant, but let that pass.)

Certainly *Jane Eyre* is a source, but there are others. Menabilly is one, although it is not the house described in the book, which is based more closely on the grand Milton House visited by the du Maurier sisters as children. The similarity between Menabilly and the Manderley of *Rebecca* is in its position and its surroundings – indeed, Daphne's 'blood red' rhododendrons still bloom alongside the twisting, overgrown and disused old drive just as when, first Daphne and Angela, then May Sarton, saw them over sixty years ago. Daphne also recollected from those early trespassing days the scent of azaleas lingering in the air, the owl flitting across the lawn as darkness fell. It all helped to create the atmosphere surrounding the imaginary Manderley. It had also been rumoured that the same Dr Rashleigh, who had left the house empty, had married a beautiful wife who ran away and left him and that years later, after her death, he had married a girl much younger than himself.

In her collection of essays, *The Rebecca Notebooks*, Daphne writes: 'I wondered if she had been jealous of the first wife, as I would have been jealous if my Tommy had been married before he married me. He had been engaged once, that I knew, and the engagement had been broken off – perhaps she would have been better at dinners and cocktail parties than I could ever be.' It was the nearest she came then to admitting that she was sufficiently insecure about Tommy to feel jealousy. In an interview she did over the radio from London to New York when the American Booksellers' Association gave her a prize for their favourite novel of 1938, she was asked if there was a real person who had inspired the character of Rebecca. She said there was not, that people who knew her in Egypt when she was working on the book had often asked coyly and hopefully if she were putting them into the book she was writing, but that 'truthfully', she had not. Rebecca never existed in real life, she was a woman so completely a creature of Daphne's imagination that she herself doubted if anyone else would really know or understand her.

Yet, years later, she was to tell a friend, Michael Thornton, that one day not long after her marriage she had opened a drawer in Tommy's desk and found a bundle of letters, which she had read compulsively. They were from Jan Ricardo, the woman to whom he had been engaged, who was witty, self-assured and strikingly beautiful. They aroused in her the unspoken fear that she was not either sufficiently good-looking or outgoing to hold a man so obviously attractive to women as Tommy. It was a long time before she could bring herself to acknowledge that he, like Gerald before him, had had several extra-marital affairs including one with a very close friend, and that she had cared about his infidelities – still did – even though she had never shown it. It was after reading the intimate love-letters from that earlier liaison, written in the bold, confident handwriting she was to give Rebecca, that the personality of the character was born, alongside that of the narrator of the novel, the mousy, self-effacing, unnamed girl, the girl based on those inner fears which fed a deep-seated lack of confidence.

Some of those who have delved into the psychology behind *Rebecca* and its triangle of Maxim (the older husband), the second unnamed wife and the beautiful dead, but ever present, Rebecca, see overtones of Freud and, in Maxim, portraits of Gerald, Tommy Browning or a mixture of both; but if that is so, then Daphne seems genuinely unaware of it although she was more conscious of the seeds of this particular novel than she was of those behind many of her other fictional works. For instance, there was the wreck she had seen off Pridmouth Cove, just below Menabilly, years earlier which gave her the idea for the discovery of Rebecca's sunken yacht after just such another wreck, and the Rashleighs' old disused boathouse on the beach.

The sinister housekeeper Mrs Danvers, she said, had been in her mind long before she started the story, possibly born in a picture she had seen as a child, or in a long-forgotten nightmare, but most probably as a memory of a genuine housekeeper Daphne had seen on the terrace of one of the great houses they had visited when she was child, a woman who wore a long black dress which touched the ground and who had a pale, gaunt face. Why did the narrator never have a name? 'I did mean to intrigue people,' she told me 'and it was so much easier writing in the first person but I have to admit, I never did have one in mind.'

Obviously there were a number of influences behind *Rebecca*, but what is apparent is that Daphne was once again gripped by a good idea that had to be put on paper. She describes how, during the earliest stages of working out the story, she paced up and down the living room of the house near Alexandria, notebook in hand, biting first her nails and then her pencil. But by the time she returned to England and her children, she had worked out the rough outline of the plot – the ex-patriate couple (like many she must have encountered herself), homesick for England, having to live where they did because of some unnamed tragedy. Should she, she thought, attempt a device she had never tried before, that of starting at the end of the story and then going back in time to work towards it once again?

Tommy was stationed in Aldershot and he and Daphne rented a beautiful Tudor house called Greyfriars, near Fleet. Once again the furniture was put into its correct position, the personal possessions were arranged as before and the children and their nanny were installed, along with household staff, so Daphne returned to *Rebecca*. This time she wrote straight on to an old typewriter from her notes.

If there is anyone who still does not know the plot of the novel then, in view of what was to happen next, here is a brief synopsis. A middle-aged, ex-patriate wife, living in the South of France with her older husband, relives the events that brought them there. She was a mousy, diffident orphan, the daughter of an indigent artist who had had to take a post as a paid companion to a monstrous, but rich, American woman. They were on holiday in Monte Carlo when she met the older, extremely attractive, Maxim de Winter, owner of the famous Cornish mansion, Manderley. She hears he is a widower and that he had had a beautiful young wife, Rebecca, who had been drowned tragically in a sailing accident. Maxim, to her surprise, takes an interest in her, she falls madly in love with him whereupon, to everyone's amazement, he proposes to her and then marries her.

Maxim takes her back to the magnificent Manderley with its hosts of forbidding servants presided over by the sinister housekeeper, Mrs Danvers, who had been Rebecca's personal maid. It soon becomes apparent that the household still revolves around the dead Rebecca and the narrator feels more and more inadequate by comparison with such a paragon. She finds dealing with a large household beyond her competence and has difficulties with Maxim's friends and relations, although they appear to be fairly sympathetic to her. She also runs into Rebecca's unpleasant cousin, Jack Favell who hints at a mystery, and a simpleton who lives in a cottage on the beach and speaks of the strange woman who was so cruel to him. Matters come to a head when Maxim gives the famous annual fancy dress ball which she attends in a costume taken from one of the portraits in the picture gallery, an idea suggested to her by Mrs Danvers. When she appears it causes a sensation for it is revealed that Rebecca portrayed the same character in the last ball given before she died.

Maxim is furious; she is desolated and fears Maxim has never got over his love for Rebecca. Then there is a storm and a shipwreck in the cove near by, during which the wreck of Rebecca's yacht is discovered with her body still in it, despite the fact that Maxim had identified a woman's body found further up the coast just after she had been lost at sea. At this point Maxim tells his wife that the body is indeed that of Rebecca, that he had never loved her, had come to hate her and that he had shot her when she had told him she was expecting Favell's child. He had then taken her body down to her boat, sailed it out to sea and sunk it with her on board.

At the subsequent Inquest evidence is given that the boat appeared to have been sunk deliberately. Was it suicide or murder? Rebecca had no reason to take her own life. Favell is deeply suspicious as, indeed, are the police. Desperately the couple search through Rebecca's papers to see if there is anything there that might give Maxim an alibi and discover she had an appointment with a Harley Street specialist in the name of Mrs Danvers. They, and the now openly vindictive Favell, visit the doctor who tells them that Rebecca had had terminal cancer, along with a uterine malformation which meant she could never have carried a child. Maxim is off the hook, even Favell agrees terminal cancer would be sufficient reason for suicide. Maxim and the narrator set off for home. Meanwhile Favell has rung Mrs Danvers to tell her what they had found out and, as Maxim's car nears Manderley they see a red glow in the sky. Realizing that Maxim is going to get away with what she was sure was murder, Mrs Danvers has set fire to Manderley and is herself burned to death.

In her earliest version of the novel, recorded in the published jottings, Maxim was called Henry and the narrator is not an orphan, but has a father living, although he is not an artist but a hard-up general practitioner. The housekeeper, Mrs Danvers, is present, but is by no means so menacing, as is the caddish cousin and the man who lives in the boathouse, but he is merely old and confused rather than simple. The girl still chooses a dress from the picture gallery, although in this early version it is an unfortunate mistake, not the suggestion of Mrs Danvers. Then, however, the story differs widely because, following the uproar which greets her appearance and the obvious anger of 'Henry', the girl attempts suicide by drinking the disinfectant, Lysol. Only after this does Henry tell her he never loved Rebecca and that he had killed her.

The plot of the early version then follows relatively closely that of the published one; a storm and a wreck bring about the discovery of Rebecca's yacht with her body still in the cabin, there is an Inquest at which it transpires that the boat must have been sunk deliberately and the wicked cousin, called 'Astley', attempts to blackmail Henry by accusing him of murdering Rebecca, who had been going to divorce Henry and marry him. The mysterious doctor's appointment made by Rebecca in the name of Mrs Danvers is followed up and the doctor tells them that Rebecca's time was limited as she had terminal cancer. With a feeling of tremendous relief Henry and his young wife get into their car and set off home for Manderley; but in this earlier draft, they do not arrive to find the house in flames; instead, both haunted by the spirit of Rebecca whom they fear will yet destroy them, they turn into the drive to see a car with blazing headlights, coming towards them. Henry swerves to avoid it but fails, and the two cars crash head-on. 'It came at us, rearing out of the ground, its huge arms outstretched to embrace us, crashing and splintering above our heads.' Whether Daphne originally intended to kill them both we do not know.

At the end of her notes she put 'epilogue', with a query, and a list of priorities – atmosphere, simplicity of style, keep to the main theme, characters few and well defined and build it up little by little; to all of which she would faithfully and successfully adhere.

Before embarking on the final version she did write an epilogue to her original story. The couple have survived but Henry can hardly walk as a result of the car crash; like Mr Rochester, he is also badly scarred and disfigured. The wife has become faded and dumpy and wears dark glasses to conceal her eyes. Mrs Danvers is still not the nightmare figure she was to become, but is remembered with pity because she was so fond of Rebecca, and as for Manderley, it has been sold. It will shortly open as a country club, for which they have just been sent a prospectus; there is now a swimming-pool, a night-club complete with jazz band, much of the garden has become a golf course and the bedrooms have *en suite* bathrooms. On its opening night a famous film star will dive into the pool in evening dress.

By the time she came to write the final version Daphne had taken her own advice and simplified the story, relying on the creation of atmosphere rather than filling in every detail of the characters and their lives. So Henry became Maxim, Maxim de Winter; the narrator remained nameless, but Mrs Danvers had taken on a life of her own – and had become far more sinister. 'When I first read it,' says Dr Rowse, 'I thought at the beginning how ridiculous it was; that no old Cornish family could possibly have had a surname like de Winter, that there was no house in Cornwall, not even Lanhydrock or Antony, as grand as Manderley and that certainly no-one in their right minds would have spent a night under the same roof with Mrs Danvers, let alone choose to live there permanently. Yet I had to admit, when I finished the book, that I had been gripped by it. She did show a marvellous gift for narrative in *Rebecca*.'

While Daphne was working on it, *The Du Mauriers* was published and was generally well received. Ivor Brown in the *Observer* was quite carried away by it, and in a review which actually carries a byline – a rare event then – describes it as 'fragrant', finds the mixture of imaginary dialogue and fact to his taste and bemoans only a lack of illustrations.

It took Daphne about four months to complete *Rebecca*. She delivered the typescript to Victor Gollancz and worried that he would think it foolish or over-melodramatic. Her anxiety was misplaced; Victor could recognize a winner when he saw one. Whether it is because of the emotion she felt so strongly when she read the bundle of old love letters or because of her skill as a story-teller, or a combination of the two, *Rebecca* remains a book which once read lingers in the mind, readily defying the inherent improbabilities apparent when the plot is summarized. She was to spend the rest of her life hiding from its popularity, from becoming the public property its massive success would try to make her.

Although some of the reviews were unusually critical, that did not alter its impact on the reading public. *The Times* reviewed it in tandem with a book by another bestselling author, Margaret Mitchell – not *Gone With The Wind*, but the now unknown *Meat for Mammon*. 'JS' finds that *Rebecca* leans heavily on *Jane Eyre*, but that Daphne's material is of the humblest. 'There is nothing in this book beyond the novelette,' he continues, 'the de Winters, by any sophisticated standards, are poor creatures and as a girl of twenty the narrator is oddly inexperienced, sentimental in a full dress way, regarding her husband with doglike devotion. Nor is de Winter himself much help since he is a stick of a man who broods upon the past, bringing himself back at times to show his wife a rather patronising tenderness or an insufferable rudeness.'

Yet, grudgingly, the reviewer admits that Daphne had evoked an atmosphere of genuine terror in her simple tale especially in the character of Mrs Danvers. 'For the sake of this Victorian spectre and its equipment of panic and foreboding, it is easy to overlook the equally Victorian weaknesses of the novel, the freakishly constructed characters, their odd behaviour and Miss du Maurier's somewhat individual grammar.'

Rebecca is hardly the first novel and is certainly not the last to become a bestseller in spite of its reviews in the quality press. For the first time Daphne found herself in the full glare of publicity, the subject of gossip columns and feature pieces in the national press and women's magazines. However diffident she might feel about herself and her relationship with Tommy, it is obvious from what we know of her that she was not what the press wanted to make her. She never was and never would be a romantic figure. Although, in spite of her own doubts, she was very attractive, she was also physically tough and competent, otherwise she could hardly have sailed a large sailing-boat single-handed, fished for conger eels with eel hooks, shot rabbits or walked for miles on end accompanied only by her dogs. She did not fit into any convenient category and from the earliest interviews made no secret of the fact that she disliked parties and any kind of social round.

What it cost her to give those early interviews can only be imagined and one of the first of them was with Tom Driberg, who was then a journalist on the *Daily Express*. In an introduction guaranteed to make any woman cringe he begins: 'Daphne du Maurier is a successful novelist, colonel's wife, actor's daughter. All three, as feminine types, can be forbidding. She is not at all like any of the types. When I first saw her, crouching by the fire in her conventionally comfortable green-walled drawing room she looked more like a subaltern's wife than a colonel's wife – any nice subaltern's pretty little wife.' It becomes marginally better after that and it is interesting that it was years before any interviewer could extract from Daphne any more than she was to give to Driberg back in 1938. She told him she hated London, liked gardening, was not interested in food, drank little ('well, I might have a gimlet, that's as far as I get'), that she did not cook ('well, I did once do a grilled chop . . .'), was uninterested in clothes and enjoyed a humdrum, comfortably-off country life, 'the duller the better'. By this time she was certainly 'comfortably off', because *Rebecca* was the first of the huge money-spinners with which she was to underpin the family and, as Dr Rowse says, 'keep Tommy in boats'.

She confided to Driberg that she disliked entertaining or being entertained or any kind of public appearance, and that she disliked most modern novels, reading and re-reading favourites such as those of the Brontës, Trollope, Somerville and Ross's *Memoirs of an Irish RM*. She was seriously considering a novel based on the '45 Rebellion, although she felt 'Mr Gollancz would never publish it.' She was disciplined, working every day from 10 a.m. until 1 p.m. and again in the afternoons, six days a week, leaving only Sundays free when she went to church, because it was close and the local vicar preached such good sermons. According to Driberg she said she could not spell and that her copy editor at Gollancz, Norman Collins, put it all right for her and also suggested ways of changing phrases if he thought they would be improved. Ideas for new books usually came after the holiday which followed the completion of the last one.

Gollancz, we learn, expected to sell over 100,000 copies of *Rebecca*. (In the event it was far more and the American sales of the Doubleday edition alone ran to two million in four years.) Reviews in the popular press had been good, but Daphne was annoyed with the papers and magazines which said the story was set in Devon instead of Cornwall, or suggested that she had forgotten to give her heroine a name. Driberg asked her if there was anything of Gerald in either Max or the heroine's father. Daphne said no to both questions. 'The father was only put in because I thought he might be coming in later on in the book, but he didn't.'

Browning had been present throughout the interview and Driberg also asked him a question. '"No", he replied, "there has never been a Rebecca in my life", said the Colonel firmly, getting up and stretching, straightening his canary-coloured pullover, examining his red leather slippers. He had been working on a script for the BBC, a one-hour broadcast about his regiment.' It is a pity Daphne did not write up what she thought of Driberg.

The popularity of *Rebecca* surpassed anything either Daphne or Victor Gollancz could have imagined. A year later she adapted the story for the stage and later sold the film rights to the Selznick International Picture Corporation for £10,000. She had wanted John Gielgud to play Maxim de Winter in the stage version, but in the event she had to settle for Owen Nares. Celia Johnson played the girl and the famous character actress, Margaret Rutherford, Mrs Danvers. It ran successfully at the Queen's Theatre until the building was bombed. One item rescued from the ruins was a little bronze statue of Gerald that she had lent the cast for luck.

Before the play had reached the stage events in Europe were already drawing towards their inexorable end. In September 1938, Prime Minister Neville Chamberlain flew on his ill-considered mission to Hitler in Munich, in search of 'peace in our time'. In his briefcase he carried, for light relief, a copy of the new novel, *Rebecca*.

After the release of the film in 1940, and the publication of the book all over the world in a host of different languages, Daphne was twice to be accused of plagiarism, although only the first claim ever reached court. It was by a Mrs Edwina

Macdonald who claimed Daphne had taken the plot of *Rebecca* from a short story she had written some years previously, entitled *The Black Windows*. Daphne had never heard of either the lady or her book and when she was sent a copy could not understand how she could possibly have been accused of plagiarizing it, as just about the only similarity between the two was that the hero had been married twice.

The lady's lawyer had appeared in the offices of Doubleday Doran in New York almost immediately after *Rebecca* had been published in the United States, announcing his client would be suing and, indeed, suits were brought against both Selznick International Pictures and Doubleday Doran. There followed a protracted legal wrangle. The suit against the publishers first came up in a lower court, Daphne producing the necessary sworn affidavits, documents and everything else it was felt was needed. It did not succeed but the plaintiff did not intend to give up and appealed against the decision. Delays mounted, lawyers were ill, judges busy and, of course, there was a war. In 1946 Mrs Macdonald died and it might well have been thought that that would see the end of the matter but it was not to be, for her family enthusiastically took up the case. There had been a number of plagiarism suits in the United States in the late 1930s and early 40s and *Rebecca* was seen as something of a test case.

Finally, in 1947, with the war well and truly over, the case was brought before the courts for the last time, much to Daphne's fury. She had stated that she saw no reason why she should appear herself, but she was finally persuaded to do so by Doubleday Doran whose lawyer urged the firm to ask her to be present on the grounds that the best way to dissipate any notion that there had been plagiarism was to have Daphne take the stand and deny it in open court. Otherwise the lawyer felt there might always be a lurking suspicion that she feared to testify. The stake, he pointed out, was tremendous. The book had had the widest possible distribution through the Book Club, the trade and numerous reprints, and the film had been an enormous success. However slim the chance might be that an astute lawyer could persuade the judge in favour of the Macdonald family, it was not a risk worth taking in the light of the enormous damages that would be claimed if he succeeded. The plaintiff's lawyer had little to lose by pressing his claim and everything to gain.

So, early in October 1947 Daphne, accompanied by Tommy, paid her first visit to the United States. The notebook in which she had made those early jottings in Alexandria in 1936 was presented in evidence, and she stood up to cross-questioning by the judge very well. The case was dismissed. The Brownings had stayed with Nelson and Ellen Doubleday and after the successful conclusion of the matter Daphne gave the notebook to Ellen Doubleday as a memento. (On her own death, thirty years later, Ellen left the notebook to her daughter who returned it once more to Daphne.) Shortly after the case was all over, the Brownings returned to England on the *Queen Mary*, Daphne being seasick throughout the entire crossing.

The second charge of plagiarism was, however, far stranger. Sometime early in the 1930s a Brazilian writer called Carolina Nabuco wrote a novel called *A Successora*. As she was bilingual in Portuguese and English she translated it herself into the latter and an agent submitted the manuscript to a number of American publishers. Towards the end of 1932 Miss Nabuco's agent, Nannine Joseph, sent a copy to the English agent Audrey Heath who offered it to a number of publishers; none of them took it up and the manuscript was returned to the United States. It is not recorded if Gollancz was one of the publishers concerned. *A Successora* was published in Brazil in 1934 and was a great success. Miss Nabuco, like Daphne, came from a very distinguished family, in her case a family of Brazilian aristocrats; her father was a well-known politician and statesman. She had been much feted on the success of her book in part because of her family background.

In March 1940 Nannine Joseph received a letter from Miss Nabuco pointing out distinct similarities between *A*

Successora and *Rebecca*. Miss Joseph agreed but did not think that this amounted to more than coincidence and there was some further correspondence. Nothing more might have been heard of the matter had not *The New York Times* taken up the story early in November 1941. The story appeared in the paper's Books Section and was written by Frances Grant. Miss Grant concentrated on the Brazilian book, drawing attention to the similarity of its storyline in general and picking out individual incidents. Both heroines take refuge in flowers and trees, both are oppressed by portraits of a dead first wife, both have a scene where the young heroine is brought to her new home. 'To an extraordinary degree the return to Roberto's Palacete in the Rua Paysandu is filled with the same dramatic interest as in the return to Manderley. For the palatial mansion in Rio – like Manderley – becomes almost a protagonist in the story.

'Here in *A Successora* are the servants waiting to greet the new mistress – and much the same servants they are. First comes Antonio who, like his English counterpart, Frith, has a kindly face, is old and has been long in the family. Here too is the housekeeper, in *A Successora* she is the wife of Antonio. In both books it is the housekeeper who gives the welcoming message for the household staff. There follows the first visitor in both books, in both cases a dominating sister-in-law, only sister of the husband. "Germana" in *A Successora* is tall and handsome like Roberto, with the robust looks that come from their Flemish ancestry. Little wonder then that Germana reminds Brazilian critics of Maxim's sister, Beatrice, "tall, broad-shouldered, very handsome, very much like Maxim about the eyes and jaw". Germana, like Beatrice, regards it as her personal mission to "civilise" the young and gauche sister-in-law who, as she reminds her, is so unlike her predecessor.

'So numerous are the parallels that one may find them on almost every page – from the set of bruises which both wives can proudly exhibit before the scrutiny of their sisters-in-law, to the cookery notes of both dead wives. About the only differences,' concludes Frances Grant, 'is that at the end of the Brazilian book the young wife discovers she is pregnant.'

There is no doubt that there are very real similarities. Each has as a heroine a shy, inexperienced second wife who marries an older husband and who is taken by him to his great house where she is daunted by the grand staff and frightened by an unpleasant housekeeper. Both wives break antique vases and try and hide the result and in both cases there is a masked ball leading to a dramatic denouement. In the Portuguese book the house does not burn down but the young wife wishes it would.

Doubleday Doran immediately published a denial of any plagiarism on behalf of both themselves and Daphne who, because of the Macdonald case, had been advised that she could not reply to the charge in any detail. She stoutly denied however that she had heard either of Miss Nabuco or the book. On 29 November the prestigious *Saturday Review of Literature* entered the lists with an article by Harrison Smith entitled 'Was Rebecca Plagiarized?' His answer was almost certainly no. He thought both had drawn on the same source, *Jane Eyre*, for their inspiration and that anyway the problems of a second wife who had had a beautiful predecessor is a common enough storyline in romantic fiction; in fact he went further and said, 'the story is as shopworn as any story ever written and the parallels discovered by Brazilian literary patriots between *Rebecca* and *Successora* are the normal and inevitable results of variants of this ancient plot.' He also pointed out that while Daphne's story ended in the couple having to exile themselves from the country and their home, Miss Nabuco's heroine triumphed over the sterile first wife by becoming pregnant and living happily ever after. He did not believe that even had Victor Gollancz seen the Nabuco book that he would have sent it to Daphne as an idea for a novel of her own. He was, he said, 'profoundly indignant' that *The New York Times* had recorded a literary scandal which had been simmering below the surface for two years.

On 2 January 1942 the basic details of the story were cabled

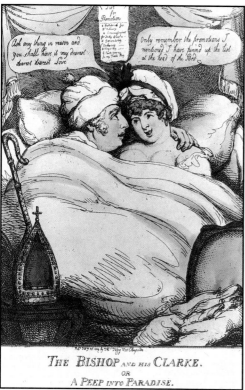

Daphne's infamous ancestress Mary Anne Clarke was the subject of considerable scandal and there were many scurrilous cartoons such as this one

Ask any thing in reason and you shall have it my dearest dearest dearest Love

Only remember the promotions I mentioned I have pinned up the list at the head of the Bed

THE BISHOP AND HIS CLARKE.
OR
A PEEP INTO PARADISE.

George Louis Palmella Busson du Maurier, Daphne's grandfather and the author of *Trilby*, with his wife and daughter in a photograph taken by Julia Margaret Cameron

The 1904 production of J.M. Barrie's *Peter Pan*, with Gerald du Maurier as Captain Hook

Daphne's father, Gerald du Maurier

Muriel Beaumont, Daphne's mother, in 1916

Daphne (*on the left*) with her sisters, Jeanne and Angela

Daphne (*on the right*) and Jeanne with their mother at Hampstead in 1922

Daphne in 1922, when she was fifteen

Daphne and Gerald du Maurier in 1925

Carol Reed (*on the left*) in *The Calendar* at Wyndham's Theatre in 1929

Fowey Harbour c.1900. Daphne's first novel, *The Loving Spirit*, was inspired by the life of a shipbuilding family in Fowey, the Slades

The du Maurier's house, 'Ferryside', at Bodinnick, seen from across the river at Fowey

Frenchman's Creek on the Helford River, setting for one of Daphne's best-loved novels

The Helford River, where Daphne and Tommy Browning spent their honeymoon aboard his yacht, *Ygdrasil*

Lanteglos Church where Daphne was married. The Slade family, whose history was the inspiration for *The Loving Spirit*, are buried in the graveyard

Daphne with her daughters, Tessa and Flavia, in 1937

Jamaica Inn as it is today

Charles Laughton playing a leading role in Alfred Hitchcock's film of *Jamaica Inn*

Celia Johnson as the second Mrs de Winter and Margaret Rutherford as Mrs Danvers in the 1940 stage production of *Rebecca*

Joan Fontaine, Laurence Olivier and Judith Anderson in Alfred Hitchcock's film of *Rebecca*

Daphne on the staircase of her beloved Menabilly in 1947. Behind her are portraits of her father and herself as a young girl

Daphne at her desk in the little wooden hut in which she wrote. In it there was nothing except her type-writer and a chair and she could look through the window at the often stormy sea

The Browning family at Menabilly in
1945. Playing with the train set are
Christian (Kits), aged 4, Flavia, aged 7
and Tessa, aged 11

POPPERFOTO

POPPERFOTO

Daphne about to give
an archery lesson to
Christian and Flavia,
1947

Daphne on the beach near
Menabilly, 1947

POPPERFOTO

Daphne at Menabilly, 1947. The skeleton of a Cavalier found at the foot of this flying buttress was the inspiration for *The King's General*

POPPERFOTO

Daphne in the Long Gallery at Menabilly, 1947

POPPERFOTO

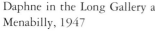

POPPERFOTO

Daphne and the children strolling in the grounds of Menabilly, 1947

THE RAYMOND MANDER & JOE MITCHENSON THEATRE COLLECTION

Daphne (*on the right*) with Irene Hentschel, the producer, and Gertrude Lawrence, the star of *September Tide*, which played at the Aldwych in 1948

Daphne with Vivien Leigh and Laurence Olivier, arriving at a dinner given by Douglas Fairbanks, Jr, in 1952

POPPERFOTO

A still from Hitchcock's 1963 film of Daphne's short story, *The Birds*

Alec Guinness and Bette Davis in *The Scapegoat*, directed by Dennis van Thal

Daphne and Tommy sailing in the late 1950s

Daphne and Tommy at home, 1959

Tessa Browning arriving at her wedding to Captain Peter de Zulueta at St James's, Spanish Place in 1954

Daphne unveiling a plaque to George du Maurier in Great Russell Street in 1960

Lieutenant-General Frederick Browning addressing his men in 1944

Dirk Bogarde as Tommy Browning in the film, *A Bridge Too Far*

Daphne in later life

to Britain by the Press Association and so appeared in the British press, while the conflict raged on in the letter columns of the respective papers in New York. On one side were those who pointed out that all authors draw on previous material to some extent, there is no patent on ideas, and that there have been countless variations on the theme of the 'Cinderella' wife and the triangle of one man and two women. On the other were those who felt there was no smoke without fire or, perhaps, that the whole business had been dreamed up as a publishers' publicity stunt.

Daphne became more and more annoyed. 'Would it not be possible', she finally wrote to *The New York Times* with regard to both Miss Nabuco and Mrs Macdonald, 'to let these two authoresses fight it out as to which of them wrote my book. Can nothing be done by the Authors' Societies in England or the USA to protect quite innocent authors like myself from the troubles and heavy legal costs of such raids without the slightest prospect of damages?' She admitted that there were similarities but pointed out that, as the same idea had obviously occurred to both authors, there were bound to be such similarities and that her American publisher had actually offered to publish *A Successora* to enable readers to judge for themselves. (In the event this never happened.) On 9 January 1942 Miss Nabuco visited the United States as one of a group of Brazilian literary figures but she declined to comment on the controversy, refusing to give any interviews on the subject. Her family meanwhile had said they considered themselves to be above the vulgar need to sue.

Daphne swore to the end of her days that she had never read *A Successora*. It was pointed out at the time of the controversy that there have been other cases of two authors dreaming up a very similar plot and the example was given of Elinor Mordaunt who had delivered to her publisher a book based on the murder of Elizabeth of Austria, only to find to her horror when she read a crime novel by Georgette Heyer called *Envious Casca*, that there were very great similarities, not least in the murder methods used; and how she had had to ask her publisher to explain the coincidence to Miss Heyer.

Years later Daphne was still confessing herself mystified and wishing she knew the answer. 'I shall never understand it,' she said, 'I've never seen it to this day but I realise that if it had been that one which had come to court rather than the Macdonald thing, I might have been in trouble – although how the hell could I have known? I wonder why she didn't do anything about it when she heard about the other case?' She wondered what had happened to Carolina ('poor woman'), if, in fact, she were still alive.

Oddly enough it would seem that in some ways the original storyline of *Rebecca*, as outlined in the *Rebecca* notebooks, bears more of a resemblance to *A Successora* than the final version. It is all, anyway, water under the bridge now and the latter is long forgotten.

After over fifty years, it would seem that the story of *Rebecca* and its *doppelgänger* is likely to remain one of literature's mysteries.

CHAPTER 15

War and the Oxford Group

Daphne was never a writer of letters to the papers, venturing into print only rarely and usually in *The Times*. Shunning publicity as she did, she needed to be much moved to take such a course. In the November after the publication of *Rebecca* and shortly before she moved again, this time to Hythe, she wrote a letter to *The Times*, which was published on 26 October 1938 on the subject of Armistice Day. The paper that particular day contained a number of letters on the growing strength of Germany ranging from those who appear broadly to support Hitler, through others suggesting various types of resistance to him (like George Lansbury), to fulsome praise for the stand taken by Neville Chamberlain from a Mr Thomas Rice of Galveston, Texas which ended: 'Permit me to add that all people who call themselves Christians, throughout the world, should thank God that England is still creating men of whom Mr Neville Chamberlain is a magnificent type.'

No-one could quarrel with the main thrust of Daphne's letter, that we should all share a fervent desire and determination to work for the better understanding of the peoples of this country with the peoples of other nations to avoid a war. But the last paragraphs have a ring which would have been familiar to many at that particular time, when she writes of the coming of 'a new era when fear, and hate, and criticism give way to faith and hope and charity', hoping that all those who appeared to be so willing to give their services to National Defence should give the same assurance and ardour to seeking international goodwill.

The phraseology used is that of the Oxford Group, or Moral Rearmament, and for the next two or three years at least she was to become caught up with it and, eventually, used by it. Frank Buchman, MRA's founder, had the kind of charismatic personality that goes with simplistic evangelism of which there are plenty of present-day examples. He was born in Pennsburg, Pennsylvania in 1878 and in his early days worked as a conventional missionary in China. Shortly before the 1914–18 War he had undergone some kind of spiritual revelation in a church in Keswick where, in the words of his hagiographer,* 'he realised his own sin and experienced Christ's forgiveness, he never again considered that any other human being, however corrupted, was beyond the reach of grace which had healed his own hate and pride.' As a result Buchman wrote a seven-page treatise, citing Biblical precedents, for the practice of personal two-way communication with God, and founded his movement, based on a commitment to search for and follow the will of God, living in the light of 'His Absolute Standards' – honesty, purity, unselfishness and love. Adherents submitted themselves to the five-fold test – a willingness to obey, to examine personal circumstances, to compare their thoughts with the highest moral standards known, to take the advice of friends also living by God's guidance and to rely on the experience and teaching of the Church, as revealed by Frank Buchman.

He soon had a large following in the United States and then decided that his next priority must be England and, to that end, set up a training-centre in Oxford in 1932 to propagandize his beliefs. Some three hundred people came forward for MRA training in the first year, determined to join the fight for Christianity and against Communism.

* *Frank Buchman – A Life*, Gareth Lean, Constable 1985

They became know as the Oxford Group. Buchman's ideas became quite popular, particularly in middle-class previously apolitical circles, although MRA even at its most fashionable never achieved the pervasive influence in political life which it enjoyed in America.

It is likely that Daphne came into contact with members of the Oxford Group, both where she was living in Hampshire and when on holiday in Cornwall. According to Dr Rowse, MRA had quite a vogue in Cornwall just before the Second World War. 'People were upset by what they feared was to come, wanted some reassurance and belief. A number of people fell for it down here at the time, people I knew, but none of them what I would term thinkers. Daphne was not an intellectual, or a thinker in the abstract sense.' Rowse saw Buchman as a man who peddled an unpleasant brand of Christianity while at the same time making himself very rich indeed, a view in which he was not alone.

Passions still run high over MRA, depending on whether you concur with the reverent biographers of Buchman or those like Tom Driberg, who subsequently set out to investigate and expose it; but, apart from a brief resurgence in Britain after the war, MRA and the Oxford Group have long since ceased to make any real impression in this country.

Certainly two years before Daphne's letter to *The Times* and her early involvement with MRA, Buchman had provoked enormous hostility in Britain by visiting Germany. He failed in his attempt to see Hitler, but did speak to Himmler. On his return he gave his now-notorious interview to *The New York Times* on 19 August 1936. 'Hitler or Any Fascist Leader Controlled By God Could Cure All Ills of World, Buchman Believes', was the headline over what followed:

'To Frank N.D. Buchman, vigorous, outspoken, 58-year-old leader of the revivalist Oxford Group, the Fascist dictatorship of Europe suggests infinite possibilities for remaking the world and putting it under "GOD" control. "I thank heaven for a man like Adolf Hitler, who built a front line of defence against Communism", he said today in his book-lined office in the annexe of Calvary Church, 4th Avenue and 21st Street.

'"My barber in London told me Hitler saved Europe from Communism. That's how he felt. Of course, I don't condone everything the Nazis do. Anti-Semitism? Bad, naturally. I suppose Hitler just sees Karl Marx in every Jew. But think what it would mean to the world if Hitler surrendered to the control of God!"'

To say this pronouncement aroused a great deal of anger is an understatement; it ensured that MRA was viewed by a growing number of British people with ever-increasing suspicion thereafter.

No-one would suggest that Daphne herself subscribed to such sentiments, but it does seem that MRA appealed to her emotionally. Like any other young wife with small children she viewed the increasing possibility of war with horror, not least because she knew that Tommy was bound to be deeply involved, as indeed he was. There was hardly a theatre of war from North Africa, through the Normandy landings to the South Pacific in which he would not participate, including Arnhem; especially Arnhem. Possibly it was at this point that MRA put her on 'hold' as it were, seeking to make use of her when the time was appropriate.

So to 1939. International events appear to have concerned Angela less; she notes that while Hitler marched on across Europe she and Jeanne continued their round of visits to Covent Garden, Wimbledon, the Richmond horse show, Ascot and Lord's and Buckingham Palace Garden Parties. For her the announcement of the outbreak of war was overshadowed by the death of her much-loved dog, the same peke which had accompanied Daphne and herself on their first expeditions to Menabilly. She wrote to Daphne about her misery from Mull where she had gone to stay with a close friend.

Daphne wrote back and, after commiserating with her

sister on the death of her dog, moved on to matters which obviously affected her more closely. She wrote mockingly about how nerves kept driving her to the lavatory whenever the post was delivered, for fear it contained the order which would take Tommy away. The British Expeditionary Force was leaving for France that very week and many of their close friends would be going with it. Tommy had been kept behind temporarily in order to continue the training programme at the Small Arms School. Daphne had volunteered for civil defence training, as she felt the commandant's wife should set a good example and had been asked if she would become a Gas Decontaminator. This would consist, she informed Angela, of rushing off to the Gas Contamination Centre on the first alert, dressing in oilskins and seaboots and sprinkling casualties with bleaching powder. It also meant she had to get out of bed when the sirens went and sit around 'in a draughty sort of workhouse with a trio of stalwart VADs . . .'

It was hard to reconcile what was to come, she wrote, with the beauty of the countryside around where they were living, and her soul quailed when she saw statements in the Press about the need to fight to the last ditch; politicians, she thought, presumably 'getting some kind of a kick' out of playing power politics. She had been reading Churchill's *Aftermath of the World Crisis*, and could see only too well how the lack of economic assistance to Germany after the First World War had sown the seeds of the second.

Angela had been attempting to write a book of her own and Daphne asked her how her 'muse' was going. She did not feel much like 'musing' and was quite unable to lose herself in a fictitious story while living in such uncertain times. She found herself swinging wildly between joining the WAAFs once Tommy was sent abroad or going off and finding some isolated Pacific Island on which she could sit out the hostilities.

Shortly after she wrote again, relaying with humour her experiences at the First Aid Post and of the 'incredible' gas practices where they had to dress themselves up in heavy oilskins and then undress 'unconscious' patients, something she deemed impossible, imagining rather a scene where, if the real thing happened, the clothing would have to be torn off. On one occasion a woman she described as '*a maniac*' came to lecture them, a humourless individual who went into all the awful details of gas poisoning. In an extremely amusing passage Daphne describes the woman, with her high-pitched voice and huge gestures intoning, 'at all costs do not let gas vapour penetrate the nooks and crannies of your body', before whipping out from her bag little phials filled with poison gas which, with a wild gleam in her eyes and muttering savagely she thrust under their noses saying they smelled like curry.

The denouement came when she personally demonstrated how to pull an unconscious person out of a gas-filled room. Instead of doing it the obvious way, crawling in and dragging them out by their heels, the woman made a VAD lie down and then straddled herself on top of her, clasping the VAD's arms round her own neck before heaving her violently along the floor by the pressure of her knees. It was, wrote Daphne, 'the most indecent thing I've ever seen in my life!!!', and all the while the woman's face was set, grim and impassive. Daphne tried later to make a drawing of it, but had failed. In a postcript she asks if it is true that Fowey has become a munition dump and that Muriel is building an air-raid shelter.

1940 and the phony war came, with Tommy still at the Small Arms School and the family in Hythe. In 1939 *Rebecca* had gone into production with Alfred Hitchcock as its director. At first he had not wanted to do it, nor had he particularly wanted to work for Selznick. He read the book and thought it would not make his kind of a script, it lacked humour and was too much of a Cinderella story; he was always to think he would have made a better film in England even though most of the cast were, in fact, English actors.

Selznick, on the other hand, had been fascinated by the

novel. Laurence Olivier was working in Hollywood at the time, making the string of pictures which was to establish him as a cinema star. They included *Fire Over England*, *Pride and Prejudice* and, of course, *Wuthering Heights*. His romance with Vivien Leigh had reached its height at about the time she had been chosen to play the most coveted female role in the cinema of the day, Scarlett O'Hara in *Gone With The Wind*. There had been talk of Olivier playing Rochester in a film of *Jane Eyre*, but the role had gone to Orson Welles. As Selznick read *Rebecca*, particularly the description of Maxim, 'his face was arresting, sensitive and mediaeval in some inexplicable way . . .' he pencilled 'Olivier' in the margin. Olivier always suspected that he would have preferred Ronald Coleman, but was only too happy to lend them his face – medieval or not – and his considerable talent.

Afterwards Selznick was to express his doubts about the way Olivier played the role, finding him slow. 'His pauses and spacing in the scene with the girl in which she tells him about the ball are the most ungodly, slow and deliberate actions I've ever seen. It is played as though he were deciding whether or not to run for President instead of whether or not to give a ball.' Most of the film critics did not agree and Olivier had an excellent press, resulting in his being nominated for an Oscar. The majority can be summed up by the review in *Cinema*, which said: 'Rarely has any writer had a book translated to the medium of the screen with the care and attention obviously lavished on Daphne du Maurier's *Rebecca*. Not only the facts of her intriguing novel have been pictorially expressed but the very atmosphere of her rather strange story is recreated in an arresting fashion.'

A dissenting voice was that of Otis Fergurson, in *The Republic*, who said it was not really a 'bad picture' but was not a healthy one. It suffered from 'a wispy and overweight femininity . . . a boudoir film. All this absurd nightmare of helplessness in the first half turns out to be mere preparation for an unsuspected angle of murder, mystery and blackmail and the things fermenting beneath the surface of this proud estate in Cornwall. They could have made the last half first and then saved the first half for a Guy Fawkes bonfire . . .'

The public did not agree, as can be seen from its popularity which continues even to this day, a popularity much assisted by the extremely classy acting, not only of Olivier, but of Joan Fontaine as the wife, George Sanders as the cad and, of course, Judith Anderson as a wonderfully sinister Mrs Danvers. *Rebecca* was to win Hitchcock his only Hollywood Oscar, the Award for the Best Film of 1940. Olivier did not win the Best Actor Award, that went to James Stewart for *The Philadelphia Story*.

Daphne herself liked the film very much. Only *Rebecca* and *Don't Look Now* were really to meet with her approval, and she was always saddened that a better version of *Jamaica Inn* was never made in her lifetime ('it could be filmed so much better now and Bodmin Moor is still unspoiled . . .').

In April her own stage adaptation of *Rebecca* opened at the Queen's Theatre with one of the last, grand West-End first nights before the dark descended. It was a great success, all three principals – Owen Nares, Celia Johnson and Margaret Rutherford – receiving good notices.

The young Browning family were still all living together in Kent, and as there had yet to be any air raids it seemed a good place for the children who were very happy. Daphne did not wish to disrupt their lives before it became necessary, although she realized the calm could not last much longer as, by that time, the Germans were moving into Holland and Belgium. She was also pregnant again, something she kept carefully concealed from the family, as she did not wish to worry Muriel unduly.

Her relationship with her mother had improved greatly after Gerald's death, when she had found her mother in tears, crying out, 'he loved you so much'. There might never be quite the full confidence that she had shared with Fernande, but neither was there any of the old hostility or misunderstandings. Possibly the separation from Fernande caused first by her marriage and then by the war had helped.

If Fernande was invited to leave France for England she did not do so and she spent the years between 1940 and 1945 in unoccupied France.

In March 1941, following Dunkirk, everything changed and Tessa and Flavia were sent down to Fowey where they were looked after in a cottage near Ferryside, soon after which, ironically, Fowey received one of the only bombs which ever fell on the town. The event worried Angela and Muriel sufficiently for them to find a home for them further out. Tommy was still awaiting orders to go abroad and Daphne wrote and told the family that if this happened she would come down to Ferryside straight away. Several of their close friends were killed at Dunkirk, others were taken prisoner. She was finding it impossible to write and had been angered by a letter she had received from her American publishers saying that they had prospects of getting 'vast' sums for the serialization of her next book and couldn't she give them some idea of what it would be and when it would be ready? She responded brusquely asking them if they had realized that the country was facing one of the biggest crises in its history, would possibly be invaded, that Tommy was about to go abroad, and that 'vast sums for the next novel' seemed irrelevant, not to say sordidly commercial, in the circumstances.

In July Tommy was given command of the 24th Guards Brigade Mechanised Group, and moved to Hertfordshire where Daphne was allowed to join him, and coped well with having to share a house with another family. The family concerned turned out to be sympathetic and friendly without being intrusive.

While she may not have been able to write fiction she had in fact worked on another book, one which is rarely listed with her others. Moral Rearmament had found a very real use for Daphne. Buchman had continued to have a remarkable influence on American politicians and was claiming that Franklin D. Roosevelt had 'specifically endorsed' MRA. Roosevelt was later to repudiate this, but certainly at a time when America was beginning to realize that they might have to fight, he managed to get the Selective Service Committee in the United States to exempt MRA members from military service, on the grounds that they were needed in civilian life to boost morale. It therefore followed, so far as Buchman was concerned, that MRA-workers in Britain should be similarly exempted. This, understandably, was not a popular move and so Buchman felt that something had to be done urgently to change public opinion.

What was needed, therefore, was for MRA to publicize to the nation the essential work its members were doing, to help 'boost morale' and who better to do this than the author of the bestselling *Rebecca*? So Daphne produced *Come Wind, Come Weather*. Not surprisingly this was not published by Victor Gollancz who would have been just about the last man on earth to offer MRA a platform. Instead she turned to her old publishers, Heinemann.

Come Wind, Come Weather takes its title from one of the versions of the first verse of Bunyan's famous hymn. It is a dreadful book. In its introduction she says that all the stories in it have been taken from actual newspaper reports, which is quite unbelievable, but in a letter to Angela she says that the material had been provided, 'by my despised Groupy friends and which I have re-written for them.' Daphne, at her very best, was never able to write convincing working-class dialogue and her attempt to cope with that of miners, trade unionists, Welsh working women, Yorkshire villagers, soldiers and local councillors is an unmitigated disaster. The stories are patronizing, unreal and simplistic; workers give up their demands and turn to God, a worker for women's rights becomes a gentle conformist, black-marketeers see the light, all these and many more turn to Moral Rearmament and are saved. The text is punctuated with words in capital letters and strings of exclamation marks which are the hallmark of the cranky leaflet, not a book by an established author.

At the front of the book is a dedication in which Daphne says: 'I want to thank all the workers for Moral Rearmament among whom are the living characters in these stories. The work they are doing up and down the country in helping men and women to solve their problems and prepare for the great struggle that lies ahead will prove to be of national importance in the stormy days to come.' She concluded it with a little homily based on the teachings of MRA.

Buchman and MRA were delighted. It was just what they wanted and they could trail the book as having been written, 'by the author of *Rebecca*'. If they are to be believed it sold 650,000 copies within the next year in Britain alone, Daphne giving her royalties to the Soldiers', Sailors' and Airmen's Families Association. She seems genuinely to have felt that MRA members should be kept home for reasons of 'morale', yet it was obvious that she had not really thought through the political philosophy behind Buchmanism, because in the same letter in which she tells Angela that she has written the book, she also says that it would surely be preferable for France to go 'Red', rather than collaborate with the Germans through Laval. She goes further in fact, and says that Laval would probably be prepared to go along with some kind of French Fascist dictatorship and would get the support of French big business, and 'those bloody silly royalists', and that everyone else would be kept down, 'to the tumbrils, I say'. Politically she was obviously very naive.

It was to prove academic anyway. When, later that year, Ernest Bevin became Minister of Labour and discovered that his predecessor, Ernest Brown, had inserted a clause into the Conscription Act granting deferment to 'lay evangelists', including MRA, he gave the Group short shrift. Although MRA did its best to mobilize support for its point of view – that its members were too important to risk being conscripted – and persuaded high-ranking church officials to write to Bevin telling him that MRA workers were true evangelists, he remained unimpressed and, after heated debates in both the Commons and the Lords, the deferment was withdrawn. MRA has never forgiven Bevin for what he did to this day although Driberg remains the ultimate enemy in its demonology, not least because whiffs of what was happening in Britain slowly drifted over to the USA. Driberg, who had spent a long time investigating the origins, funding and methods of Buchman and MRA, spent six months in the United States, time which he had put to good use and MRA's profile was not enhanced when copies of the *Daily Mirror* were circulated, accusing British men working for MRA in America of being 'draft dodgers'. Buchman anyway was under attack from within and had quarrelled with Sam Shoemaker, who had provided him with his luxurious New York office accommodation. His most loyal lieutenant then broke from MRA on the grounds that he now had grave misgivings because of certain policies and points of view which had arisen in MRA's development. He therefore gave Buchman immediate notice to get himself, his staff and his belongings out of Calvary House.

Whatever Tom Driberg's failings might be in putting over an interview with an intelligent woman author, he was a good investigative journalist and he was later to put his research on MRA into a book, *The Mystery of Moral Rearmament*. Only relatively recently he was described in vitriolic terms in an apologia for Buchman, a description which included calling him 'a notorious homosexual' (which he would be the first to admit he was) and either a committed KGB-agent or a double-agent for the KGB and MI5, which requires some substantiating.

Daphne's involvement with MRA and her public support remain an aberration in her life. She never mentioned *Come Wind, Come Weather*, when discussing her work, and it is not listed with her other titles in any of the current editions of her books, fiction or non-fiction. If there were some 650,000 copies of it printed back in 1940, then it is remarkably difficult to get hold of; specialist booksellers mark it 'scarce'!

CHAPTER 16

A Dream Fulfilled

Throughout all the moves Daphne was to make with Tommy whether in England or abroad, she had never lost sight of Menabilly, still going to visit the house until the war broke out, wandering round its grounds (with the blessing of the Rashleighs) and dreaming about it. While she was still living in Hythe, she had had a letter from Angela telling her that there was to be a sale of the entire contents of Menabilly and was there anything she might like?

She would, she says, have liked the lot, every stick, from the Jacobean chests to the Victorian bamboo odds and ends, but it was just not practicable. They were about to move to a shared house and her existing furniture would have to go into store as it was. She had made some tentative enquiries about buying Menabilly, but both it and the estate were entailed, which would always make that an impossibility. Reluctantly she wrote back and said there was nothing she could do in the circumstances. In fact one of the buyers was A.L. Rowse who bought, among other items, a rare dutch print of Sir Francis Drake and an ornately decorated wardrobe which had been made by his grandfather who had been a carpenter on the Rashleigh estate.

Meanwhile Daphne had the new baby to consider. She finally told Muriel about three months before it was due, which she thought would be somewhere round Armistice

Day. She had made no plans, she wrote to Angela, beyond telling her gynaecologist and the nurse who would be employed to look after her, and she was prepared to have the child anywhere which was safe and convenient, from the local military hospital to an air-raid shelter. She wondered if it would be safe to take a flat in London as she had for Flavia's birth, but decided to leave decision making until nearer the time. Tommy, it seems, had been delighted from the first at the idea of another child and hoped for a boy.

In another letter, written in September from Hertfordshire, she described the light raids they were experiencing, saying that she had watched a flight of German bombers high overhead on their way to bomb Luton; how, in spite of its implications, it was a strangely exquisite sight, the remote and unreal silvery creatures humming above her like birds. To her relief her cook had decided to stay with her and she had set about advertising for a nursery maid for the new baby; the two small girls and their nanny had returned, for the time being.

Tommy was leaving for the East Coast, a Defence Area forbidden to wives and families, where his passion for flying and interest in the military use of gliders was to put him in command of the country's First Airborne Division. Otherwise, so far as was possible, life was normal. She visited her London hairdresser and a new gynaecologist in Hertfordshire, as her own female specialist did not want to leave London. She bemoaned this fact because not only was the new doctor a man, but a specialist who seemed only interested in all the possible complications of childbirth. She did not find male doctors particularly sympathetic – a view with which many of her readers would heartily concur even today. Tessa had been informed of the impending event, but Flavia was considered to be too young. Expressing her fears that Flavia might have 'frightful emotions in her teens', she fervently hoped for a 'Christian' rather than a 'Gloria'.

Neither Angela nor Jeanne had volunteered for military service but Jeanne, almost from the beginning of the war, had turned to working on the home front, and after some training on a farm, she had taken on a large piece of land near Bodinnick which she turned into a market garden. She and Muriel had been living at Ferryside while Angela continued her peripatetic round of visits to friends, but the house was likely to be commandeered at any time, so it was decided that it should be given up voluntarily before it was taken anyway. Besides, Muriel was not well, so a rented house was found on the Esplanade in Fowey, a decision which upset and annoyed the absent Angela resulting (reading between the lines) in some pretty sharp correspondence from Jeanne who accused her of only ever thinking about herself. Jeanne did work very hard on her land, long days which began with taking the ferry across the river, followed by a three-mile walk, and all this before getting down to breaking virgin ground to make it ready for growing vegetables.

Christian was born on 6 November in the house Daphne had rented in Hertfordshire, news first broken over the telephone, which Daphne then followed up with letters to Jeanne in Fowey and to Angela, who was staying with a friend on the Isle of Mull. She noted that her telephone call to their mother had resulted in Muriel expressing concern about her, as she had thought Daphne sounded 'depressed'. Tommy, of course, had returned to the East Coast and the command of the First Airborne Division, and she was feeling tired and 'slack', but she was thrilled with 'the creature', a small fair-haired son, with what she described as a shrewd and clever little face. His birth had been precipitate, beginning with backache on the Sunday, the day after the nurse had arrived, leading her to take a cup of tea up to her bed at teatime, an event followed immediately by violent pains ('like people in books'). By the time the midwife had handed her the gas and air (which she found useless), and they had sent for the doctor, the baby literally 'shot out', howling lustily and weighing-in at six-and-three-quarter pounds. She decided that must be the way it should be done. Flavia and Tessa were delighted with their new brother, as was Tommy, who had returned thrilled to his base. The little boy was christened Christian Frederick du Maurier Browning.

In spite of the war, the resultant anxiety and the new baby, an idea for another novel was steadily beginning to grow. Unfortunately it coincided with one of the few times in her life when Daphne was to be swamped by domesticity. Just as she intensely disliked being portrayed as a gentle wispy lady novelist, neither did she consider herself to be a writer of romances. But this particular book, written under such very unromantic circumstances, can only be described as such, and is one of the reasons for its continuing popularity, especially with young women. For *Frenchman's Creek* she returned again to the Cornwall of her imagination and to the beautiful river on which she had spent her honeymoon. The title had been bequeathed to her by 'Q' (who had used it for a short story), and who said he would be interested to see what she did with it.

Gone were the carefree days of Ferryside, the hours spent writing without even having to worry about cooking supper, for no sooner had she embarked on the new book than Tessa went down with measles, swiftly followed by Flavia, and within no time at all the whole household was plunged into chaos because the Nanny also became ill. Fortunately the Nanny was able to continue looking after the baby, thus leaving Daphne free to care for the two little girls, but whatever the cause of her illness might be, it left her prone to sudden fainting fits. For Daphne it was a crash course in domesticity as she rushed around with bed pans, brewed up hot drinks, made up feeding bottles and wrestled with dirty nappies; but however exhausted she might feel, if there was a gap of any kind during the evening, she would go to her typewriter and hammer away at *Frenchman's Creek*. Flavia had the measles particularly badly with a range of complications, screaming the nights away with pains in her head. Daphne, admitting in a letter to Angela that she was by nature indolent and liked her sleep, found herself for the first time with days that started with the early-morning feed at six, and ended with the last one somewhere around midnight. There was also a pair of evacuee twins to consider, who were being looked after by the cook. In the circumstances, she suggested to Angela, who had wanted to come on a visit, that she left it until things had quietened down.

The Navy had finally taken over Ferryside and so when Angela returned to Fowey, it was to the small house in the Esplanade which had become the home of Muriel and Jeanne. Angela spent the next few months helping Jeanne on her smallholding, but she, too, had had a book published in the spring of 1941. It was called *A Little Less* and caused something of a minor sensation, as it had a lesbian theme.

Daphne, writing to congratulate her, was still up to her ears in family illness. This time everybody, including the unfortunate Nanny, had gone down with 'flu; Flavia was running a temperature and the baby had a hacking cough, for which Daphne was having to dose him with special medicine. Angela's book, she said, had been received with mixed reactions by her friends and her own view was that possibly Angela's talent lay in short story writing rather than in novels, as *A Little Less* was more 'a series of episodes than a continuous novel' – the objective view of the professional writer, rather than that of the soothing sister. As a footnote to Daphne's domestic problems, while she was wrestling with measles and influenza in Hertfordshire, Plymouth was undergoing its first and most terrible blitz. A vivid memory of many who were there at the time was of a cinema audience which refused to leave even at the height of a raid, as they were riveted by the film, *Jamaica Inn* and they insisted on seeing it through to its end.

Its says a great deal for Daphne's professionalism and overwhelming urge to write that she managed to finish *Frenchman's Creek* on time, enabling it to be brought out the same year. There is no hint in the writing of any sense of strain from the difficulties she had encountered and most readers assume she wrote it in the peace and quiet of Menabilly. She was never happy with it herself, describing it as 'more or less pure Jeffrey Farnol', a reference to a writer of coy romances who was, even then, out of vogue. It is certainly a romance, but its rather obvious theme is saved by her evocation of the Helford River at the height of summer, of the creek she had first discovered in the carefree days spent with Foy and Lady Vyvyan, and to which she and Tommy had sailed on their honeymoon. While Daphne identified herself very closely with the heroine of the subsequent novel, she did not see herself in Dona St Columb, the spoiled young wife of a wealthy, absentee, Cornish landowner, who has fled the Court and the pressing attentions of both Charles II and the evil rake, Lord Rockingham, to seek refuge in her husband's house on the Helford River. The house has been empty for years, its only occupant William, an unconventional servant. For weeks Dona is happy going for walks and playing with her children, unconcerned by the rumours of piracy, until one day she finds her way down through the woods and comes upon a secret, hidden creek.

She is soon aware that things are not as they seem and, after watching William talking to a strange man in the middle of the night, she follows the track they have made down to the creek and there, on the high tide, is a sailing ship. At this point she is captured, bundled into a boat and taken on board to meet the handsome captain of the vessel, a Frenchman with a *tendre* for ornithology. The inevitable happens; she falls in love with him and, after several weeks of dalliance ashore, sails away on his next piratical venture, which includes stealing a merchant vessel from Fowey Harbour under the eyes of its enraged owners, an event followed by a passionate interlude afloat. When she finally returns home she discovers her husband, Lord Rockingham, and a party of friends have arrived, brought down by stories of the activities of the Frenchman who has become the scourge of the Cornish coast.

Events move swiftly thereafter, the pirate is captured after a duel with the deeply suspicious Rockingham, William is badly wounded and she herself kills Rockingham before helping her Frenchman escape without her. She is left watching his ship sail away into the dawn, knowing that before her lies a humdrum life as the wife of a boring Cornish squire.

Reviewers in Britain were non-committal and the book did not have the success of *Rebecca*, although it has remained a firm favourite with readers. But even in America, where the reviews were poor and the reaction of the book trade far from enthusiastic, it soon sold forty-three million copies and it was hoped sales would, eventually, touch a hundred million. The best said of it was that it was a good yarn and excellent 'escape' literature. Tommy, who gave her unstinting praise for every book she wrote except one, was particularly fond of *Frenchman's Creek*, because of its association with his first romantic days with Daphne.

The book was made into a film with Joan Fontaine, the shy mouse of *Rebecca*, as Dona; the then-popular Mexican actor, Arturo de Cordova, as the pirate; and the popular English actor, on whom Daphne had had a crush years before, Basil Rathbone, as the wicked Lord Rockingham, a role in which he stole the film. It was a lavish, technicolor production and one of the most expensive Hollywood films yet made, but once again Daphne disliked the result, 'that awful Californian coast, not a bit like the Helford River'. Tommy loved the film as well as the book, most especially the music used for it, Debussy's haunting 'Claire de Lune'. It remained a favourite piece ever after.

The joys of finishing the book were swamped for Daphne, who was now coping with Christian's teething, and merely noted that her relief that Victor Gollancz had liked the book was somewhat tempered by the sleepless nights she was having to undergo. To remove some of the pressure, she sent the two little girls and their Nanny to Tommy's mother, but the baby seemed quite demoralized under her care, screaming all night to come into her bed, then struggling against her when he got into it, leaving her covered in scratches. It was necessary, she writes, to pander to his every little whim, and she lusted after going and doing something nice, quiet and restful, like making Bren guns.

She had been blessed with the good health and sound constitution of Mary Anne Clarke, rather than that of the Busson du Mauriers, but even so the fraught winter and spring, with its succession of childish ailments, influenza, a new baby and a book to finish, finally took their toll, and in the late spring she collapsed with pneumonia and was seriously ill. It took her some time to recover and, during her convalescence, she detailed her day, sleeping until ten, after bouts of insomnia that even sleeping pills did not alleviate, coming down in time for lunch ('like a jaded actress'), resting on the sofa all afternoon, followed by a short walk. She notes that she, who had hitherto hardly touched a drop of alcohol, had newly discovered wine and was enjoying the bottles of claret left behind by Tommy. She started to hanker after France, had re-read her grandfather's *Peter Ibbotson* and this had triggered off a nostalgia for Paris, a city which she could not imagine ever being able to visit again; a state of mind which made her feel even worse.

Apparently during her illness her temperature had soared, resulting in delirious ravings which, she joked, might leave her open to blackmail for years. She wrote to Angela asking her if she could get hold of any Pond's skin cream, telling her that she now did not have to lift a finger, that the children were back and blooming and that she was reading Hemmingway's *For Whom the Bell Tolls*, which contained the best descriptions of love she had come across, apart from *Lady Chatterley's Lover*. She wondered if Jeanne might make her a birthday cake and, as she had developed a taste for wine, anything in that line would make a welcome present. As she recuperated she began work on her next book, *Hungry Hill*.

Although by this time almost anything with the words 'du Maurier' on the cover would sell, *Hungry Hill* is certainly not one of her better works of fiction. As in *The Loving Spirit* she decided to write a saga spanning a long period – in this case no less than five generations of an Irish copper mining family. Possibly it was because she was so obviously mentally and physically tired that this very long book drags as it does, but it is also in equal part due to the fact that she set it somewhere she quite clearly did not know, and it therefore lacks that sense of place which makes her best work so successful. Her Irish families are never convincing and she also manages to reach almost the end of the story still avoiding the political tensions which have torn the country apart for centuries and which, in the long period she covers, so bitterly divided the Protestant Ascendancy from the indigenous Irish Catholics.

Back in Fowey, her sisters were able to stand with others watching the sky to the east of them glow red as Plymouth burned once again. Angela had written to Daphne about how she was much in demand opening, 'War Weapons Weeks', eliciting the response that Daphne found the idea of any bombs raining down on innocent women and children anywhere so dreadful that she could not imagine what she herself would say, even though it might be vitally necessary. Angela, who had spent some time assisting Jeanne with her market garden, interspersed with trips to Scotland, had found the 'powers-that-be' becoming less sympathetic so that for a while she had to work on a farm until, after some months off through illness, she was allowed to join Jeanne again. She also joined the Home Guard.

By 1943 Tommy was in Tunisia in North Africa, heavily involved in the North Africa campaign, where he was putting to good use the knowledge of the terrain he had acquired when he had been stationed in Alexandria before war. He was working, too, under the command of the man he was always to adore and who never lost his unstinting loyalty, Montgomery. With a husband fighting the desert war and most of her friends scattered, Daphne returned again to Fowey with her three children, not this time to her beloved Ferryside but to the rented house on the Esplanade where Muriel was now living. The Navy had moved out of the old house and Angela and Jeanne had returned as it was so much nearer to the market garden. It was a long time since Daphne had visited Menabilly and when she did so what she saw appalled her. The spring of 1943 had been a dreadful one for Cornwall; the gales had been so severe that even the sheltered Fowey – Bodinnick ferry had been unable to run and, in a place where snow in the depths of winter is rare, it had snowed hard as late as May. The house looked as if it had been blitzed. The shutters were open and hanging loose, the windows broken, and when she climbed in through one of them it was to find a scene of total desolation – the wallpaper had fallen off the damp walls, there were fungal growths on the ceiling and everything was covered in dust, cobwebs and mould.

Her unhappiness at the sight was coupled with anger, and she decided to take what she realized was probably a vain step. She rang her solicitor and asked him to contact the owner of Menabilly and ask him to rent it to her. To her amazement, a week later the lawyer came down to see her and told her that the Rashleighs were willing to allow her to have a twenty-five-year lease on the house, but that she must treat it as something of a 'whim', not least because of the state it was in. Possibly the best she could hope for would be to camp out there during the summer. It was, however, made crystal clear to her even then that there would never be any question of Menabilly being sold either to her or anyone else as it, and its surrounding land, was entailed. There has been much surmise over the years as to why Daphne preferred to rent first Menabilly, and then Kilmarth, when she could so easily have bought an old house of her own. One can only surmise but it does seem as if she identified so totally with Menabilly and the Rashleighs, that she wanted to become part of it and of a family which could trace its origins back six hundred years. No amount of money could have bought her either.

So, while Tommy conducted his war against the Germans in Tunisia, she attacked the years of neglect which had almost ruined Menabilly. Fortunately she was by now an extremely wealthy woman in her own right; royalties poured in from all the books, especially from *Rebecca*. Everyone thought she was mad. It would cost a fortune, they said. There was no electricity, no water, no heating, the roof had fallen in in places and she would never get any staff to work there. Like a general with an army she marshalled her troops – an architect, builders, a plumber, an electrician – and when they told her that something could not be done, she begged and pleaded with them at least to try.

First the flowering japonica and ivy were stripped off the front of the house, then the roof was repaired and the windows mended. The carpenter set to work on the floors and reset the doors while the electrician wired the house for electricity. A well was discovered in the kitchen of the old house and the plumber set about finding a way of ensuring a water supply. Chimneys were swept and fires lit in the grates and Daphne seems to have had no trouble getting staff, for she writes that 'relays of chambermaids' scrubbed, brushed and mopped with buckets and swabs. It should all have been impossible in war time, but it was not. The work went on throughout the whole of the summer and autumn of 1943.

She had written to Tommy telling him what she was doing and he had encouraged her while remaining doubtful that she could possibly make the place habitable for when he returned home on leave that Christmas. But it was, she says, like a fairy-tale. At the beginning of December the furniture vans arrived bringing all the household goods that had been in store for so long and were placed, 'like fairy things', in the rooms of a glowing and repaired Menabilly.

Tommy returned imagining they would be spending their days huddled around the fire and the nights in camp-beds, only to find Menabilly immaculate, down to the Christmas decorations, the tree, and the holly behind the pictures, a hot bath waiting for him and even the telephone installed.

Writing about it two years later she was to say even then that she had to keep pinching herself to make sure it was true, that her love affair with a house had reached its consummation. She belonged to it and it to her. She wondered if it was wrong to love 'a block of stone' so passionately, as if it were a person and worried that the feeling might not endure. Also there was the underlying fear that the house could never belong to her, that one day the Rashleighs might want it back, but that had to be put to the back of her mind. For the time being, however, the house was hers and, in the still of the night, she felt it told her its secrets, secrets she could turn into stories, and that 'in a strange and eerie fashion we are one, the house and I.'

From that moment until the summer of 1969 when she finally had to leave there was hardly anything that would persuade her away from it. She would leave Menabilly only for holidays, for research for future books and when she considered it absolutely necessary, and it would always be with the utmost reluctance.

Her love affair with the house lasted until her death.

CHAPTER 17

The King's General

The move was a watershed for Daphne. At thirty-six years old she had finally realized her dream and was living in Menabilly. She was enormously successful; professionally she could do no wrong. In the twelve years which had begun with the publication of *The Loving Spirit*, she had written and had published nine full-length books and the public was still greedy for more. She was also writing short stories, although these are harder to date; while they began to be published in anthologies in 1952, various permutations of the same stories were to appear under different titles for the next twenty-five years. She had also sold the film rights of *Jamaica Inn*, *Rebecca*, *Frenchman's Creek* and *Hungry Hill*. Professionally she was at her peak.

She was also an immensely wealthy woman, well on the way to becoming what the headlines in the popular press would soon proclaim, 'the highest paid woman writer in Britain'. Writing about this success in 1958, she said that she believed that both it, and the enjoyment of it, were very personal and private matters, like saying prayers or making love. She found the outward trappings an embarrassment, feeling that in some way they negated the effort that had gone into writing each book, the dull but necessary grind which all authors experience as they wrestle with making their story work. For her the satisfying moment of triumph was immediately after the task has been finished. She loathed the way writers were supposed to become public figures, open hospitals and fêtes, crown carnival queens, appear on the radio and the newly emergent television, and cynically mused that no doubt if there had been television when *Jane Eyre* and *Wuthering Heights* were published, the two sisters would have been persuaded into Leeds to visit an art gallery, only to find themselves taking part in 'Charlotte and Emily Brontë – This Is Your Life!'

She always remembered clearly a time when, stranded for an evening in London with nothing to do, she had found herself with little money on her, not even the price of a taxi back to the railway station, and it was pouring with rain. She came out of Piccadilly Underground Station opposite a cinema where she saw her name in lights above the advertisement for the film of *Rebecca*. Long queues of people stood outside waiting to go in. She did not join them. For her the incident was to remain a salutary one.

Domestically she was in a position that any writer, but especially any woman writer, would envy. In spite of the war her wealth enabled her to live with sufficient basic staff to run the house, cook and look after the children, now aged ten, six and two. She had all the time she wanted to write or to research, to work the hours that suited her best.

Menabilly was now the centre of her life, the point around which everything else revolved. It was, says Dr Rowse, 'her own personal paradise and she never wanted to come out of it. She was never what you might call a family woman, the centre of her life was never there.' The world of the imagination, which had always meant far more to her than the real one, could now be kept firmly outside the gates of the large Menabilly estate. She had all she wanted.

Whether Tommy felt the same is another matter. She now had three children, including a much-wanted son, and the sexual side of her marriage, never the vital element for her as it was for him, would steadily diminish in its importance for her over the years, leaving only a deep, abiding fondness and affection. It is evident that he returned both but was driven by a need to find physical fulfilment elsewhere. Temperamentally they were remarkably unalike in other ways, too. She had never made any bones about her intense dislike of almost any kind of social life or public gatherings, doing everything she could to stay out of the limelight. Tommy was the complete extrovert, a very physical man, as shown by his keen interest in such a wide variety of sports and in flying. He had succeeded brilliantly in his army career and as a result was to be picked out for high office after the war; in the normal course of events it would have been expected that his wife would be at his side playing an important and supportive role. His was to be a world of people, national events and royal protocol, a world which she was only very rarely prepared to share. 'When Browning went to the Duke of Edinburgh,' says Rowse, speaking of his appointment to the Royal household after the war, 'the only concession Daphne would make was to go to Balmoral twice a year.'

That might well be something of an exaggeration – for instance, she herself records that she was at Clarence House drinking coffee with a lady-in-waiting while Prince Charles was being born and was aware that 'history' was being made; but it is not too far from the truth. Tommy had also to reconcile the fact, both difficult and in some ways humiliating for a man like him, that his army pay could never have paid for their life-style and the upkeep of Menabilly – on several occasions he had to appeal to her to help clear his overdraft. But the life she chose and from which nothing would deflect her, meant that for a considerable number of years they were to spend a large proportion of their time apart, a pattern which, on the whole, meant that they spent only weekends and holidays together. Given that Tommy was a highly sexed man, attractive to, and attracted by, women, it was hardly a recipe for fidelity; but they would remain fiercely proud of each other throughout all their lives – he of her books, she of his professional expertise.

In January 1944, following that first Christmas at Menabilly, Tommy's 1st Airborne Division became expanded
into a full Corps and he was promoted to the rank of
Lieutenant-General. He was now forty-seven years old. He
was soon closely involved in the detailed planning of the
forthcoming invasion of Normandy. In the May of that
year the now defunct London evening paper, *The Star*,
ran a little gossip story about the Brownings. Under the
headline 'The General's Phone Call', it noted that however
busy he was, Lieutenant-General F.A.M. Browning, Chief of
Britain's airborne troops and officer commanding the Glider
Pilot Regiment, had 'an appointment every evening which
only the most urgent affairs could make him miss. That is to
telephone his wife, Daphne du Maurier, the famous novelist,
and his three children . . .' It continued: 'We both write every
day, too,' Mrs Browning told me today. 'We don't see much
of each other though, in fact we've only seen each other
once since Christmas. Then we spent a few days together,
wandering about the countryside with the children.' She was
then quoted as saying that she hoped he might get home for
her thirty-seventh birthday on the 13th. She and her children,
burbled the columnist, live in a seventy-room (!) house three
miles from Fowey in Cornwall. 'The house is called Menabilly
and figured as Manderley in her novel *Rebecca*, Menabilly is
haunted or supposed to be "but we have seen nothing so far of
the lovely lady in a blue gown who is supposed to look out
of one of the bedroom windows," said Mrs Browning. "The
house was empty for twenty years and that is probably why
it is reputed to be haunted."'

At the time of the newspaper report she must have been
in a considerable state of apprehension, fully aware what
Tommy was about to face. Fowey, like other west country
ports, was full of small naval vessels and landing craft ready
for the Normandy landings the following month, while every
boarding house, hotel and empty villa was crammed with
American troops. At that time it was impossible for those living in the west country ports, from Exmouth to Falmouth, to

have been unaware that the invasion of France was imminent. During that May Daphne was asked to give a secret party for the American war correspondents hiding out in Fowey, and it seems that she had to send the entire staff of Menabilly out on a picnic for the occasion, the American high-command providing everything from the food and drink to the cutlery, crockery and Negro naval staff to wait at table. There were, it seems, around sixty American journalists present.

On 6 June, D-Day, Angela recalls how they were to look across the River Fowey and find the harbour had, quite suddenly, completely emptied. Tommy's own Corps had been allotted a vital role, that of seizing and holding the left flank of the salient between Caen and the sea, the open flank upon which the counter-attack of the Panzer Divisions would be launched with the object, as one of the war reporters was to put it, 'of rolling up the whole bridgehead before the seaborne troops could be securely established.'

Browning assigned the duty to Major-General Richard Gale's 6th Airborne Division, which was dropped soon after midnight on 6 June, along the estuary of the River Orme, in time to give it six hours of darkness before the arrival of the seaborne troops during which it could accomplish its task of blowing up bridges, destroying German guns, and seizing defensive positions. All this was done, continues the report, 'with skill and gallantry, and repeated enemy attacks were driven off.'

There was to be a space of three years between the publication of *Frenchman's Creek*, and Daphne's next novel, *The King's General*. Obviously the war and her own anxieties played a significant part in the gap, but the new book required a considerable amount of historical research of the kind she had not needed to undertake when writing the history of the Bussons and the du Mauriers. She had used the atmosphere and position of Menabilly in *Rebecca*; this time she would repay her debt to her inspiration by using the house itself.

She had long been fascinated by the background of the Civil

War and intrigued, indeed almost obsessed, with the legend of the skeleton dating from that era, which had supposedly been found in the wall of the house when the Victorian William Rashleigh had built on his new kitchen wing. For months on wet days she would spend her time in a fruitless search for the place where she thought the secret room might be. The skeleton was the starting point for her story, the rest a mixture of fact and fiction – the facts of the Civil War itself are reasonably accurate, and most of the people featured in her novel did exist, but the story she wove around them is almost totally fiction.

She began her research by writing to the then, present-day William Rashleigh, who lived at the Rashleigh property of Stoketon House, just outside Saltash. She asked him if it were possible for her to have access to family papers. Apparently he refused, not even being prepared to go as far as discussing the matter with her in person, the reason being that he had deeply disliked her biography of Gerald, whom he had greatly admired, finding it cruel. However, his daughter, Oenone, kindly came to the rescue and copied out some of the papers for her, along with all kinds of family details. The notes still exist, carefully written in red ink in an old exercise book, and they throw a fascinating light on the family. She gave Daphne a copy of the relevant portion of the Rashleigh family-tree, with details of the members of the family who were directly involved in the Civil War and the families into which they had married, like the Harrises of Lanrest and Radford, and the Courtenays. There were also copies of correspondence between some of the most important protagonists of the Civil War, such as that of King Charles I and Jonathan Rashleigh and between the Rashleighs and the Grenvile brothers, Sir Bevil and the notorious Sir Richard who was to become 'the King's General in the West' and the subject of her new historical novel. The Rashleigh papers are a most remarkable archive.

Although *The King's General* is not entirely successful and rather falls off in its middle section, where Daphne had to wrestle with military strategy and the course of the war in the west, her decision to tell the story solely in novel form rather than mixing fact with imaginary dialogue works. She begins her story in 1620 when her heroine, Honor Harris, is a child of ten waiting for the return of her older brother Christopher, who has just married Gartred, the only daughter of the famous Grenvile family, whose grandfather had been the famous Sir Richard Grenvile of the 'Revenge', and the friend of Francis Drake. The marriage is a failure and sows the seeds of betrayal, distrust and enmity between the old families of Cornwall which will bear bitter fruit during the Civil War. Honor grows up the beauty of the family, willingly allows herself to be seduced by Gartred's brother, Richard, but is crippled for life on the day before she is due to marry him, in an accident engineered by Gartred.

When Daphne takes up the story again, fifteen years later, the Civil War has been fought for two years and Honor has taken refuge with the Rashleighs of Menabilly, her sister Mary having married the widowed John Rashleigh. When Richard and Honor meet again she is paralysed and confined to a wheelchair, he is the King's General in the West, and a man with a reputation for ruthless cruelty. He had married a wealthy and rapacious widow whom he has discarded, but he has with him his two sons: the first, Dick, the legitimate child of the marriage who he despises as a milksop; Joe, the second – his favourite – a bastard fathered on a local milkmaid during his courtship of Honor. Honor has been given rooms in the Menabilly Gatehouse and has discovered a secret staircase behind the panelling, leading down to a small secret room where Jonathan Rashleigh hides money and plate for the Royalist cause or, occasionally, himself. From there a narrow tunnel leads out into the grounds.

The Parliamentary troops march towards Menabilly, drawn by Grenvile into a trap, and he leaves the house asking Honor to hide his son Dick until he returns. It is historically true that Lord Robartes of Lanhydrock, Commander of the Parliamentary forces, did take Menabilly as his headquarters, treat the family with extreme severity and sack the house, and that his forces were then slaughtered on the marshes at Par after a battle fought on Castle Dor, the site of an Iron Age fort about a mile from Menabilly. Whether anyone hid in the secret room as the boy does in the novel we do not know. After Grenvile's successful battle, Daphne plots the history of the war through Sir Richard's abortive attempt to break the siege of Plymouth – during which Robartes hangs his bastard son – to his ultimate disgrace and imprisonment at the hands of his own superior officers.

The last section of the book takes place after the war has ended, at the time when there was a genuine attempt to start an uprising in the West. Once again she brings all her protagonists to Menabilly – Honor, her brother Robin, Gartred, who is now his mistress, the new man on whom she has her eye, the rake Sir Peter Courtney, whose wife, Alice, is a Rashleigh relative and the Rashleighs themselves, and their respective children. Richard Grenvile, who was allowed to escape with Prince Charles, returns with Dick Grenvile, now an embittered young man, to head the rising. But Dick betrays them all. Once again the secret passageway and room is used by Honor, this time to aid the escape of Richard and Dick before the Parliamentary soldiers arrive, but the passage is in a parlous state and the door out of the room can now only be held open by a piece of fraying rope, the old mechanism having broken. She sends them off to hide until the following night when, under cover of darkness, they can make for the shore and a waiting boat, but two days later she is told that only Richard was waiting on the shore. A note from him informs her that Dick had found his own way to salvage his honour, by sacrificing his own life to allow his father to escape from the secret room, holding the rope until it broke and knowingly bringing on himself certain death by suffocation.

So how much of The King's General is really based on fact? Certainly, as already mentioned, the people in the novel existed – Honor, Robin and Jonathan Harris, Jonathan and

Mary Rashleigh, John and Joan Rashleigh, their cousin, the attractive rake, Peter Courtney and his wife, Alice; Lord Robartes and, of course, the Grenvile brothers, Sir Richard and Sir Bevil although there is no proof that Richard ever had a bastard son. Honor Harris, however, was never crippled either in a riding accident or in any other way, and she may or may not at one time have been Richard Grenvile's mistress. Jonathan did collect plate for the Royalist cause and it was most probably hidden in the secret room which, with its passageway, had been built primarily for the purpose of smuggling. The small room had also been used to secure his older brother who was mentally disturbed and who was subject to fits of violence. Gartred Grenvile was real enough, did marry Christopher Harris and later Antony Dennis, but there is no reason to believe she ever played the part assigned to her by Daphne, although she was one of the few of the book's protagonists who, in real life, survived to see the Restoration, dying in Taplow at the ripe old age of eighty-five. There was also an uprising in the West after the Civil War had ended, but there is no proof that Richard Grenvile came back to lead it or that his son was even alive at the end of the war; records show only a daughter who survived and who looked after Sir Richard during his long exile in Holland.

Honor Harris and her brother Robin are buried inside Tywardreath Church (the skeleton cavalier is supposed to lie in an unmarked grave outside it), at the end of the aisle under a plaque which says:

'In memory of Robert Harris sometime Major-General of his Majesty's forces before Plymouth who was buried hereunder the 29th day of June 1655. And of Honor Harris his sister who was likewise here underneath buried, the 17th day of November, in the year of our Lord 1653:

'Loyall and stoute; thy Crime this – this thy praise, Thou'rt here with Honour laid – though without Bayes.'

Both died young and, like Richard Grenvile, did not live to see the Restoration.

On the walls of Menabilly there still hang the portraits of the shadowy originals of Daphne's story, an eerie experience for the visitor. How close their personalities came to those Daphne gave them is not known, but certainly the young John Rashleigh seems to have been unlike his heroic, fictional self, as he was considered at the time to have been, as they say, not quite the full shilling. On the other hand the portrait of his wife shows a woman of great beauty who would have put Daphne's Gartred to shame. Sir Peter Courtney was, indeed, the rake she made him and appears to have made a bigamous marriage in France while Alice was still alive.

And what of that skeleton? Was it true that William Rashleigh had really found it behind a buttress of the old Gatehouse, along with its hat, sword and other effects? And that he had been so shocked that he had had it buried secretly in the local graveyard? Certainly Daphne and Browning believed so and, indeed, Browning showed this writer exactly where he thought it had been found. In fact he was not quite right. At which point an intriguing footnote can be added, for I have seen proof of its existence. In 1980 when the Victorian wing was demolished, the Gatehouse had to be removed as it had become structurally unsafe and, contrary to the story, the remains of the room still existed. (They do so no longer.) The artefacts found with the skeleton certainly date from the right period, but the Rashleighs do not think it was a son of Richard Grenvile as there is no proof that he ever returned to lead the uprising. It was not a Rashleigh as all the family could be accounted for at the end of the war. The later William Rashleigh, who spent a good deal of time researching the family background, thought it was probably the remains of a Grenvile cousin, either Roger or George, who had returned to Cornwall to raise forces for the rebellion on behalf of the Prince; and that whoever it was, was hiding in the room when the Parliamentary forces came to Menabilly for the second time.

On this occasion no chances were taken and the women of the household were kept locked away upstairs. The Rashleighs think that possibly the door to the room could only be opened from the outside and that, as neither Mary nor Joan Rashleigh could get away to feed the young man or give him some air, he either starved to death, or more likely suffocated, before they were able to reach him in his terrible prison.

Apparently when the book was published in 1946 some of the older members of the Rashleigh family were shocked and upset by Daphne's use of real family names in a largely fictional story. All that is far in the past and the novel is now regarded with great affection. As Mrs Veronica Rashleigh says: 'I don't think it matters in the least. It's a really good and entertaining story. It just doesn't matter that it's not historically accurate,' though Daphne, she said, did 'worry about "crippling" Honor!' Presumably William Rashleigh was brought round to the idea as Daphne thanks him for his help in her book, along with 'A.L. Rouse' (spelling was never her strong point) and Oenone.

Perhaps those amateur psychologists who delve into *Rebecca* should also turn their attention to *The King's General*. Daphne often said that Honor was an extension of herself, her own persona in the past; that she felt the 'shadow of the buttress' lying on her as it had on Honor, haunting her with the imagined voice of the terrified boy crying out to her as he suffocated to death behind the wall. Like the crippled heroine of her novel she felt frustrated and helpless in the face of a situation she was unable to prevent, an 'invalid of time'. But Honor's crippling had another effect as well.

Daphne was to tell her publishers in America that there were points in common between Sir Richard Grenvile and Tommy. One she mentions is that both were strict disciplinarians – although, she jokes, Tommy did not shoot his officers for insubordination, as Sir Richard had and anyway Tommy's were too well trained to be insubordinate. There are also other similarities. Her description of the sunburned, green-eyed, physically attractive Richard Grenvile is very like that of Tommy as she wrote about him when they first met, and, like Tommy, he is ten years older than her heroine. She makes Grenvile a great womanizer who could happily court (and seduce) the daughter of a fine local family, while at the same time going home to bed a milkmaid; and even when he marries for money and other practical reasons he chooses a woman with a strong sexual appetite. Yet, when he meets Honor again, one gathers her crippled condition precludes her from consummating the reunion, and that from then on he remains faithful to her, although their relationship has to stop short of complete physical fulfilment.

Daphne finished the book and sent it away to Gollancz and Doubleday Doran. She wrote that she now finds it very difficult to find staff to help her run the house and that she spends her time in corduroy trousers and old sweaters hacking back the brambles and chopping wood for the fire. But she is happy. She sees as few people as is practicable, hiding on the roof if anyone calls uninvited. She leaves Menabilly only with great reluctance but when she does, does so in style, taking a suite at Claridges . . . Tommy, she says, had not seen *The King's General* because of being overseas. She had, however, dedicated the book to him. It says: 'TO MY HUSBAND – Also a general but, I trust, a more discreet one.'

There is no trace of Tommy in that side of Richard Grenvile which is historically accurate and which, to some extent, she also portrayed – the bitter, hard man who was capable of extreme savagery and who, in the end, estranged himself even from his own side. But she did make him that flamboyant, physical extrovert, who could genuinely love her heroine while at the same time making love to other women. Was she expressing her own fears?

For whatever reason *The King's General* is the only one of Daphne's books that Tommy disliked.

CHAPTER 18

A Bridge Too Far – and after

Daphne achieved something else shortly after the Brownings moved into Menabilly. Slades Boat-yard – the boatyard of *The Loving Spirit* – had come up for sale and she and Tommy had bought it. She now had not only the house, but the source of her first inspiration as well.

Tommy had always been interested in boat design and they both felt that owning their own yard would enable him to try out his ideas after the war, starting with a boat of his own designed to take the whole family sailing. *Ygdrasil* would be retired and become a plaything for the children on the lawn outside the house. The yard would concentrate on yachts and, as she told her local paper in September 1944, add to Fowey's amenities as a yachting centre, especially if a proposal to widen Fowey's narrow old streets were to be carried out (something which, happily, has never come to pass).

As well as the early research on *The King's General*, she was also working on two plays, *The Years Between* and *September Tide*. The idea for the first was sparked off by a true story. Before the war she and Tommy had been friendly with the Conservative MP for Bodmin, John Rathbone, and his young American wife. He had achieved junior government rank, becoming first PPS to Colonel J. Llewellin, Civil Lord of the Admiralty, and then Parliamentary Secretary to the Ministry of Supply in July 1939. However, like Tommy, he was mad about flying, had his pilot's licence and, as he had already joined the Royal Air Force Volunteer Reserve, immediately war broke out he volunteered for the RAF.

Sometime in December 1940 he was reported missing over Germany, his plane having been shot down and it was some considerable time before it was confirmed that he had been killed and not taken prisoner of war. The young widow married again, a friend of his. John Rathbone was truly dead but, thought Daphne, just suppose it had worked out differently? Just suppose the wife had married in all good faith and then the husband had turned up again after all? It also had overtones of a play Gerald had adapted from a book by Rebecca West, *The Return of the Soldier*. The second play was purely an imaginative work. Meanwhile Tommy was about to be plunged into what was to become the most controversial event of his career as a professional soldier.

The landings in Normandy had succeeded and it was towards the end of August that Montgomery came up with his idea for what was to be known as 'Operation Market Garden'. As the Allied forces drove on towards Belgium, sections of the German army began to retreat, in fact it almost became a rout. Montgomery's idea was to follow this up and push up through Holland, entering Germany by the Ruhr, the industrial heartland. It was an extremely daring idea. The airborne part of the operation, called 'Market', was a vast undertaking involving about 5,000 fighters, bombers, transports and gliders in a daylight assault. They would drop or land paratroopers and their equipment (including vehicles) behind the German lines. The main route up from the border was a long, straight road running beside the Rhine, which was crossed by five bridges, the last being the Arnhem Bridge. The task of the airborne troops, some 35,000 of them, was to secure all the bridges leading to the German border right up as far as Arnhem.

Meanwhile a ground-force column, the 'Garden' section of the operation, would drive through at top speed in the wake of the retreating Germans, preceded by artillery and led by rocket-firing fighters, and make the dash to the Arnhem Bridge.

A good many people had severe misgivings about such a plan, some voicing them at the time. Later, in his memoirs, Major-General Roy E. Urquhart, Commander of the 1st Airborne Division, was to a tell a story whose punchline became the title of Cornelius Ryan's definitive work on the Arnhem disaster, *A Bridge Too Far*. He said:

> 'On the narrow corridor that would carry the armoured drive, there were five major bridges to take. They had to be seized intact by airborne assault. It was the fifth, the crucial bridge over the lower Rhine at a place called Arnhem, that worried Lieutenant-General Frederick Browning, Deputy Commander, First Allied Airborne Army. Pointing at the Arnhem Bridge on the map he asked: "How long will it take the armour to reach us?" Field Marshal Montgomery replied briskly, "Two days". Still looking at the map, Browning answered, "We can hold it for four". Then he answered, "But, sir, I think we might be going a bridge too far".'

He was to be proved all too right but his loyalty to, and admiration of, Montgomery was such that he never spoke of his misgivings again. Browning was brought back from France not only because of his experience of airborne warfare, but also because of his enthusiasm for the use of gliders. He had never lost his faith in their military use even though, when they were used during the Sicily landings, there had been severe loss of life, as many of them had crash-landed.

For obvious reasons, Tommy could give Daphne only limited information as to what was about to happen. Rumours of something spectacular about to take place flourished however, but when she was contacted by a local paper asking her if her husband was taking part in this latest 'adventure', all she was prepared to say was that she had not heard from him for several days and that when she had he was suffering from a bad cold in the head.

On 17 September, in the words of Cornelius Ryan:

'Shortly after 10 a.m. on Sunday, September 17th 1944, from airfields all over southern England, the greatest armada of troop-carrying aircraft ever assembled for a single operation took to the air. In this, the 263rd week of World War II, the Supreme Allied Commander, General Dwight D. Eisenhower, unleashed Market-Garden – one of the most daring and imaginative operations of the war. Surprisingly, Market-Garden, a combined airborne and ground offensive was inspired and carried through by one of the most cautious of all the Allied Commanders, British Field Marshal Bernard Law Montgomery.

'That Sunday afternoon, at exactly 1.30 p.m., in an unprecedented daylight assault, the entire Allied airborne army, complete with vehicles, began dropping behind German lines. The target for this bold and historic invasion from the sky: Nazi-occupied Holland.'

With his own reservations put aside, Tommy Browning had delivered an optimistic summary of what was to take place shortly before the operation was launched. He was remembered as being in high spirits and delighted that at last it was all about to happen. The object of their part of the exercise, he had said, was to lay down a carpet of airborne troops over which the ground forces could pass. He also told them that he believed the operation was so important that it held the key to the duration of the war. He had, said his colleagues, the kind of picturesque confidence that had always made him 'a heroic figure to his men'.

For Market Garden to succeed Montgomery needed two things: first, everything had to go exactly to plan with all the reinforcements being in the right place at the right time; second he needed a lot of luck. In the event he was to get neither.

The supposition that the Germans would continue in their headlong retreat turned out to be incorrect for, when the German High Command realized what was happening they pulled out troops from elsewhere, brought in reinforcements from Germany, and prepared to fight to the death. Information from the Dutch Resistance that the situation was changing rapidly and that German troops were on their way back to northern Holland was ignored by the Allies, as were offers by well-trained units of the Resistance to start diversionary activities which would assist the incoming Allied troops while they were still able to do so.

The first part of the operation did go off relatively smoothly, and Browning and his airborne troops were dropped safely. All the men who had anything to do with Tommy during Market Garden were to remark on his coolness and his ability to appear immaculate whatever the circumstances. Apparently, as soon as he had landed and his jeep had been unloaded, they came under sporadic shelling. Unperturbed, Browning stopped and undid a small tissue-wrapped parcel he had brought with him. Inside was a silk pennant with the pale-blue 'Pegasus' insignia of the British Airborne division on a maroon background. This he fixed to the jeep's bumper. Afterwards there were stories to the effect that Daphne had stitched the pennant with her own hands, a myth she was to put right herself in a letter to Cornelius Ryan. 'I am sorry,' she wrote to him, 'to disappoint the mythmakers, but anyone who has seen my attempts to thread a needle would know this was beyond me. It is a delightful thought, however, and would have greatly amused my husband.'

The safe arrival of Browning and the first wave was just about the only success. They discovered that the Germans had destroyed the bridge which offered the best of all the crossings of the Rhine, which made the capture of the Arnhem Bridge absolutely essential. After that it seemed that everything was to go wrong. Although the weather was clear in Holland, fog descended on the airfields of eastern England, delaying reinforcements and back-up support, and when it did clear many of the gliders never got through. In the second wave 385 men arrived out of 454, with fifty-four of their pilots killed or missing. The long, vulnerable column of ground troops, stretching right back to the Belgium border, ground to a halt as German resistance stiffened and they came under heavy fire.

Communication between the different sectors varied from the poor to the non-existent, and Browning was only one of the commanders involved who had to dash about in person to try and find out what was going on. Newspaper reports of the time do not, of course, give any idea of what was happening on the ground, but they must have been sufficient to worry all those who had family and friends involved in the exercise.

The end was disaster. The brave paratroopers who had finally taken the Arnhem Bridge in the belief that when ground reinforcements arrived they would soon be relieved were to fight fruitlessly for sixty solid hours, the light forty-eight-hour ration supply they had brought with them running out early on. The losses were terrible. Meanwhile the ground column found itself fighting all along its length. Browning, who was in his headquarters at Nijmegen, soon became uneasy. Although the breakdown in communications meant that he did not know what was going on, he suspected serious trouble. In his book, Ryan exonerates Browning completely from what happened at Arnhem. He had been correct in saying that, at a push, Arnhem Bridge could be taken and held for four days but not longer. In fact it was 19 September before he knew the true position, ten days after the first drop.

Back home, limited as the news was, it was becoming apparent that Market Garden had run into trouble, although the scale of the disaster was not revealed. On 25 September the decision, with which Browning 'dejectedly' agreed, was taken to start trying to evacuate what remained of the survivors.

Early in the morning of 29 September, while she was still in bed, Daphne was woken by a telephone call from a young female newspaper reporter. Was it true, she was asked, what was being said on German Forces Radio, that Tommy had been captured? Had she heard officially, and was it correct? Daphne was obviously shocked, she had heard nothing at all from Tommy since the landing on the 10th, and anyway she never listened to the German radio. That was just the beginning. From then on, the telephone never stopped ringing for the rest of the day as reporters from all the national papers asked her the same thing. Desperately she tried to find out herself if this were true; meanwhile the story had already appeared in both the daily and evening papers, even in her own local *Western Morning News*. As well as the reporters, she was inundated by calls from friends and family also asking her to confirm the story.

It was late in the evening before a friend of Tommy's in the Airborne Division rang and told her that he was safe and the story quite untrue, and the next day's papers carried the fact, the War Office having issued an official communiqué to that effect. Tommy, fit and well, had been landed 'in the Midlands', by a US troop-carrying plane, with others of the force evacuated from Arnhem, including Urquhart. With them came other troop-carriers, full of exhausted and wounded men from Nijmegen. Those at Arnhem were either dead or had been taken prisoner.

On 3 October Daphne had a letter published in *The Times* complaining about what had happened to her, enquiring if there was not some information-centre in London where the Press could have found out what had or had not happened to Tommy officially. She emphasized how upsetting it had been for his family and friends, not least the pressure put on her by the continual telephone calls. Far more tact and thought should have gone into contacting her, she wrote, even had it been necessary to contact her at all – which she doubted. The incident had caused her many unnecessary hours of great anguish.

The cost of Arnhem was appalling. The Allied forces suffered, as Ryan notes, more casualties in Market Garden than in the first days of the mammoth invasion of Normandy. Total

Allied losses for the twenty-four-hour period of D-Day are estimated at between 10,000 and 12,000 men. In the nine days of Market Garden combined losses – airborne and ground forces – in killed, wounded and missing amounted to more than 17,000 men. The British casualties were highest – 13,226. Only a handful of those who held Arnhem Bridge survived to tell the tale. The Dutch, who felt they had been treated like idiots by the Allied forces, suffered gravely too – estimates differ as to how badly. Some were killed in the fighting between the opposing forces, some fighting with the Allies, others in the bitter German reprisals which were to follow.

A brief summary of the story of Arnhem has been necessary because, much later, it was to return to haunt Daphne, when Richard Attenborough made a film of Ryan's book in 1977. Tommy never deviated from his support for Montgomery. Montgomery in his own memoirs said: 'In my – prejudiced – view, if the operation had been properly backed from its inception, and given the aircraft, ground forces, and administrative resources necessary for the job – it would have succeeded in spite of my mistakes, or the adverse weather, or the presence of the 2nd SS Panzer Corps in the Arnhem area. I remain "Market Garden's" unrepentant advocate.'

Prince Bernhard of the Netherlands took another view. 'My country can never again afford the luxury of another Montgomery success.'

A couple of weeks after his return, and a brief reunion with Daphne, Browning gave a press conference on the Arnhem affair. At no time did he ever mention his initial misgivings about Arnhem being 'a bridge too far'. The operation had been, he said echoing Montgomery's words, '85 per cent successful', and he claimed that it had saved the Second Army 25,000 casualties. Montgomery's request to him to lay an airborne carpet from Eindhoven to Arnhem had given him 'a chance of doing something I'd always wanted to try – a daylight operation with full air support. We were convinced it could be done. Some people have criticised Field Marshal

Montgomery for saying that it was 85 per cent successful. It was exactly that or rather more. It punched a hole through a strongly held German line, and when the First Division was withdrawn it was within a mile of the final objective.'

Every effort had been made to reach the Arnhem Bridge, but 'our attempts, though gallant, failed to link up with the division', and he eventually had to recommend the withdrawal, Montgomery had had his carpet and no military operation could ever be 100 per cent successful. 'If one or two things had gone right we should have got the Arnhem Bridge. That is a tragedy of war, and a lot of first-class men were lost. Otherwise I have no regrets.'

The most likely outcome of Arnhem would have been that Tommy would return to the war in Europe and see out the final crossing of the Rhine, but only a few weeks later he was posted to the Pacific. Owing to illness, Lieutenant-General Sir Henry Pownall had to relinquish his post as Chief-of-Staff of the South-East Asia Command, and Browning was sent to take his place. He had been sent, said a *Times* war correspondent, because SEAC was being reinforced with young and capable officers in the higher ranks. In his new post Browning would be Chief-of-Staff to Admiral Lord Louis Mountbatten.

For two years between 1944 and 1946 Daphne and Tommy were to see little of each other. A friend recalled having tea with Daphne while the three-year-old Christian played gliders and dive bombers with a toy horse and how, in spite of everything and her obvious concern over Tommy and the progress of the war, she had kept doggedly on with her own work.

She had made her own routine. She wrote, not in the house where she might have had a splendid study, but in a hut in the garden, heated by an oil heater. Here she hammered away on her typewriter working almost office hours, sometimes all day, sometimes until lunchtime. She had plenty to occupy her. *The Years Between* was to open in London in January 1945, and there was the continuing research on the Civil War, although she had not found the place where the skeleton had been immured. Domestically, matters were on an even keel and the children were safe and happy.

Tommy remained out in the Far East until the Japanese surrender, in which he played a prominent role. When Lt.-Gen. Tazako Numata, Chief-of-Staff of the Japanese Southern Army signed the preliminary agreement for facilitating the surrender, the document was also signed by Browning. He subsequently told the Press on 29 August 1945 that the attitude of the Japanese had been very correct throughout, though they had asked 'a great number of unnecessary questions.' He had also clarified the details of the final, definitive surrender.

A contemporary report describes Browning, immaculate as ever, heading the British deputation and describing the details of the surrender plan to the Japanese in front of representatives from Holland, China, France, the USA and Australia and how one of the Japanese, Rear-Admiral Chudo, was 'seen to be gulping back tears.'

Shortly afterwards he returned to Britain and became Military Secretary to the Secretary of State for War, a post in which he served for only a year before he retired from the Army. He was given a knighthood in the 1946 New Year's Honours List, making Daphne Lady Browning. But after those hectic years away, he was not to settle down happily with Daphne at Menabilly and design yachts for their boatyard. On his retirement from the Army, he chose rather to accept the post of Comptroller and Treasurer to the household of the young Princess Elizabeth, a post which, by its very nature, would ensure he was kept busy elsewhere.

CHAPTER 19

Theatre

Daphne had indeed been working on her two plays. The first of these to be presented was *The Years Between*. It opened at The Opera House, Manchester, on 20 November 1944 and then transferred to the West End on 10 January 1945 where – shades of Gerald – it opened at the Wyndham's.

Looked at now it reads like a play of the 1930s rather than the 40s, and it was not received with enthusiasm by most of the theatre critics. The story-line did follow that of the real-life MP, John Rathbone, up to the time when he was reported missing, but the play supposes that afterwards his docile and rather dependent wife has actually stood for Parliament herself and become a Conservative MP representing his old constituency. When the play opens she is about to marry a sympathetic farmer, an idea she has to give up when her supposedly dead husband reappears who, after behaving in a singularly churlish fashion, departs again leaving them all resigned, it seems, to a life of celibacy.

'Miss du Maurier,' wrote James Agate in *The Sunday Times*, 'does not help by starting the play off with a whopper – or rather three whoppers. First, we are to believe that Captain Wentworth didn't really crash, but only pretended to do so, so that nobody would suspect him of being the chief organiser of the Underground movement in Europe. Second we are to believe that Diana is not allowed to know any of this because

195

she is Ibsen's Nora all over again, a tweeting song-bird who is to chirrup all over the house except when her lord and master is at his desk writing his books and speeches. Third, we are to believe that, his mission concluded and the war ended, the Colonel returns to find the canary turned bird of wisdom and representing the constituency in his stead! Well, I don't think Miss du Maurier can have it all three ways any more than I believe that a heroine wearing three rows of whacking great pearls cares threepence whether working-class houses are provided with baths or not.

'Eventually we get to a lot of chaffering about the magnanimities, and finally the Colonel accepts the Government's offer to return abroad and look after Germany. Whereupon Diana, who has become the complete Mrs Pardiggle, proposes to devote the next few years to seeing that the working classes take baths – one gathers by forcible immersion if necessary – and Richard (the farmer) decides to start farming Cader Idris.'

Beverley Baxter in the *Evening Standard* appears to have agreed. He found the characters totally unbelievable, from the husband who was an author (what did he write?, asks Baxter), and an MP of whom we were given no picture as 'a politician save that he was a Tory which perhaps Miss du Maurier thought was enough for us to get on with', through Diana (elected without a contest!), to Richard the farmer who apparently 'had a farm which seems to look after itself'. He thought the end of Act II was rather well written, but that by Act III 'unhappily, Miss du Maurier had shot her bolt. Having created an admirable situation, she could do nothing to resolve it. So she decided to end the war, which was accomplished by the use of the radio and, one has to record, to the titters of people in the audience.' *The Years Between* did, however, have a modest success.

Her next play was *September Tide* which was to star Gertrude Lawrence. The family connections went back a long way. Although Gerald had not liked, or appeared to advantage in films, his most successful performance had been in *Mr Camber's Ladies* directed by Alfred Hitchcock, in which he played a nobleman who marries a music-hall actress, the role being taken by Gertrude. The two later had a major stage success playing opposite each other in a melodrama entitled *Behold, We Live*. Gerald played a barrister dying of cancer, whose wife refuses him a divorce to enable him to marry his mistress, the role taken by Gertrude Lawrence. Charles Laughton recalled that the scene in which Gerald took farewell of his mistress without informing her of his terminal illness was one of the most affecting he ever saw on stage.

Gertrude Lawrence's name was an enormous box-office draw, and in July 1948 Daphne had the opportunity of discussing the play with her in New York, as Daphne had been persuaded to accept an invitation from *Ladies Home Journal* to visit the United States. She noted with delight that they would be paying her fare and giving her expenses while she was there. Domestically she was having some problems, as Muriel who was in failing health was installed with a nurse at Menabilly for a few weeks.

It seems that Daphne was away from Menabilly a good deal during the spring and summer of 1948, first in France, where she was still picking up the threads of her pre-war experiences, then visiting her children in their respective schools (Christian had gone down with chicken pox). She also notes that Tessa, who seems to have been burning the candle at both ends with Cambridge May Week, the May Balls and 'Commem. Week' at Oxford and Ascot, had made Tommy anxious when it seemed she had disappeared for a day or two only to surface in Oxford having been taken there by a new admirer. In a self-revealing paragraph in a letter written to a friend, Daphne says that she hopes that her various American editors will take her out to dinner in turn while she is in New York, as she could not be expected to sit around in Gertrude's dressing room every evening while she was on stage; also, that she hoped she could get away at weekends without being accompanied by Gertrude; she was one of those people who could not bear to mix up her friends, preferring that each should always remain firmly sealed in their own watertight compartment.

The new play, *September Tide*, was produced first at the New Theatre, Oxford, in November 1948, transferring to the Aldwych Theatre in December of that year. The story-line is unashamed romantic tosh. Stella, the beautiful, gifted and sensitive mother-figure, lives in a house which is obviously heavily based on Ferryside. She is the widow of a naval commander and has long been pursued by the stalwart and unimaginative Robert. As in *The Years Between*, in spite of the war, there is a faithful servant who does the heavy work about the house. To the Ferry House comes Stella's daughter, Cherry and her new husband, Evan, who is fifteen years older – a hard-drinking, womanizing, but terribly talented artist. Cherry had been at art school when she met him for the first time in a pub on the King's Road. After a further series of evenings spent consuming vast amounts of whisky, they both get blind drunk and wake up together in Cherry's flat and, although nothing untoward seems to have occurred, Evan does the decent thing and marries her.

Stella welcomes the couple. She is always tiptoeing about making things comfortable. She has prepared a studio upstairs for Evan to paint in, while she cooks delicious meals for them, mends their clothes and tastefully arranges the roses. Evan, we are to believe, sleeps alone in the studio. Time passes and, while painting a portrait of Stella he falls desperately in love with her. Cherry goes to the cinema in Fowey with a friend and is unable to get home as a storm and the strong September tide mean that the ferry is unable to undertake the river crossing. Stella and Evan admit their love for each other and there they are, left together all night in the Ferry House. Do they or don't they make love? It seems they do not, but nothing can ever be the same again. Shall she marry Robert and let Cherry and Evan live in the Ferry House? No, that sacrifice is too much, says Evan. So he accepts a convenient offer to go to New York, taking Cherry with him and leaving

Stella behind with her son, Jimmy, who suddenly turns up with a broken leg . . . As the ferry bears the love of her life away, Stella watches mistily through the window, pensively smoking a cigarette. All the characters in *September Tide*, like Daphne and Gerald, smoke like chimneys throughout the play.

The production was immensely assisted by having Gertrude Lawrence as Stella and the young Michael Gough as Evan. From all accounts Lawrence could make audiences believe just about anything. *The Times* loved Gertrude, but lacked enthusiasm for the play. 'We are troubled little or not at all that the mother's passionate love for her daughter's husband should seemingly leave the relations of mother and daughter quite unstrained. It would be vain, perhaps, to scrutinize the dialogue for adequate reasons why the painter's manners should so rapidly improve and why he should suddenly grow, in his own words, to man's estate quite capable of playing his part in the necessary renunciation. To love the leading lady is (shall we say) a liberal education, and that explains everything. Yet, in justice to the author, one must say that she pours the treacle with a technically expert hand: the story, even if we do not believe it is, in general, good theatre.' Matinée audiences adored it. In 1975 it had a brief revival at the King's Theatre in Edinburgh and the critic from *The Stage* thought it might profitably be put on in London as a charming period piece. But too much had happened in the theatre since *September Tide*. Audiences reared on Osborne, Pinter and Beckett, let alone McGrath, Brenton and Barker, would find *September Tide* hard going and, alas, Gertrude Lawrence is no more.

The King's General was published in 1946 and was particularly successful in the United States. Interviewed about it Daphne emphasized the amount of research she had had to do and also that most of it was historically accurate; which it was with regard to the actual events of the Civil War, but it has certainly left some misunderstandings behind about the authenticity of the people involved – most readers firmly believe that Honor Harris was crippled the day before her marriage to Richard Grenvile, and that the skeleton in the wall was that of his traitor son. Like the wreckers of *Jamaica Inn*, the myth has firmly become entrenched as reality.

With the ending of the war her life settled into a well-defined pattern, which would remain virtually unbroken for the next fourteen years, a pattern based around Menabilly where she would stay apart from brief forays abroad – such as the two trips to the USA, visits to Balmoral or London (in both cases, usually in connection with Tommy's royal duties), brief trips for research, and holidays including visits once again to France. Now that Europe was at peace, she was able to revive her friendship with Fernande, although obviously never on the intense basis of those early years. Fernande had sat out the war in Vichy (unoccupied) France and Tommy, knowing how fond Daphne was of her, actually arranged for an officer and a handful of men to be sent to see if she was all right once France had been liberated.

At the end of the war Daphne's daughters were sent to an Anglican convent in Surrey and Christian to a boys' boarding school. One of Tessa Browning's contemporaries remembered her vividly as being very much the lively centre of her particular group. All the girls were very well aware of the Brownings' famous mother, but Daphne only rarely appeared in the school during the years Tessa and Flavia were there, preferring to meet them outside. On one occasion she came to see Tessa play Laertes in an all-girl production of *Hamlet*. Apparently she was very good and her contemporary also recalled the fuss made by the staff over Daphne's visit. Once Christian Browning was old enough, he followed his father to Eton.

Daphne used to recall how, when she was only four, she told her governess, Miss Torrance, that she could not only write but had written a book, *John in the Wood of the World*. The story proved to be prophetic for someone who would so single-mindedly turn her back on the wood of the world now that she had found her own rural, private paradise, her Garden of Eden. The twenty acres of famous cultivated gardens had long since become overgrown and she was happy to let the whole estate return to the wild. She would walk for miles through the woods, across the fields, down to the cove at Pridmouth where, long ago, she had seen the wreck of the coaster which was later to figure in *Rebecca*. There would always be a dog or several dogs at her heels for she never lost her love of them. Her first puppy, Jock, was a West Highland terrier who had been given away by Muriel when the family moved to Cannon Hall, something Daphne had been slow to forgive. Later he had been replaced by a mongrel she called Brutus, after the play *Dear Brutus*. Unfortunately, after a visit to the vet, Brutus had transferred his affections to him and would spend his days sitting on the Vet's doorstep. Eventually Daphne had had to give in and Brutus moved in with the vet.

There followed another West Highland terrier, also called Jock, who had come to a sad end, having been found drowned in a rain-water tank after chasing away a cat; he seemed to be an accident-prone animal for she had had to rescue him once before from what was nearly another watery grave in Cumberland. The deaths of Brutus and Jock seem to have provoked an odd reaction in her for when, during one of those idyllic pre-war holidays in France with Fernande, Gerald had written to tell her of Jock's death, he told her that by some eerie coincidence Brutus had returned from the vet's to Cannon Hall looking for her that very same day. He had been run over and killed on his way home. In tears she had told Fernande that the dogs had made some kind of sacrifice as they had known they would not see her again. Neither then, or later, was she ever to explain what she had meant by this.

Ideas came unhurriedly as she walked the woods and if they no longer crowded in on her, one after the other, as they had in those early days, she knew better than to try and force the pace. Just as holidays, usually those taken abroad, would trigger off ideas for short stories, so a place, a house, an inn, a portrait would start the seed growing that would develop into a novel. She still found fictional characters easier to deal with than those based on real people, unless a gap of centuries made them sufficiently distant. Questioned frequently as to where her characters 'came from', she would search her mind for answers. From memories suppressed or events long forgotten? Certainly, as with all authors. From dreams perhaps? From books or poems read years previously? What writer does not draw on past sources – look at William Shakespeare. She gladly acknowledged her debts to the Brontës and Thackeray, and those robust Victorian historical novelists like Harrison Ainsworth and Charles Kingsley.

She never pretended otherwise than that every 'original' character in her novels was almost certain to have had its origins somewhere, possibly deep in herself like Honor Harris, even if it was impossible to trace them.

As we carry our genetic inheritance from our parents, she would say, so the fictional characters develop as they must, 'and without control', albeit nurtured and formed by the writer.

She never worked to a plan and never wrote to commission always refusing to guarantee when 'the next du Maurier' would appear. She was content that her writing pace had slowed to a book about every two years. After some months of brooding over the new book, working out the story-line in her head and creating the characters, the next stage was to plot carefully each chapter in synopsis form in a notebook (using George's old black book whenever possible), as the ideas matured. Then it was back to the hut, a converted summer-house, which Daphne always used for writing, with its splendid view across the Channel for a day of regular office hours, to the old typewriter and the obsessive chain smoking.

Dialogue still came easiest to her, description and narrative slower. Sometimes she revised chapter-by-chapter as she went along, more often leaving it until the end, when she had finished the book. Modestly she would admit to her grammar still being poor, and her spelling even worse, and that although she owned an *Oxford English Dictionary* she never could be bothered to stop to look up words. She relied on her publishers to put obvious mistakes right and was only too well aware of the criticisms levelled at her, especially that she was always prone to use what were described as 'tired' adjectives. She was able to live with criticism, not only because it never affected her popularity or her sales, but because she truly regarded herself first and foremost as a story-teller not a writer. 'There are people who can polish,' she would say, 'and people who can't. A really frightfully good writer like Charles Morgan can do it but if I tried, God knows what would happen!'

Even working as she did for a set number of hours, six days a week, a book now took between four and six months to complete, and she wondered if this was because she was getting slower or because she was delving deeper into characterization. She would finish each book totally drained of energy.

The success of any du Maurier novel was assured, for there were few novelists with such a faithful following and an article in *Books and Bookman* dating from 1952 quotes Victor Gollancz as saying that, while other bestselling writers went up and down in public esteem, she remained an extraordinary constant. Hardback editions of her books usually sold anything up to 200,000 copies, to say nothing of the enormous book-club, cheaper edition and paperback sales, foreign sales and serial rights. Yet she still felt diffident as she finished every book, sending it to Gollancz feeling much like a schoolgirl submitting an essay to her teacher.

With the girls now away she could live even more intensely in her head, inside the private paradise that was Menabilly and, once Christian had gone too, even meals were of little interest until the evening except when Tommy was home. After a day of writing she might have a last walk before it was dark, and then would settle down with a couple of slices of cold ham and a salad before an evening spent in Menabilly's beautiful 'long room', which she had furnished with Chippendale furniture and other appropriate pieces. Visitors to Menabilly in the winter months found it a chilly place in spite of the large open fires, central heating – what there was of it – being confined to an ancient system in the Victorian wing. By her own choice Daphne owned no car.

Apart from her trips to London she would dress neatly but casually, telling her rare interviewers that she saw no point in spending a fortune on what went on her back. She was still a very attractive woman, and had lost the roundness of face of the 1937 photograph which had come with young motherhood. She was blessed with excellent facial structure and those remarkable eyes, but was never vain about either. 'Do you know,' she was to say on one occasion when looking into a mirror, 'my son tells me I have the face of a murderess . . .'

Yet the first fruit, after *The King's General*, of those walks in the woods absorbing the Cornish landscape, was a novel which was not about Cornwall at all, but one in which she was to return in spirit to the London she had known before she had married Tommy, and to a family whose life, like that of her own, was centred around the theatre. *The Parasites*, she was to say, was the nearest she ever came to self-analysis, and that its three leading characters are all reflections of herself. If this is true then she is ruthlessly self-critical. It is dedicated: 'For Whom the Cap Fits', followed by the *Encyclopaedia Britannica* definition of the word 'Parasites'. After describing what they are and how they operate, along with some examples, it concludes: 'Parasites affect their hosts by feeding upon their living tissues or cells and the intensity of the effect upon the hosts ranges from the slightest injury to complete destruction.'

The 'Delaneys' of the novel are very obviously based on the du Mauriers, as the fictional family, too, has descended from several generations of famous artists of various kinds. Beloved 'Pappy' Delaney is a world-class opera singer, 'Mama' a

204

ballerina. Beautiful Maria is the illegitimate child of Pappy and a Viennese actress who died in childbirth, leaving him a daughter. Niall is Mama's son, possibly the child of a pianist who lived with her for a few weeks, and who was then sent away to die as he was found to have TB. Celia alone is the child of Pappy and Mama and the only legitimate one of the trio. Maria becomes a famous West End actress, Niall a successful composer of musicals, while Celia sacrifices her own talent in order to stay home and look after Pappy. Mama is given a relatively early death in an incident reminiscent of that of Isadora Duncan. Like the real-life dancer, Mama, too, drapes herself in long, floating chiffon scarves, and while the family are on holiday in Brittany she slips on a cliff while picking sea pinks, falls over the edge and is hanged by her long scarf, an event watched by a horrified Niall.

All three, in their different ways, are parasitic. Maria, spoiled and successful darling of the London stage, marries, after a string of lovers, the quiet, dependable, straight-forward Charles, heir to a large estate and a title, because he reminded her of the character Simon in J.M. Barrie's *Mary Rose*, in which she was playing the name-part at the time. But her true and lasting emotional attachment is for Niall, child of her stepmother, and it is to him she keeps returning while still enjoying the comfortable life provided for her offstage by Charles. Not even her children have a strong enough hold to keep her either from acting or from Niall.

Niall lives for a long time off an older woman in her flat in Paris, and continues to do so even when his musical comedies are successful. An additional twist is that the woman has at some time in the past been Pappy's mistress. But he, too, is emotionally bound by his relationship with Maria. Celia willingly gives her youth to Pappy, her emotional development stultified by him. When, in early middle age, she is given a chance to escape from domesticity through her paintings, she rejects it, preferring to look after Pappy until his death. Even that does not liberate her – once again she prefers to live at second hand, this time through the eldest of Maria's children to whom she intends to stick like a leech.

There are obvious overtones of Daphne's own early life. The Delaneys are well off and very successful, and the children are brought up to have virtually anything they want. Places from her childhood and adolescence recur: Maria has a flat in Church Row, Hampstead, where Gerald was born; Niall moves into Freada's flat on the Avenue de Neuilly, near where Fernande had her school. Niall has a sailing-boat. There is no high drama in the story. It begins at the point where Charles has had enough of all of them, and particularly of a wife who has little or no interest either in him, the children or the estate and whose personality changes with each part she plays; who will take all he can give of affection and financial security, while reserving what love she is capable of for Niall. Charles is tired, too, of keeping Niall and Celia for long periods of time and pandering to Celia's need to be needed. The three then tell their own stories up to the 'present', at which point Charles announces that he is going to divorce Maria and marry a neighbour, who lives nearby in the country, and who will be happy to look after him and his children and they can all get out and manage as best they can.

Maria goes back to London and a part in a new play, only marginally upset at the way things have worked out. She'll still have Niall and there will always be other wealthy lovers. Celia plots how she can steal the affection of Maria's oldest daughter from her new stepmother, and Niall sets off for France in his leaky yacht; whether he makes it or drowns on the way over is left open.

In many ways *The Parasites* is an unsatisfactory book. The characters are so unpleasant and two-dimensional that, as with *The Progress of Julius*, it is difficult to care what happens to them, nor is there any feeling of reality in the life they lead. If Daphne really did feel that Maria, Niall and Celia represented three aspects of herself, then what does one make of it? She gives Charles the words that sum them up: 'A parasite. And that's what you are, the three of you. Parasites. The whole bunch. You always have been and always will be. Nothing can change you. You are doubly, triply, parasitic; firstly, because you've traded ever since childhood on that seed of talent you had the luck to inherit from your fantastic forbears; secondly, because you've none of you done a stroke of ordinary honest work in your lives, but batten upon us, the fool public who allow you to exist; and thirdly, because you prey upon each other, the three of you, living in a world of fantasy which you have created for yourselves and which bears no relation to anything in heaven or on earth.'

It would seem that, somewhere inside that paradise garden, Daphne was reviewing her life to that point – the indulged daughter of a famous family whose reputation had given her a head start, the writer whose adoring public enabled her to do as she wished, the woman who was happiest living in the world she had created for herself, cut off so far as was possible from the reality outside.

What she had, though, which her fictional parasites did not, was the ability to work hard and with discipline, an ability which had turned her into a true professional; so far from being a parasite, she was the main provider for the family. She also had a gift conspicuously lacking in her three uninteresting protagonists – a sense of humour.

Looking ahead to her later life, though, it seems as if she gave prophetic words to Mama. Just before she dies, Mama has been talking to Niall, telling him that she is terrified that she has developed some incurable illness about which she dare not consult her doctor. She could not live, she says, if she could not dance again. 'It's me,' she says, 'it's my whole life. Nothing else matters. It never has done.' Niall considers this, and realizes that is why she has never been to him what he wanted her to be – she has never been unkind, angry or cold, it was just that dancing had come first and, as her first child, he had expected too much of her, hoped for 'things that did not happen.'

Mama continues: 'It's queer how a woman is made. There is

something deep inside that can't be explained. Doctors think they know all about it, but they don't really. It's the thing that gives life – whether it's dancing, or making love or having babies – it's the same creative force in a man but a man can have it always. It can't be destroyed. With us, it's different. It lasts only a little while, then goes. It flickers and dies, and you can't do anything about it. You have to watch it go. And once it's gone there's nothing left. Nothing at all . . .'

'It does not matter to a lot of women,' she said, 'but it matters to me.' If 'writing' is substituted for 'dancing' then this truly does seem to be some form of self-analysis.

As a footnote, Angela, writing in 1950, notes that Gerald was only able to read Daphne's first three books. She did not think he would have enjoyed those she describes as 'historical novels'; but he would have loved *The Parasites*.

CHAPTER 20

Fame and Fortune

Throughout the late 1940s and into the 50s, Tommy was heavily involved in the itinerary of the Royal Household. Princess Elizabeth and her husband, the Duke of Edinburgh, were undertaking many foreign trips, in part to make up for the years of the war and Tommy, as Comptroller of the Household, almost always accompanied them. In that capacity he had been to Canada and Australasia, among other Commonwealth countries, and it is hard to imagine a life more alien to that of Menabilly. In 1952 events took a dramatic turn, for he was in Kenya when the news came to the Princess of her father's death, George VI, and he accompanied the royal couple when they flew back to Britain. Obviously they had become very fond of the 'sophisticated and elegant ex-guards officer', as the popular press described him, and did not want to part with him when Princess Elizabeth became Queen. So Tommy was appointed Treasurer to the Duke of Edinburgh, receiving a KCVO in 1953. In the February of that year he and Daphne were honoured guests at the Coronation; and had the privilege of keeping their chairs which had been specially made for the occasion.

Meanwhile everything else remained the same, with Daphne at Menabilly, and Tommy feverishly commuting at weekends. The *News Chronicle* noted, when he received his KCVO, that 'he travels from London every weekend he can spare from his duties. Miss du Maurier rarely returns the compliment.'

After *The Parasites* came the stylish and popular thriller, *My Cousin Rachel*. Again the setting is Menabilly and the twisting, overgrown, and unused drive of Menabilly leads off the old crossroads of Four Turnings, which is now a small roundabout. When Daphne was writing *My Cousin Rachel*, the gibbet which had once stood there had obviously been removed years previously, but there used to be, on the spot where it had been, a tall standing stone, known locally as 'the Tristan stone'. The legend carved on it seems to suggest that it once marked the grave of 'Drustans', son of 'Cunomorus', otherwise known as Mark, and she was to make use of the Tristan stone when she came to finish Q's novel *Castle Dor* in later years. It has since been moved some yards further on and is now to be found by the roadside, tradition having had to give way to the needs of modern tourist traffic. But the home farm of Menabilly Barton is there on the brow of the hill, by the path which leads down to Pridmouth Cove, and the hospitable waters of Fowey Harbour still give shelter to ships from all over the world.

If, as Daphne so often said, old incidents and long forgotten stories surfaced later as ideas for books, then it does seem likely that the story of Madeleine Smith's husband, as retold by Foy Quiller-Couch in a melodramatic manner, did provide certain characteristics of Rachel. There is also, so far as the names used are concerned, another source. Daphne and Tommy were friends of Sir John Carew-Pole of Antony House, near Saltash. In one of the bedrooms hung a portrait of an attractive dark lady painted by a Mary Beale. She is Rachel Carew, an ancestress of the Carew-Pole family, who married an Ambrose Manaton, son or nephew of another man of the same name who plays a leading role in *The King's General*.

Over lunch one day Daphne told Sir John how she liked to try and incorporate members of the great Cornish families into her stories when she could and that she would like to use Rachel Carew as a model for the 'heroine' of the new book on which she was working, at least so far as her appearance went. 'I wouldn't want to use her surname,' she told him, 'because my Rachel is a possible poisoner and I wouldn't want to be sued!' Sir John told her that he did not mind at all – and anyway the lady was long dead, but Daphne thought it better to be on the safe side in case some member of the Carew family decided to christen their daughter Rachel. 'Anyway she set her book in quite a different period to that of the original Rachel and her story was total fiction,' says Richard Carew-Pole. 'Our Rachel was most respectable and actually died well before her husband.' Rachel's Italian home, the Villa Sangalletti, is also based on a real house, glimpsed by Daphne while on an Italian holiday.

For the second time Daphne was to take on a male persona in a book. Like the narrators of *I'll Never Be Young Again*, *The Scapegoat*, *The Flight of the Falcon* and *The House on the Strand*, he is emotionally dependent on an older man, in this case his cousin, Ambrose. Somewhere, lost in all these books, as Daphne was to confirm, is that imaginary Eric Avon, the cricketing wizard and talented extrovert invented by that teenage girl so many years earlier. But since Eric Avon was always so dominating and masterful, he appears to mirror more closely the guides and mentors of these often inadequate and emotionally immature male narrators, than those characters themselves. Sadly, only one of them, the narrator in *The Scapegoat*, ever really becomes his own man.

My Cousin Rachel opens with the young narrator, Philip, remembering how when he was a boy he and his cousin Ambrose had passed the gibbet at Four Turnings on which swung the body of a man, Tom Jenkyn, and how he asked Ambrose what had brought him to this terrible death. 'He killed his wife, so Ambrose said. And that was all.' Ambrose, to whom she gives a dominating and charismatic personality, seems remarkably emotionally inexperienced for a man who is supposed to be in his forties, but be that as it may, he is sent off to Italy for the winter as he is suffering from chest trouble.

There he meets the beautiful and fascinating Rachel, a second cousin of the family and the widow of an Italian nobleman called Sangalletti. Ambrose falls passionately in love with Rachel, marries her, and remains in Italy. After a while he begins to send increasingly alarming letters to Philip. He is ill with sickness and vomiting, suffers from terrible pains in the head, which Rachel doctors with herbal drinks. Finally he asks Philip to come out to him for he is convinced she is trying to poison him.

Philip leaves Menabilly at once but arrives in Italy too late. Ambrose has died, Rachel has gone, and their affairs are in the hands of a sinister lawyer, Rainaldi. Philip is told that Ambrose died of a brain tumour, the same condition which had afflicted his father. Grief-stricken, Philip returns home convinced that Rachel has killed his cousin and determined to bring her to book somehow, though he is unable to persuade anyone else that Ambrose's death has been caused by anything other than natural causes.

To his amazement, Rachel herself arrives in Cornwall bringing home Ambrose's personal belongings. Ambrose had intended to leave her the estate and its income until her death (when it would revert again to Philip), but never had time to change his will. Among Ambrose's effects is another letter accusing Rachel of profligate extravagance and broadly hinting that she had had a reputation for immorality even when she had been married to Sangalletti. It also informs Philip that she had miscarried their child and could never have another. Rachel, however, proves to be so fascinating that in no time at all Philip has fallen for her, just as Ambrose did, and she finally allows him to make love to her. He loads her with precious family jewels, makes over the estate to her, begs and pleads with her to marry him, but she refuses. Soon he discovers she is meeting Rainaldi secretly and, shortly afterwards, Philip becomes ill, with exactly the same symptoms as those exhibited by Ambrose. He also has been given herbal medicine by Rachel. As soon as he recovers, he searches her room and finds in a drawer a packet of the highly poisonous seeds of the laburnum, a tree he knew also grew in the garden of the Villa Sangalletti.

Yet he can find no other 'proof' and there is no certainty she has ever used them. Warned that the bridge which has been built across the new sunken garden designed by Rachel is structurally unsafe, he says nothing when she tells him she is going to see how the work is going on. While she is out he finds packets of other, innocuous, seeds, a letter to Rainaldi which is quite innocent and another to the family lawyer (and his own godfather) returning the jewels and telling him she will soon be going back again to Italy. There is also a picture drawn by Ambrose, bearing the message 'remember the good times'.

As he realizes that it is quite possible that Rachel is, after all, quite innocent he is told that she has suffered a fatal accident when the bridge gave way beneath her. He rushes to her and she dies in his arms, calling him Ambrose.

Was she or wasn't she a poisoner? Daphne was always being asked. 'I just don't know,' she would reply. 'Sometimes I think she did, sometimes I didn't – in the end I just couldn't make up my mind.'

Whether or not her readers made up their minds as to the guilt or innocence of Rachel, as they pondered if her beautiful face was indeed that of a murderess, they certainly had no doubts over the merits of the novel and bought it in their tens of thousands.

In an article in *The News Chronicle*, timed to coincide with its publication, the 'highest paid woman writer in Britain' was reported as having been paid £50,000 for the film rights alone. The young and up-and-coming Richard Burton, 'acclaimed as the outstanding actor at the Stratford Memorial Theatre last year', was to play Philip, and Vivien Leigh had been approached for the part of Rachel. In the event it went to her female co-star in *Gone With The Wind*, Olivia de Havilland, and this time the film was actually made in Cornwall, around Fowey and Carlyon Bay.

In 1952 Gollancz brought out a collection of her short stories under the title *The Apple Tree*, which enabled her devoted readership to see her, for the first time, in a very different guise as an exponent of the sinister and macabre. Some of these stories and others that followed have a night-marish quality, showing people in, at best, a cynical, and, at worst, a truly repellent light; their study might well provide a fruitful field for a psychologist. In this first volume they are set variously in the Alps, on the Riviera, in Hampstead and in Cornwall.

A young, aristocratic woman encourages an affair with a simple country photographer, murders him when he becomes an embarrassment, and gets away with it; a man chops down an apple tree and dies as a result; a young woman in wartime London is found to be a female version of Jack the Ripper; the murder of a boy turns out to have taken place among a family of swans. The collection also includes 'The Birds', out of which Hitchcock was to make one of his most famous films.

The idea for the story had come to her one day when she was walking across to Menabilly Barton farm from the house. A farmer was busy ploughing a field and above him the seagulls whirled and dived. She wondered what it would be like if all birds suddenly became hostile to the man and banded together to attack him. In the story the birds begin to attack after a harsh winter which leaves them without enough food, first the seabirds, then the birds of prey, the buzzards, falcons, sparrow hawks, finally even the small birds, all turn against their old enemy. They pierce human flesh with their beaks, tear their way into houses and flats, cause aircraft to crash, reducing the human population to a state of siege, barricaded in their houses behind their boarded-up windows, waiting for the horror they know is now inevitable. The story ends with one of the characters musing on how many million years of memory had been stored in their little brains, how many years of man's cruelty to his own and other kinds now gave them 'their instinct to destroy mankind with all the deft precision of machines'.

It is obvious that such a nightmare subject would appeal to Hitchcock who, in spite of his having turned three of her stories into highly successful films, she never actually met. She thought the resultant film was overblown and particularly disliked the translation of the setting of the story from Cornwall, with its small fields and stone hedges, to small-town America.

The stories were part of a collection written over many years and, with the knowledge that an anthology of them was to appear in 1952, she concentrated her energies on her next book, the story of her grandmother, Mary Anne Clarke. For this she had much of her research close to hand, in the documents and letters the du Maurier family had never been able to bring themselves to throw away, the excellent resource into which she had been able to dip when she was writing *The Du Mauriers*. She also had help from two researchers. One, Oriel Malet, was to undertake a good deal of work for Daphne during the years that followed, and she was despatched to the British Library and Public Records Office to trace what she could of the career of Mary Anne. The other, Derek Whiteley, went through books, papers and other documents of the period to help with the political background and also advised her on books that she should read.

It was during this research that she made one of her rare visits to be with Tommy while he was attending the Queen and the Duke of Edinburgh at Balmoral. The subject of Mary Anne and her connections with the royal family came up and the Queen Mother was particularly intrigued. When Daphne wondered as to how much of the scandalous connection she should put in her book, the Queen Mother told her, 'put it all in. Don't leave anything out!'

Before its publication, however, there was to be a major event in the family, the marriage of Tessa to Captain Peter de Zulueta of the Welsh Guards. It was just the kind of wedding Muriel had imagined for Daphne, with the ceremony taking place at St James's Church, Spanish Place, in London. *The Times* of 3 March 1954 notes that the bridegroom was the son of the late Senor Don Pedro de Zulueta and the late Marchioness of Bath, and that the ceremony was performed by the bridegroom's cousin, the Reverend Alphonso. In total contrast to Daphne, Tessa walked up the aisle in oyster-satin brocade and a full-length veil, with a fine complement of bridesmaids (including Flavia) attired in gold satin, and when the happy couple left the church it was to walk under an arch of swords held by Welsh Guards Officers. It was followed by a reception for several hundred guests at the Savoy Hotel (of which Tommy was one of the directors), including Prince Charles' Nanny, Nurse Lightbody. The de Zuluetas then flew off for a honeymoon in Switzerland, before settling down in a house near Ascot.

Unfortunately *Mary Anne* is a book which, for all the liveliness and notoriety of its subject matter, is hard to read, for once again Daphne was to try and mix hard fact and real historical happenings with poor fictional dialogue and imaginary events. The gift for story-telling, usually her strongest card, so often seems to become laboured when she turns to non-fiction, and even the *Western Morning News*, struggling to be kind, suggests that some of her readers may find it a little disappointing. While she was writing it, the suggestion was made that it might be turned into a stage play, and Gertrude Lawrence was approached to play the lead. It would have been fascinating to see what she might have made of the role, but she was to die two years before publication.

Disappointing or not, Gollancz printed 125,000 copies of *Mary Anne*, even if it was, as the *Daily Herald* was to say, a book which 'will bring delight to the hearts of circulating libraries and acute nausea to critics.'

In the publicity surrounding the publications of *My Cousin Rachel* and *Mary Anne*, a strong subtext begins to emerge. First there are the beginnings of the 'recluse' legend, as Daphne is variously described as living a 'hermit-like existence', 'hiding behind the seclusion of Menabilly with its rhododendron screen', and 'turning her back on the world'. There is also the question of money. She had inherited her attitude towards it from George – certainly not from Gerald – but it seems that no matter how much the earnings poured in, she lived in continual fear that somehow there would never be sufficient.

Part of the fear was because she was ferociously and heavily taxed but, that having been said, it was a theme which was to recur whenever she could be persuaded to talk to journalists. In an interview following the publication of *My Cousin Rachel*, she points out that of the £50,000 she received for the film rights she would only have seen £1,300 of the money the Americans paid for the book, had she not managed to evade the issue by paying it into a trust fund for Tessa. Similarly, a further £20,000 for the serial rights went into a similar trust for Flavia. She was alarmed, she told the interviewer, that her only 'capital' was in her head, and there would never be enough income to store against the day when her typewriter might no longer be a money spinner. 'That might happen any day,' she said. 'How can I say when this gift – for it is a gift for I've never studied how to do it – of producing bestsellers will leave me?' Yet as each book was published, so its predecessors continued to produce a flood of royalties.

She claimed that she had paid £123,000 to the Inland Revenue, in one year alone, and that of the money from the first hundred thousand copies of *The King's General* that she had sold, she had seen virtually nothing. She was to continue to make over much of her income to family trusts and later, in 1958, she turned herself into a limited company, by which time she had truly become, as the old *Sunday Graphic* put it 'the highest paid woman writer in the world.'

Her behaviour and attitude to money might well be put down to journalistic licence, except that it coloured so much of what she did and said, and it became an obsession; it was always there as a rider to her success. By the time she reached her early thirties, she could have invested her earnings, lived off the proceeds and, had she been so inclined, never worked again, never written another word. Yet she lived as if in constant fear that the magic source of her inspiration might one day cease, and that very source had become inextricably bound up with the money the source provided. Even before Tommy's death she lived comparatively modestly at Menabilly; there was no spectacular expenditure on entertaining, no collecting of antiques or paintings, other than for use or pleasure, no Rolls-Royce nor designer clothes; and her children were rapidly growing up.

She once made a strange off-hand remark to the effect that she was fearful that one day the creative gift would leave her and that 'when it does, I hope my daughters, with their Trust Funds, won't disown me like King Lear's!'

CHAPTER 21

France Again and Family Matters

F ollowing the research into the family history that she had undertaken for *The Du Mauriers* and *Mary Anne*, Daphne became fascinated to see how far back she could go, particularly into the origins of the Busson-Mathurins, the glass-blowers. As she grew older she became intensely interested in, 'where "I" come from', from whence her talent derived. The glass-blowers had crafted beautiful pieces of engraved glass designed to endure and last for years; George had been an artist, engraver and writer, and Gerald, of course, an actor. As she was a writer she felt that something of the original talents of the glass-blowers had come down to her, a gift she hoped in some way she would also bequeath to Christian whom, of all her children, was the one she felt most likely to inherit the du Maurier talent.

So in October 1955 she went over to France to see what traces of the family might remain, and to this end visited la Sarthe which, before the French Revolution, was part of the old provinces of Anjou and Maine, the area so heavily fought over in the Hundred Years' War of the fourteenth and early fifteenth centuries. The area's principle town is Le Mans, now somewhat better known for motor racing than medieval cavalry charges.

Daphne thoroughly enjoyed discovering the villages and small towns which had been so familiar to her ancestors, as she traced the sites of the various eighteenth-century

219

foundries. She found all of them – La Ville aux Clercs, La Pierre, Courdrecieux, Plessis Dorin, Cherigny and, indeed, the farm of le Maurier. It was an uncanny experience for her. She had had handed down to her from George, through Gerald, a glass designed by Michel Busson which had been blown at La Pierre before the time of Louis XV. At Plessis Dorin she found to her surprise that the little house in which one of her ancestors, the Master of the Foundry had lived, was still standing some two hundred years later.

Overcome with nostalgia, she wandered about the ruined buildings, among the remains of dusty broken glass, looked through the old windows and imagined the lives of that great-great-grandfather and the great-great uncles and aunts who had lived out their lives here so long before. She found a grave of one of them at Vibraye. They had lived through one of the most dramatic and turbulent periods of history before, during and after the French Revolution in which many of them had taken a very real part and, apart from Robert who founded the 'du Maurier' line, had been on the side of the Revolutionaries.

The idea of the trip had been to discover as many of the sites as she could, soak up the atmosphere of the place, trace the family back through existing records, and seriously research the history of the times. In the normal course of events she would have returned home to set about her task with enthusiasm, the new book taking precedence over everything else. But it was not to work out like that at all and it would be seven years before that particular piece of work would see the light of day; she would find herself needing to employ at least two researchers out in France to undertake much of the essential work, sending the material back to England for her to work on.

Part of the reason for this was to do with events in the family, but the overriding cause was that she had become subsumed by the plot of a completely different book. One evening while wandering round one of the small towns in the area she happened to glance idly into a lighted, uncurtained window. Inside a French family were sitting around the fire in the dusk and she found herself wondering – as most of us have when passing such a window in the street or looking into a house from a moving train – who they were, what they were like, how they lived; but Daphne went further. She imagined herself suddenly transported into their midst, listening to their conversation, even perhaps becoming one of them.

The idea took a firm hold in her mind, removing for the time being the desire to write another family history. Once again she turned to the little notebook and started to plot out a story-line, that of an English man in France who unexpectedly meets his double, his *doppelgänger*, a French count, and who, through an unforeseen and unwanted set of circumstances, finds himself living the count's life instead of his own.

The Scapegoat is an underrated book, a truly compulsive piece of story-telling. Once again she tells it in the persona of a male narrator though John is not the young ingenuous protagonist of *I'll Never Be Young Again*, or *My Cousin Rachel*, but a rather retiring, older, college lecturer. While wandering around in Le Mans in the rain, John is accosted by a Frenchman who says he knows John. John tries to put this strange incident out of his mind, but later, in the station buffet, he sees before him his double or, as north-country legend would have it, his own 'fetch'. His French counterpart speaks like him, has his mannerisms, and even introduces himself as Jean, the Comte de Gué. He invites the reluctant Englishman back to his hotel, offers him a drink (which he has drugged) and the unfortunate John knows no more until he wakes up the next morning wearing the Comte's clothes and with the Comte's chauffeur waiting to take him home.

He finds he owns a château, a glass-making business (on the verge of bankruptcy) and an extremely complex personal life; an ailing, pregnant wife, a ruthless sister-in-law who is also his mistress, another mistress in the local village, and a highly intelligent, precocious young daughter with whom he soon becomes involved in an intense father-daughter relationship. At first he keeps attempting to explain what has happened but, in the end, lets matters take their course. In the circumstances he is not surprised that Jean has taken a God-given opportunity to escape, but gradually he acquires a confidence he never had before as he tries to put the business to rights, reassure his downtrodden and hopeless sick 'wife', breaks off his relationship with his sister-in-law, but sleeps with his other mistress with whom he genuinely begins to fall in love. Then everything starts to fall apart, not least when he discovers that Jean has a price on his head, as he is suspected by surviving members of the French Resistance in the area at best of being a collaborator and at worst an outright traitor.

Desperately trying to keep his head above water, he is finally overwhelmed when the wife, overcome by depression, either falls, or throws herself, out of a window killing herself and the expected baby. She is an heiress and her money will revert to him, enabling him to pay off all the family debts. At this point the real Comte Jean turns up, as everything has now worked out so nicely for him, at least as far as the family is concerned. John is left with nothing for Jean has taken his name, resigned from his college and spent all the small capital he had in the bank. Unpleasant and egotistical to the end, he takes up the reins of his life again, as the 'scapegoat' wanders off into the dark countryside, possibly to become a monk. Whether the Resistance finally take their revenge on the Comte is left unresolved.

The plot is certainly not a new one, *The Prisoner of Zenda* and *Rupert of Henzau* are among the books Daphne notes were favourites in her youth and there are many other examples. But the book, within its own limitations, does work, and in the relationship between John (as Jean) and his supposed small daughter, Marie-Noel, Daphne manages to portray a relationship which is intense and strange, but is also affectionate and believable, and nothing like the twisted, not to say perverted, feelings existing between Julius and *his* daughter in her earlier novel.

The Scapegoat took Daphne six months to write and during

that time, she says, various strange things happened to her. At the beginning of the book she mentions, in passing, German Measles and within a month went down with it herself, for the first time in her life. When she came to the part in the book where the sick, pregnant wife, Francoise, has to have a blood transfusion, Tessa gave birth to a son who had to have two transfusions. Daphne began to find it all rather frightening.

She was rarely to find any book so obsessive and wrote the last chapter, where Jean returns to take up his place as the Comte de Gué once more and poor John is ruthlessly turned out, jobless and penniless into a hostile world, at such a fever pitch that afterwards she collapsed, stiff and aching, with a temperature of 102. She had to stay in bed for a fortnight to recover.

The manuscript was duly sent off to Victor Gollancz who, in turn, sent it to Hollywood as it seemed a natural for a film. Offers poured in, most in excess of £100,000, but this time she decided to do something quite different. If there was to be a film, then it would have to be made her way and she knew just the actor she wanted for the leading role. She had recently seen Alec Guinness playing the role of the dissident cardinal in the film of *The Prisoner* and had greatly admired his performance. She had not seen him in anything else but, acting on a hunch that he would like it, she sent him a copy of the finished manuscript and asked him what he thought. He was, he says, somewhat surprised to receive it, but read it through, and it seems her hunch was right for he liked it.

So, for the first time, the two met and Daphne found him very compatible. She got on with him, she said, because she recognized in him the same shyness from which she suffered herself. 'I was fond of her,' he says, 'and after the film we used to meet from time to time for a meal, but I don't think I ever felt I knew her really well.'

The two of them agreed that they would see if it were possible to get the film into production themselves, and both felt that the man to produce it would be Michael Balcon. But, having laid the foundations, it was to take a long time before their painstaking negotiations were to bear fruit. In part, this was due to the fact that finding the necessary backing for an independent film always has been notoriously difficult, but there were other, more personal, reasons.

The first was a happy one, for in 1956 there was another grand family wedding, this time that of Flavia – an event which mirrors almost exactly that of her elder sister, even down to the groom being a Guards officer – this time in the Coldstream Guards. On 17 July 1956, Flavia married Captain Alastair Tower at St Peter's Church, in fashionable Eaton Square. Once again it was a full-dress occasion with the younger Miss Browning, attired in white lace over tulle, attended by four bridesmaids in delphinium-blue organza. The 'something borrowed' was Daphne's pearl tiara which, given her dislike of formal functions, was unlikely to have seen a great deal of wear.

The second major event of 1956 was very different. On 28 November, Muriel, 'Mo', du Maurier died twenty-three years after her beloved Gerald. By the end of the war she was already in failing health, following a severe fall, and had a private nurse. It soon became apparent that she could not return to live in London at Providence Corner, so it was sold. After the few months with Daphne referred to previously, she and her nurse moved into Ferryside, where she spent the last seven years of her life with Angela; the third daughter, Jeanne, lived almost permanently abroad. The move did mean that she could keep in continual touch with Daphne, and be visited by the grandchildren when they were in Cornwall. Muriel died peacefully at home.

It had taken Gerald's death to bridge the gap between Muriel and Daphne, although Daphne was never able to forget the estrangement of her early years. Both had suffered from an innate reserve, a reserve Muriel had been able to overcome with the more extrovert Angela and Jeanne; but for Daphne it went deeper, back to the days when the sight of Muriel's loosened hair had made her hysterical, to her identification of her mother with the Snow Queen.

On Muriel's side, Gerald's extreme attachment to Daphne would have been hard for any mother to come to terms with, let alone a conventional one who had also had to cope with passing infidelities, and with a man who became increasingly insecure as he grew older.

Daphne's marriage had naturally relieved the pressure a good deal. Gerald's death had done the rest. From then on, Daphne and her mother were able to establish a far more ordinary relationship, assisted doubtless by Muriel falling into the conventional role of loving grandmother; and she must have thoroughly enjoyed the two elaborate society weddings. But Muriel's death resurrected the past for Daphne, bringing back feelings she was finally to reveal when she wrote her short autobiography of those early years at Cannon Hall and Ferryside, years succinctly summed up by the emotions she had felt when she tried to comfort her mother on Gerald's death, holding her close 'twenty-five years too late'.

However, professional life goes on and, afterwards, the negotiations over the production of the film version of *The Scapegoat* continued, but progress was still very slow as Michael Balcon had to grapple with the complexities of making a film independently of Ealing Films, without his usual assistance from MGM. Finally, and cautiously, the plans were announced. 'At last,' burbled the *Daily Mail*, in 1958, 'the highest paid woman writer in the world has turned herself into a limited company.

'For twenty years her bestselling novels have been earning hundreds of thousands of pounds. Most has gone in tax – in just one year she paid over £120,000 to the Inland Revenue. "The new arrangement will spread the load a bit," she said, yesterday. "To sell a story outright and pay a lump sum in tax on it does seem foolish." For one book, *The King's General*, she got £100,000. And had to pay tax at 19s.6d. in the pound on it. Partner in her business venture is Alec Guinness. The object of the company is to film her novel, *The Scapegoat*. The stars will be Alec Guinness and Bette Davis.'

This way, continued the report, she would get only a small initial payment, but in time would receive a percentage of the profits so that the tax savings would be considerable. In fact the basis of the deal was that she would give her book and Guinness would give his services.

Michael Balcon, when approached, was circumspect. Asked if Ealing Films were prepared to offer for the rights of *The Scapegoat*, he told the *Daily Express*: 'The offer has come from them (i.e. Daphne and Alec Guinness) to us. Normally we'd make a picture in association with MGM, the distributors. But Miss du Maurier and Mr Guinness want to be actually identified with *The Scapegoat*. They want a very substantial interest in it. They want it to be a joint effort.' The paper was unable to drag any comment out of Alec Guinness who was in the middle of making *Barnacle Bill*, a film which leant heavily on the multi-role success he had had in *Kind Hearts and Coronets*, but which was nothing like as good.

Finally the venture did get off the ground and Daphne wrenched herself out of her seclusion to follow the fate of the film-making process from beginning to end. The script was written by Robert Hamer, who also directed it.

When the time came for the film-unit to move out to France, to shoot scenes on location, she joined them for a little while. She found it a strange and uncanny experience to return once again to Sarthe, in such an unlikely way, to watch the film-unit shooting in the square of La Ferte Bernard, the little market-town she calls Villars in the book. They used the château of Semur-en-Vallon, and she found it hard to believe that her initial glimpse through the window of a lighted room had resulted, finally, in so many people being in that one place at the same time – the actors, the director, the technicians and all the paraphernalia of film-making, not to mention the interested local people and the Comte of the real château, the Comte de Vibraye. As she sat in the sunshine eating her lunch with the film-unit, she hoped it would be as happy an experience for everyone as she was finding it herself.

There was, though, one cloud. Robert Hamer's script

deviated more and more from her original story-line, and as he was also the director, it became a very difficult problem to resolve; in the normal course of events the director could have mediated between the original author and the scriptwriter. Daphne found that the phrase in the contract which apparently gave her 'script approval' did not mean in reality that she had true control over it. 'There was,' says Sir Alec, 'great trouble in scripting it and the resultant film was far from satisfactory. Of course the fact that Daphne had "script approval" didn't mean she actually approved of the final version. Compromise always has to come into these things.'

Asked about this at the end of filming, Daphne kept much of what she thought to herself, merely pointing out that the story had been changed in several ways, although the adaptation had been done with 'great thought and care'. Hamer, like herself, was an ardent Francophile and had tried to ensure that the atmosphere and feel of the story was true to its original background.

For a little while after the film was finished, Daphne lived at Menabilly without any of the family: Tessa and Flavia were now married and living away from Cornwall, while Christian ('Kits'), aged eighteen, had just embarked on his own career in films. It seems that Daphne had not lost contact entirely with her past and so who better to give her son a good start in his chosen medium than her past love 'Carol', by then Sir Carol Reed, who had a long string of successes behind him? So Christian was installed as his personal assistant on the film *Our Man in Havana*, made about the same time as *The Scapegoat*, and also starring the hard-working Alec Guinness.

The Scapegoat was released in June 1959 and was never regarded as much of a success, even though it had the magical du Maurier name behind it and two stars, Guinness and Davis, considered cast-iron box office. Sir Alec is right, it is unsatisfactory and there seems to be no good reason why Hamer should not have stuck to Daphne's original story, other than that all too often film-makers feel the necessity to change the plot of books when it comes to adaptation for film, rarely for the better. It was probably not the sole reason for the film's somewhat cool reception; Bette Davis did not seem easy in the role in which she was cast either.

Before June, however, there was to be a drastic change in Daphne's life, a change which was to be the forerunner of things to come. Throughout the 1950s Tommy had continued his busy role with the Queen and the Duke of Edinburgh, his tiring commuting to Menabilly. Throughout that time, says one of his friends and colleagues, he was the perfect courtier, he 'not only looked like a Queen's man, he acted like one, and he would have been just as successful at the Court of the first Elizabeth.'

Increasingly, though, during the last two years he had felt tired and ill and finally, in April 1959, he announced he was retiring from Royal Service. He was sixty-two years old. He had concealed his deteriorating health so well that his decision came as a shock to most of those who knew him, both in London and in Cornwall. 'I feel Prince Philip should be served by someone one hundred per cent fit,' he said when he announced his resignation, 'not by someone who has been feeling ill and is not fully up to his job.'

He spent the summer of 1959 with Daphne, at Menabilly, recuperating gradually, while battling with constant nausea caused through problems with his liver. He particularly disliked being put on an extremely dull, fat-free diet, which could not even be livened with the odd glass of wine. The carefree 'Boy' Browning was a 'boy' no longer. He put his illness down almost equally to the strain of his life with the Royal Family and the exhaustion caused by the endless commuting. From then, until his death six years later, he and Daphne were to enjoy a friendly and affectionate companionship.

A friend who was fond of both of them says: 'I think the sexual thing between them was long gone; poor old "Boy" was always rather short changed on that. She always found it rather a bore. In those last years she came to think of him

228

mainly as her good friend, always speaking of him very kindly as if he were indeed a "boy", a loved child. I expect in some ways he never did seem very grown up to her once she had matured herself – but then, as most women know, that goes for so many men.'

CHAPTER 22

Searching for Tristan

The next three years were busy ones for both Tommy and Daphne. With retirement and the cessation of travelling, Tommy's health improved and as he was not a man who could happily sit around doing nothing, he soon threw himself into local affairs. In October 1959 he became the first Group Controller of Civil Defence in Cornwall, an honorary post to which he was made welcome by a committee largely made up of old Cornish families (its Chairman was Lady Carew-Pole of Antony), and he took on his duties with real enthusiasm. His local connections, not to mention his war record, and the prestige accorded to his having served the Royal Family for so long, ensured he would be much sought after and he soon became Deputy Lieutenant of Cornwall as well.

The Campaign for Nuclear Disarmament flourished in Cornwall and its members were used to outright antagonism, ridicule, mindless insults or all three. In Tommy they found an engaging and civilized adversary it was impossible to dislike. He became a popular local television figure too, as he put his case, well ahead of his time, in seeing that such a force could well be turned into a permanent form of civil-disaster organization. When he was elected to the county's Territorial and Auxiliary Forces Association he was given the fastest promotion on record – before he had attended his first meeting, he had been elected its chairman.

Daphne had had another collection of short stories published in October 1959, under the title *The Breaking Point* (later to be reprinted as *The Blue Lenses*). Again they lean heavily on the macabre, 'The Blue Lenses' being a particularly unpleasant tale of a woman who, after having an eye operation, is given blue glasses to wear; they cut out bright light, but also enable her to see people as they really are, in the shape of largely predatory animals – foxes, wolves, rats, hyenas. The collection also contains the strange story, 'The Archduchess', mentioned earlier, about the small golden-age European state whose royal family has always practised incest.

When writing fiction, once she had plotted her story, Daphne would work solidly until a novel was finished. Non-fiction, as shown by *The Glass-blowers*, took longer and often overlapped with other projects. Back in 1954 she had been asked to write a preface to a new edition of *Wuthering Heights*. It was something she could easily have done without leaving Cornwall, but her investigations into her own family background and that of the Rashleighs, had provoked in her something of an addiction to the actual business of research. She had never visited Haworth and therefore decided to go and see the Brontë home and papers for herself, not least because of the strong Cornish connection, through the Branwells of Penzance. She had gone to Haworth at the end of October 1954, accompanied by Flavia (then still unmarried) and her friend and researcher, Oriel Malet. The weather was kind and she was able to spend the mornings in the Brontë Museum, and the afternoons exploring the countryside which figures so heavily in the Brontë novels, especially *Wuthering Heights*. Happily, it was before the enormous tide of commercialism washed over Haworth and it was still possible to make something of an adventure of tracing the path to the ruined Top Withens Farmhouse (the model for Wuthering Heights), across the stone packhorse bridge and up over moors still purple with heather. Top Withens had featured too in less well-known books of her own childhood – Halliwell Sutcliffe's *Shameless Wayne* and

Ricroft of Withens, whose episodes of family feuding in the aftermath of the Civil War had strong similarities with *Lorna Doone*, and foreshadowed her own *The King's General*.

She found the Brontë papers absolutely fascinating, particularly those strange early writings of the precociously gifted Brontë children, the sagas of Angria and Gondal. Making sense of the manuscripts in the original is not an easy task and even Rowse, ever suspicious of the non-academic, gives her full credit for the way she unravelled and interpreted them. The trip enabled her to write her preface, but it awoke far more – a burning desire to write a biography of the neglected Brontë, the brother Branwell, who had, in his early days, seemed equally as gifted and imaginative as his sisters. A writer with an added talent as a painter, he had recklessly wasted his gifts, compounding the family tendency to tuberculosis with drink and drugs. There are overtones of the recklessness of past members of her own family in Branwell, which intrigued her, but he also appealed as being more understandable today than he could possibly have been in his own time.

Over the next few years Daphne undertook a considerable amount of research, encouraged by J. Alex Symington, editor and compiler of the *Shakespeare Head Brontë*, who shared her enthusiasm for Branwell. She went to many sources, apart from the Brontë Museum, as is shown in the acknowledgements of her book (her first non-fiction book to be properly indexed). She examined the Brotherton Collection of Leeds University and spent time in the British Library Department of Manuscripts of the British Museum. She had copies made of the manuscript of *Percy*, and two other stories, while a friend and helper looked into the local history of Sowerby and Luddenden Foot, with particular reference to the 'navigations' and the 'boaties' of the canal boats. On this occasion, too, she was to have an excellent editor in Sheila Hodges, who revised and edited her finished work with, Daphne says, 'great patience, sympathy and skill'.

The result is not a complete success as, once again, she goes into imaginary dialogue and thoughts; but it is a fascinating book, 'highly unusual,' says Rowse, 'in that for the first time it showed sympathy towards the boy and made him really important. She brought alive and rehabilitated that strange, submerged character.' Daphne made Rowse feel differently towards the boy who gave up the struggle to succeed through using his own talents. 'I'd found him so weak – I've no real time for people who waste their abilities in drink and, in this case possibly, drugs, but Daphne had a compassion and comprehension for humanity altogether wider than mine.' The book brought Daphne and Rowse together across a divide caused by his early jealousy of her easy start and fortune, and her fear of summary dismissal by an historical scholar. It was a friendship which would never again be in doubt. Some time after the book was published in 1960, she gave him a copy of it inscribed, 'To A.L. from his student, with love'.

She always had a very soft spot for *The Infernal World of Branwell Brontë*, although it never sold like the novels. 'I got,' she would say, 'frightfully worked up over him.' On Symington's death she herself bought the Brontë books and manuscripts from his library, and her book is essential reading for Brontë scholars, not least because of its comprehensive notes and index, both of which are full of information which is actually readable rather than – as all too often in works of this kind – merely gnomic. She was unlucky in that, as is so often the case after years of disinterest and neglect, another biography of Branwell was published the same year. This was by Winifred Gérin who was working her way through the Brontë family, one at a time.

In 1960 there were two events which, although quite unconnected, were to affect her deeply. Both were concerned with a death. The first was that of her cousin, Peter Davies, the third of Barrie's Lost Boys to die dramatically before their time. In 1926 Peter had set up his own small publishing house and was greatly loved by his stable of authors. (He had published Angela's autobiographical sketch, *It's only the*

233

Sister, in 1950.) For reasons that have never been understood – if they were ever known – on 5 April 1960 he left his Chelsea office as usual and went to the Royal Court Hotel in Sloane Square, where he had a modest amount to drink; he then crossed the road to Sloane Square tube station and threw himself under the first oncoming train.

Although Michael had been Barrie's favourite – to the point almost of obsession – Peter had never lived down the fact that he was, because of his christian name, thought to be the original of Peter Pan, something the press would never let him forget. He loathed his own connection with the book, and he loathed the book even more, referring to it more than once as 'that terrible masterpiece'; in fact, Peter Pan was an amalgam of all five Davies boys according to Barrie. The headlines in the papers after his death perpetuated the legend: 'Barrie's Peter Pan killed by London Subway Train,' said *The New York Times*; 'Boy Who Never Grew Up Dead,' 'Peter Pan Stood Alone to Die,' 'Peter Pan's Death Leap' and 'Peter Pan Commits Suicide,' chorused the London papers. The verdict of the inquest, held eight days later, was 'suicide while the balance of the mind was disturbed'. Friend and colleague Herbert van Thal said Peter Davies was 'an irreparable loss to the publishing trade. For here was a personality witty, astringent, with a brilliant and remarkable knowledge of literature; and, withal, he possessed a deep and kindly understanding of his fellow men.' Not too long afterwards the fourth brother, Jack, died too.

It had been a tragic family, starting with Arthur's agonizing death from cancer of the jaw, swiftly followed by that of Sylvia du Maurier at barely forty, Guy dead in the trenches and the strange drowning of the brilliant and possibly homosexual Michael.

All the du Mauriers remained loyal to the family, but Peter and Daphne had been special friends as well as cousins and he was one of the few people with whom she could happily talk for hours. On her visits to London they would meet in the Café Royal. Like her, Peter seems to have been obsessed with family, and in their intense discussions, George and Gerald lived again to their mutual delight. 'We never discussed the world of today,' she said after his death, 'only the past. Always the past.' There is a hint of what might have driven Peter Davies to do what he did when she recalls how she asked him more than once if perhaps his brother, 'Nico' Davies, of all the du Mauriers, was the only one to have escaped the streak of melancholy and depression which haunted the family. Peter thought he probably had. It suggests that this was a streak which already affected both of them, a force strong enough to drive Peter to his death, and to make Daphne's last years a misery for herself and all who knew her.

In October 1959 she had been approached by the old London County Council and asked if she would unveil one of the council's famous blue plaques which was to be put up outside the building in Great Russell Street where George du Maurier had lived. She agreed, on the understanding that there would be no crowds and that all she would have to say was that she unveiled the plaque; the ceremony was planned for March 1960. However, circumstances intervened and Daphne was unable to attend, so the event was put back to 22 April, thus falling just after Peter Davies's death and during the week of the subsequent inquest. At first Daphne said she could not do it in view of what had happened, but was finally persuaded to change her mind after having been promised that the planned celebratory lunch would be cancelled. Tommy had told her that the LCC Press Office was adept at dealing with the media, and she asked Gollancz if they could contact them, explain that there had been a highly publicized bereavement in the family, and see that there was no publicity for the event. So George's plaque was unveiled in front of a handful of people, including 'Nico' Davies and his two sons, and another cousin, Gerald Millar.

The second event was, in terms of her own life, more ominous, but at first seemed a mere cloud no bigger than a man's hand. It was another death, this time that of an almost forgotten figure, Dr Rashleigh, who had long ago inherited Menabilly, let it fall into disrepair, and allowed Daphne to lease it back in 1943.

She had had it spelled out to her from the outset that she could never own the house as, even if Dr Rashleigh had wanted to sell, and his family had agreed, the estate had been entailed to preclude such an eventuality. For seventeen years Daphne had firmly closed her eyes to the very real possibility that one day the Rashleighs might want their house back. Menabilly was and always had been 'hers', a conviction from which no-one could move her. So long as Dr Rashleigh was alive she knew she was safe, because he had expressly stated that he never had any intention of living there; now that he was dead the estate passed to his nephew, Phillip, and that opened up the serious possibility that he might feel quite differently about Menabilly and want to live in it himself. It was something she had fervently hoped and prayed would never happen, something to which she now deliberately shut her mind.

She was helped in this by being offered a project which she was to find both time consuming and fascinating. In 1959, her old friend Foy Quiller-Couch was going through her father's manuscripts ('Q' had died in 1944), when she came across his half-finished novel, *Castle Dor*, based on the Tristan and Iseult legend; she asked Daphne if she would like to complete it. Loving and admiring 'Q' as she did, she readily agreed, telling Foy she felt honoured to have been asked. Tommy was also very enthusiastic about it, and was only too happy to join her in her local research. For the basis of his version of the legend, Quiller-Couch had gone back to one of the very earliest written sources, that of *Le Roman de Tristan*, by the twelfth century chronicler, Béroul, a contemporary of Chrétien de Troyes, who had brought the concept of courtly love into the old legends of Arthur and Lancelot.

Daphne sometimes wondered over the years if she had inherited her addiction for research from an eccentric brother

236

of Muriel's, who had been convinced that Francis Bacon wrote the works of Shakespeare. He had decided, for reasons best known to himself, that Shakespeare's original manuscripts were in a sealed box buried in the bed of the River Wye. He spent years of his life unavailingly trying to find them, so that he could prove to the world once and for all that Shakespeare did not write Shakespeare.

So Daphne and Tommy took to the hills, fields and river paths of the Rivers Fowey and Fal, and the iron-age fort of Castle Dor where the archaeologist, Raleigh Radford, had undertaken excavations in 1936 and 1937, a dig which had ceased with the war. The idea for the dig had come from Professor Charles Singer who had lived at Kilmarth, and Radford was always sorry he had been unable to continue. Tommy had researched the Civil War Battle of Castle Dor and appreciated its importance as a much earlier strategic fortification which could have been held against all comers. He poured scorn on the version of the Tristan legend that had Iseult landing at Tintagel to meet King Mark, not least because it would have been impossible to bring a boat in close to the cliff below the castle – a castle which dates anyway from Norman times, far too late to have played any part in the saga of Arthur or Tristan.

Equipped with field glasses and local Ordnance Survey maps, they tried to retrace the footsteps of Tristan and King Mark, based on the early Breton legends. Béroul placed the 'palace' of King Mark at 'Lancien' and there is, below Castle Dor, a farmstead known as Lantyan. Support at least for the place names in the legend had come from Radford's excavations. Inside the concentric rings of the 'fort', he found remains of an iron-age fortified village dating from the second century BC, along with traces of artefacts which showed there had been a trade in tin, most likely with Brittany. In the early 1960s, Tommy would take any lunchtime visitors to Menabilly who showed an interest, up to Castle Dor, and mark out for them where everything had been; where in the fifth century AD, King Mark had built his great hall, the extent of the ancient fortifications and the position of the smaller dwellings by the entry gates. He would explain the differences in the past landscape, especially the rivers, and demonstrate how easy it would have been to repel invaders even with primitive weapons. His vivid interpretation of old wars helped Daphne enormously.

As Daphne herself says in *Vanishing Cornwall*, the brambles and bracken have once again taken over Castle Dor, and it is hard to see the remains of what was, if not the palace of a king as we understand it, the great dwelling place of a local chieftain. This writer is fortunate to have had it explained by Tommy himself – the ninety-foot long hall, the granaries and porters' lodges, built on top of the original iron-age village, the spring of water (so essential in the event of siege) now buried under ploughland, pointed out before new building in the Fowey Valley and Par Estuary changed the landscape beyond recall.

Daphne and Tommy walked the woods along the riverbank to St Sampson's Church at Golant (which figures in the story), noting place names such as 'Mark's Gate'. A trickle of water running into the River Fowey at Woodget Pyll used to be known locally as 'Deraine's Lake', and Daphne wondered if that was a corruption of Lac de La Reine. The walk beside Woodget Pyll, past Lantyan farmhouse, under the viaduct and down to a further creek became a favourite of theirs – it is only just about possible today, development and closed footpaths making it much more difficult. They wondered if one of the islands, which appeared in the middle of the river when the tide went out, was the basis for another part of the story in which Tristan fights a duel in just such a spot.

The Béroul version of the Tristan legend is more earthy and less romantic than its successors. Daphne and Tommy drove to Malpas, near Truro on the River Fal (now smothered with yet another new housing development, an embryo marina and an industrial estate) because, according to Béroul, this was where Tristan, disguised as a pilgrim, carried Queen Iseult across the river – a plan devised by the two of them so that he could slip and fall in the mud, tumbling them together with obvious consequences, but allowing the Queen to protest to Mark that she had lain down with no man other than a pilgrim. Tommy found this version of the legend all too unromantic and prosaic.

Romantic nostalgia was an integral part of Tommy's make-up and Daphne tells of how, as they looked across the Fal at Malpas at high tide, he remembered that they had visited the spot in *Ygdrasil* on their honeymoon, and how he had lost overboard a little dish-mop of which he had been particularly fond, part of the furniture of the boat since its launch, and which had now lain rotting in the mud for twenty-five years.

They also tried to find, near Truro, the old palace of Carlyon and the apple orchards of Avalon. Not surprisingly they were unsuccessful. Daphne became depressed and wondered to Tommy if any of it were true, if there had ever been a dying Arthur and a magic boat; but he, she said, clung stoutly to his dream of 'weeping queens'. So they struggled through the woods and floundered through mud continuing their search, trying to imagine the boat with its three queens, bearing the corpse of King Arthur down river and out into the far west. As she describes in *Vanishing Cornwall*: "What then?" I asked.

"The Lost Land of Lyonesse and the Islands of the Blest," answered my husband, lowering his field glasses, his vision of the past undimmed, his faith in the future steadfast.'

After Tommy's death, living alone at Kilmarth (apart from her devoted secretary-housekeeper), Daphne recalled those explorations in search of Arthur and Tristan with delight, a quest which had drawn the two close again after the years apart, absorbed in trying to discover the origins of legends which haunted both of them.

They were convinced that whatever the origins of the Arthur legends and the places essential to them, there was no doubt that there had been a chieftain called Mark who had lived at Castle Dor, a conviction borne out by the 'Tristan' stone standing at Four Turnings stating that it had covered the grave of 'Drustans', son of Cunomorus, also known as Mark which, if this was so, made the illicit relationship between Tristan and Iseult even more dangerous. Daphne pondered, too, on the similarities between the end of the story – where (an added complication) a second Iseult tells the dying Tristan that the ship bearing the original Iseult has black sails instead of white – and that of the return of Theseus in Greek mythology. Perhaps there were stronger links with Crete than she knew, for on rocks on the lonely path between Tintagel and Boscastle there are the scratched remains of the patterns of mazes, or 'Troy towns', found also in the Eastern Mediterranean.

The resultant novel, *Castle Dor*, is something of a disappointment simply because she had to finish a story begun by somebody else. It would have been far more interesting if 'Q' had finished it and she had written a version of her own. It has never been divulged who wrote what, but it would seem from the text that 'Q's' involvement finished less than halfway through. For a little while Daphne struggles to maintain his style, but then gradually moves into her own. 'Q' set his version towards the end of the nineteenth century and made his protagonists not King, Queen and Knight, but publican, Breton onion seller, and publican's wife; because of this Daphne was left with a story which lacked the grandeur of myth, and she seems to have found real difficulty in blending all the ingredients of the original legend into a cohesive whole. It remains an interesting exercise.

Her researches into its origins, and her recollections of retracing the physical landmarks of the story, are far more interesting. Writing in *Vanishing Cornwall* after Tommy's death, and in the knowledge that she would be leaving Menabilly for Kilmarth she says: '. . . a mile and a half seaward, overlooking the great sweep of Par Bay, there stands an old house built upon fourteenth-century foundations. It is named Kilmarth. The word, in Cornish, means "retreat of Mark". It is strange and moving to believe that this spot, once the home of Professor Singer – who was the first to suggest that Castle Dor should be excavated – was the last outpost of an ancient Cornish king who, with passion spent and jealousy forgotten, looked out in peace across the open sea.'

CHAPTER 23

Blows to the Heart

Castle Dor was published in April 1962 and treated as an interesting exercise by reviewers, rather than as a work in its own right. Several writers remarked on how 'Q' himself had finished Robert Louis Stevenson's historical romance, *St Ives*, and that the Tristan and Iseult legend, too, had passed from hand to hand, receiving embellishments and alterations on its progress through the centuries.

In a passage attributed to 'Q', one of the characters actually says: 'It is a curious coincidence that no poet, or shall we call him investigator, has ever lived to conclude this particular story. His work has always been finished by another.' Foy Quiller-Couch expressed herself as being greatly satisfied with what Daphne had achieved. It was no light thing to have been asked to undertake, she said, but 'she has done it and so cleverly has she woven her work into his that I defy anyone to discover where the shuttle has passed from his hand into hers.' Rather than Gollancz, her usual publisher, it was published by J.M. Dent, who had published Q's fiction.

The walks in the woods and the completion of *Castle Dor*, was something of an Indian summer for Daphne and Tommy. She was now a young-looking, slender fifty-five to Tommy's sixty-five. The flow of creative fiction had slowed down considerably – she was to write only three more full-length novels although she was to live a further twenty-seven years,

242

but there were to be a number of non-fiction books, a thin autobiography and two more anthologies of short stories, along with a collection of essays.

As well as coming to terms with middle age, she was also searching, as many do at this time, for some kind of meaning for life, and into whether the conventional Christian beliefs were tenable; she was unable to follow her sisters into religious certainty, Jeanne into Roman Catholicism and Angela into High Anglicanism. The 'Absolutes' of Moral Rearmament had long since gone, although she still knelt in prayer nightly as she had since she was a child, ending with the words 'let everything be all right', as if, she was to say, by expressing herself in this way she might come to terms with fate. Yet, even then, she recognized that the only prayer which is truly worthwhile is 'for courage', courage to bear the ills that will come to all of us, including those we bring on ourselves. Hell, she decided, was probably what we make it; it is not other people, as Sartre says in his play, *Huis Clos*, but ourselves.

She pondered on telepathy, whether we had all once had a sixth sense, which had been ignored by Western civilization and so allowed to die. Trying to find a way to live without the framework of a conventional religion was one of the great problems of our time, she wrote. Another, she noted, long before radical feminism hit the agenda, was one that faces all women who try to reconcile their desire for equality and the fulfilment of their ambitions, with their role within the family. Although she herself had been extremely fortunate with regard to this particular dilemma, always having had sufficient assistance to enable her to work as she wanted, and have children, it is obvious that she had doubts about how well she had succeeded as a wife and mother, in the shadow of her success as an international bestselling novelist.

Politically she saw herself as Left of Centre and on a number of occasions was to express a certain amount of admiration for Harold Wilson, a politician whose progress she had followed with some interest.

Meanwhile, she had taken up again the threads of the history of the glass-blowers of La Sarthe, set aside first for the novel, and then for the film, of *The Scapegoat*. Experience in researching *The Infernal World of Branwell Brontë* helped make this book far superior to *The Du Mauriers* or *Mary Anne*. She had also found a device whereby she could pass into the imagination of a character without using the previous clumsy form of factual content, laced with imaginary events and conversations. She began her story in 1844, when the children of the Robert Mathurin Busson, who had voluntarily exiled himself from France during the Revolution, returned home to Paris to discover that their father had not died on the journey back to France to see his family, as they had been led to believe, but had lived on there for several years. This was a deliberate decision that he had made so that he could avoid keeping his wife and children back in England; he also failed to mention to his family that they were not descended from an aristocratic family of 'Comte du Mauriers' either, that he had merely adopted the name of the farm where he had been born.

Daphne then goes into the first person to narrate her heroine Sophie's extraordinary story and, by so doing, makes the history live. Only Honor Harris of *The King's General* is as tough a woman as Sophie, a woman who remained positively in favour of the Revolution to the end of her life, but who suffered bitterly during the worst excesses of the Terror. Daphne's researches were far ranging, from Carlyle's *French Revolution* to a host of sources in French, including first-hand accounts of the time; her bilingual ability had never proved more useful. The passages which deal with the Vendéan uprising and the height of the Terror – the mindless killings, the hysteria of the Vendéan mob, the privations of the ordinary people, almost rank with Defoe's *A Journal of the Plague Year*, in persuading you into believing that this is a genuine first-hand account of the times.

Sophie Duval is a survivor, a strong woman determined to do her utmost to hold the family together whatever the odds, a woman capable of advising on the running of a glass foundry, delivering her sister-in-law's baby in appalling circumstances, coping with the death of her own child, and wrenching a musket off her sister to shoot down the man who had killed her sister's son. *The Glass-blowers* was published in 1963, and was severely underrated by the critics, who had long since written her off – or down – as a mere romantic novelist. It deserved better.

The same cannot be said for her next novel, *The Flight of the Falcon*. Italy provided the inspiration, as it had done for many of her short stories and some of the background of *My Cousin Rachel*. Once more she adopted the role of a young male narrator, living in the shadow of an older, stronger man – in this case a Fascist, older brother who was thought to have been killed in the war. He surfaces at a later date and is running a strange university in the hills, where students are encouraged to participate not only in old-fashioned duelling, but also in life-and-death war games. The idea for the plot had come to her some years earlier, when she was driving round Italy with Christian. Seeing a town perched on a hill she had asked him impulsively to stop so that they could visit it. It was surrounded by a medieval wall and they had to drive in through the gate. Then, in March 1963, when visiting Rome with Flavia, she had seen a guide taking round a party of tourists and wondered what he thought of them, 'whether the courtesy he showed veiled contempt'. Later that evening, she saw a sleeping peasant woman, half-buried in old shawls, huddled on the steps of a church. When she got back to her hotel she wondered what had brought her to the church doorstep, and the image fused with that of the city far from Rome. All three images provided the plot for *The Flight of the Falcon*.

But the striking images fail to set the book alight, it is written as if her heart is not in it. Possibly it was not, for the years from 1963 to 1965 saw her whole world turned upside down. While she might have wrestled with the conflict between family and work, or struggled to come to terms with the philosophy of belief, she had steadfastly refused to do the same about the possibility of leaving Menabilly. On the surface, therefore, life continued as it had for the last twenty years, the disciplined hours of writing, the walks in the woods with the dogs – sometimes with Tommy, sometimes on her own; lunch with selected friends, supper with Tommy before television viewing and bed in their separate bedrooms. She did not discuss leaving Menabilly.

Menabilly was *her* house, desired and longed-for ever since she had first seen it, her first love, her house of secrets which she had lovingly restored from its decay and which had amply repaid her love with the inspiration it had given her.

She recalled the old legend of the mandrake root, much used by witchcraft because of its resemblance to some kind of strange and twisted creature, which was said to shriek and then bleed when it was pulled out of the ground. She drew a clear analogy – that would apply to her if she ever left Menabilly. It was as if the Rashleighs had given her only their ghosts, the shades of themselves, along with their Blue Lady and the suffocated young cavalier, and did not exist any longer as real people.

She would show favoured visitors around Menabilly, as if it had been hers for generations, from the antique furniture she had chosen for its appropriateness, to the family portraits, and the Rowlandson cartoons of Mary Anne on the panelled walls, side by side with drawings by George du Maurier from *Punch*.

Michael Thornton, an old friend of Daphne's, speaking of her feelings when she finally came to terms with having to leave it, notes: 'The house had been, in a strange way, as much a lover as any man had ever been, and she was deeply angry. "If only I had a plastic bomb," she muttered. She remained outwardly friendly to Rashleigh but never forgave him.'

Tommy was fond of Menabilly too, but he had always been far more realistic. For him it had been a pleasant place to relax, during those snatched weekends away from the Palace, a retreat where he could now sit in his study reading *The*

Times, and ponder events. When the worst happened and Phillip Rashleigh made it clear that he was not going to extend the lease and that he wanted to return and live in Menabilly, Tommy did his best to reconcile Daphne to the inevitable.

Poor Phillip Rashleigh was in an impossible position. He had never understood why Dr Rashleigh had not wanted to live in the house, as he too loved it. It had been made clear to Daphne not only when the Brownings took on the original lease, but subsequently, that it was not just a question of the fact that she could never own it, but that it was quite likely that one day the Rashleighs would want to live in it again. When an anguished Daphne told the press how she felt, at being forced out of her magic house and how she prayed for some kind of deliverance, the unfortunate Phillip found himself cast as the villain of the piece.

So, deeply conscious of the effect his decision would have on her he offered the Brownings what he considered to be an acceptable alternative – the Rashleigh Dower House, Kilmarth, the old home of Professor Charles Singer. In her essay 'Moving House', written in 1969, there are few clues as to how Daphne really felt. She writes that, 'like a miracle', her unspoken prayer was answered by the offer of a second Rashleigh House. It is a sanitized account of what happened, and there is no trace here of the desperate attempts to make Phillip Rashleigh change his mind, the overwhelming feeling of depression which, a forerunner of things to come, overwhelmed her at the mere thought of leaving her precious Menabilly.

Why she and Tommy did not set out to find themselves a beautiful property and buy it, so avoiding any similar disruption ever happening again, remains a mystery. Daphne had more than enough money to buy any Cornish house of any size or age she might choose, especially at the prices obtaining in the 1960s.

But the knowledge that her worst fears had been realized, and that she was to lose Menabilly, was not Daphne's only anxiety. At first after he had given up his position with the Queen and the Duke of Edinburgh it seemed as if Tommy had regained his health. He had also divested himself of many of his London commitments, including his directorship of the Savoy Hotel, to avoid the travelling involved in monthly board meetings (although he retained an interest both in Claridges and the Berkeley), so that he was able to free himself to be busy with county affairs and with his role in Civil Defence. He soon achieved a high profile and in 1962 he and Daphne had entertained the Queen and the Duke of Edinburgh to 'family tea' at Menabilly, while the Royals were visiting the west country, on which occasion, Daphne noted, the Queen complimented them on their 'lovely old house'.

However, as time went on, Tommy's health began once again to give rise to anxiety, although he kept as active as before. In May 1964 they launched a new boat from their yard at Polruan, the *Ygdrasil III*, built to Tommy's own design – with a real coal fire installed in the cabin and a chimney sticking up through the deck . . . The official launch was undertaken by their friend, Anne Treffry of Place House in Fowey – an even older Cornish mansion. 'I sat on the boat with my dog and my husband made a speech thanking the men who built her. It was a very smooth launch,' said Daphne. 'Now we shall use her to cruise around the Cornish coast throughout the summer.'

During 1964 Tommy did everything he could to encourage Daphne to look positively on the inevitable move to Kilmarth, and together they made a number of visits to look over it and see what improvements needed to be done, as it had been neglected for many years. To anyone who had not lived in Menabilly it would seem an elegant old house, well-proportioned and slate-hung. Although there had been a house on that site for centuries, the present one was not as old as Menabilly, most of it dating from the eighteenth century, but with two substantial twentieth-century additions. If it was not as big as Menabilly, it was sufficiently large for two people and visiting children and grandchildren. Indeed, rooms once used to house a substantial Victorian domestic staff could be converted into a self-contained wing, where the younger grandchildren could rampage, and the older ones play pop music to their hearts' content without disturbing anybody else. Under the house was the basement where Professor Singer had carried out his experiments, still cluttered with dusty and broken test-tubes and bottles, but there were also other disused rooms – kitchens, pantries, stillrooms, a laundry. Daphne found the house 'as desolate as Menabilly had been before we lived there.' Tommy, ever more cheerful, responded by telling her that he could 'see ourselves here'.

So plans were put in hand for the work which would need to be done before the move was undertaken, discussions held with the chosen architect, estimates sought from builders; but if Phillip Rashleigh had entertained any hopes that he might move into Menabilly within a relatively short time, they were not to be realized.

Shortly after Christmas 1964 Tommy went into St Mary's Hospital, Paddington under observation and on 6 January 1965 he underwent major surgery from which, when he emerged, he was said to be in a 'satisfactory' condition. He was then sixty-eight. At the end of the month he returned to Menabilly to convalesce, and a few weeks later signed the lease of Kilmarth, an act which put paid to any last hopes Daphne might have entertained of a last-minute reprieve – although in actual fact, she would remain at Menabilly for another four years. For Tommy's apparent rally, after he returned home, was to prove short-lived. Within weeks he became so ill that he needed full-time nursing, and Daphne employed both day- and night-nurses so that he might remain at home. On the morning of 14 March 1965, he suffered a sudden collapse, and died almost immediately.

Enclosed in her own misery at the prospect of having to move, Daphne had still been aware that he was seriously ill. Even so his death came as a monumental shock to her. 'It was as if the sheltered cloudland that had enveloped me for years, peopled with images drawn from my imagination, had suddenly dissolved, and I was face to face with a harsh and terrible reality. The husband I had loved and taken for granted for thirty-three years of married life, the father of my three children, lay dead.'

Like all people bereaved she went over and over in her mind how she could have missed the danger signals, the ominous signs that the illness had been terminal. In retrospect she blamed herself for being 'heartless' when, on his last night, he had told her he was unable to sleep, and how she had replied, 'You will, darling, you will', before leaving his room, and how his eyes had followed her out. The next morning one of the nurses had come and asked her to telephone the doctor as her patient seemed to have become unusually pale, and 'I went through to him expecting possibly an increase in weakness, but inevitably the usual smile. Instead . . . he turned his face to me and died.'

She joined the nurses in trying to revive him with the kiss of life but knew, in her heart, that it was useless. His eyes were open, 'but the spark had gone'. She had described death time after time in her books; this was the real thing.

The newspapers the following day ran long obituaries, detailing his life and career, with particular reference to the Arnhem campaign, and his time with the Royal Family. He would long be remembered, said *The Times*, as 'the man who created and commanded the British Airborne Forces in the Second World War. It was he who raised and trained our parachute battalions and brigades and the Glider Pilot Regiment, welding them into swift-moving, far-ranging, and hard-hitting battle formations which showed themselves superior to the Germans' best in dash, courage and tenacity.' He had, it continued, 'a natural genius for command.'

Automatically Daphne did the things that are necessary, following a death in the family – agreeing to an autopsy to verify that it had been caused, as the doctor diagnosed, by a sudden coronary thrombosis, writing the death announcement for *The Times*, making clear that the funeral and cremation would be private, as he had wished himself, and that there would be no memorial service or flowers. Anyone who wished to make a donation should make it to the Security Fund for Airborne Forces.

Only her children and the closest friends of the family attended the cremation, after which she scattered Tommy's ashes in the woods of Menabilly where they had walked together so many times. She refused invitations to stay with any of her children, wanting to face alone whatever the future might hold at Menabilly, while she still had possession of it. 'To go elsewhere, even with them, would postpone the moment of truth.'

She forced herself to sort out his bedroom, the clothes hanging in his wardrobe, the yachting magazines beside his bed. She took to wearing his shirts, wrote at his desk and used his pens to answer the letters that came in from all over the world, commiserating with her. She had always found answering her huge fan mail a real chore, and had said on more than one occasion that she only wished she could find some way of stemming the tide, but when it came to Tommy, she sat down and answered every one. Never having been a person that cried easily, she was surprised to find how often she wept. She found the physical act of weeping strangely healing perhaps because 'as a child I seldom cried'.

Her thoughts turned once again to life after death and the philosophical musings in which she had indulged in recent years took on a new urgency, as she sought to come to terms with loss. Baptised and christened an Anglican, she did not feel drawn to seek solace in that church even though now she shared the common yearning of the human race for belief in a life after death, a continuation in some way of the vital human spirit. She wanted to be able to think of Tommy having been somehow reunited with his parents, and with the dead comrades of two world wars. She hoped that his own steadfast and simple faith in the world to come, the 'peace that passes all understanding' – a line he used to quote – would be borne out in some way she herself could not imagine. 'Yet I had seen his empty shell. I had seen the light flicker and go out. Where had it gone? Was it blown to emptiness after all, like the light of a candle, and does each one of us, in the end, vanish into darkness?' In desperation she asked A.L. Rowse what he believed. 'I said we can never know, can we? The more we know about life, the more of an incomprehensible mystery it all is. The best we can do is to be loyal to those we loved, for people do go on in our minds . . .'

For the first time in her life writing proved no solace and she was deeply annoyed by well-meaning friends who told her that at least she had her writing to turn to; she found 'the stories I fashioned once were fairy tales and they cannot satisfy me now.'

In the following months she passed through all the stages common to the newly widowed – the desire to blame the doctors and hospital for failing to cure Tommy, an anger with herself and others because they might have failed him. She noted the strange limbo in which a widow in today's society exists, 'belonging nowhere, resembling in some indefinable manner the coloured races in a world dominated by whites.' Yet, as time passed, she began to feel a kind of tranquillity descending on her so that sometimes she felt almost tangibly what she described as 'an atmosphere of love, a living presence', not in the sense of a ghost, but as if she was occasionally given a glimpse of the freedom and joy of another world.

Theirs had been an unlikely union. From the day Tommy had sailed into her life in *Ygdrasil* thirty-three years earlier, and extricated her from her involvements with Geoffrey and Carol, and severed the immediate tie with Gerald, she had given him the most of which she was capable. In the early years she came as close as she could to physical passion and physical jealousy, and she had turned her back on Cornwall and loyally followed the drum. In her own way she loved him and, as has been already noted, she was very proud of him as he was of her. Although they had spent so much time apart, he had always existed in her life, if not as a physical presence then as the one person to whom she

252

could always turn, who would look after practical matters, support her in her professional life, be the good friend in whom she could confide – a necessary outlet for a woman so self-contained.

In return, he had accepted that once she had entered the gates of her magic garden, then she had set the ground rules for their way of life. She would retreat into that world of the imagination from which he would be always barred. Yet, by so doing, she brought on herself the very fate she had feared, when she had read the bundle of love letters shortly after her marriage, the letters which had given her the impetus to write *Rebecca* – that she would be unable to hold permanently a man so sociable, so physically outgoing. Separated for such long periods, he was virtually certain to turn to other women. If she knew about all his minor involvements then she might well have accepted them, as the kind of affairs Gerald had indulged in – a brief flare and then an end. But the long-running relationship with a woman who had been her friend was not in this category. It went deep and one can only surmise as to what she, Tommy and the other woman – who also loved Tommy dearly – went through.

But in those last years they had shared companionship, affection, and a common interest in the search for those early tragic lovers, Tristan and Iseult. They had been happy and now he was gone.

Whether it was his death, or the move to Kilmarth which stopped the creative flow – or a mixture of both – she was never to know. But until the darkness of depression and confusion descended on her in the last ten years of her life she would continue to return to two things – her memories of Gerald, and to searching her soul over how she had treated Tommy. She once said she wished she could somehow swoop up into the sky and ask him how much of a 'bore' it had been to him, her always living at Menabilly, writing away five days a week, while he saw her only at weekends; whether she had 'bitched up' his career because of it, and whether it was true that he had turned down the highest command in Germany at the end of the war, because he knew she would never be able to bear leaving Cornwall.

CHAPTER 24

The House on the Strand

Tommy's death might have delayed the move out of Menabilly, but it could not prevent it. Eventually it was agreed that Daphne could remain where she was until the summer of 1969 – another four years, during which time Kilmarth would be made habitable, and the various conversions that she and Tommy had discussed before he died had been carried out.

With all the children now grown-up and married, there was no longer any need for the kind of staff at Menabilly she had had years before, especially as the devoted Esther Rowe was such an excellent housekeeper/secretary. Her children – and increasingly her grandchildren – would visit her and she would pay visits to them, also taking part in family holidays. On visits to London she would sometimes lunch with Alec Guinness, although the friendship never became a close one.

Writing about her widowhood a year after Tommy's death, she states how important it is for the one who survives to have time to plan their future, and how necessary it is to resist the attempts of friends and relatives, however well-meaning or anxious, to push the widow or widower into some hasty move which will later be regretted. 'If it is financially possible for you, stay in your own home, with the familiar things about you,' she wrote. 'We need many months to become reconciled to the loss that has overtaken us; and, if at first the silence of the empty house may seem unbearable, do not forget it is still the home you shared, which two persons made their own.' That having been said it must have been an eerie experience for both Daphne and Esther to live in such a large and isolated old house without anyone else.

The first project she undertook was a healing one. For some time she had been thinking of writing a non-fiction book about Cornwall, in part because she had written about the county only in her novels. Two of the books, *The King's General* and *Castle Dor* had, as we have seen, required historical research, and she felt that some of the material she had accumulated might well be used elsewhere. Also she felt concerned at the speed with which the old Cornwall – the genuine Cornwall – was disappearing, under the rising tide of concrete and the flood of tourism caused by rapid social and economic change. She felt very strongly that she wanted to note down something of the traditions and legends of the county before they disappeared without trace. The result was *Vanishing Cornwall*, a title chosen, she said, because she felt both she and her beloved county had reached a watershed, she in her life and Cornwall in its history.

Her idea was that it should be very much a picture book and this gave her the chance to work on it with her son, Christian, who had now turned to photography. He had married an Irish girl and had recently become a father.

Further research for the new book gave her an impetus to get out and about. Together she and Christian retraced the journeys she had made with Foy Quiller-Couch over thirty years earlier, to the Lizard Peninsula in the south, and Bodmin Moor in the north. Her love of the macabre, so much a theme of her short stories, surfaces in this book too, as she traces some of Cornwall's stranger legends, including that of wicked John Penrose whose sins are eventually found out by supernatural means, variations of which occur along the length of the north coast. But one real-life character is a match for anything which would appear in her next anthology, *Not Before Midnight*.

In a chapter on Cornish Eccentrics she tells of the Reverend Densham of Warleggan, a real village with a name which another historical novelist, Winston Graham, was to use for the villain in the Poldark series. ('Demelza' – the name of his heroine – is another village not far away.) To return to the Revd. Densham; he came to Warleggan in the 1920s, a bleak place with a church which had been blasted by lightning a hundred years earlier in 1818. He was a bachelor, and caused a small stir on his arrival when he asked around for someone to employ as a gardener to live in on wages of one penny a year and free potatoes.

This was only the beginning. Needless to say Densham did not find anyone willing to work on these terms nor, it seemed, did his congregation take to him, with the result that attendances at his services rapidly fell away. Nothing daunted, Densham made large cardboard cut-out figures which he propped up in the pews to swell the ranks. He never went into the village or visited his parishioners, had his provisions and post put in a box at the end of his drive and erected eight-foot-high fences, topped with barbed wire, to keep callers out. The parishioners begged the Bishop of Truro to have him removed, but he was unable to do so as technically Densham had broken no ecclesiastical laws. He still took all the Sunday services, although by this time they were attended solely by cardboard cut-out figures. Legend had it that a young man, who unknowingly applied for the post of organist, was locked in a room to keep him there and had to escape at night by breaking out and braving the Alsatian dogs which roamed the garden and churchyard.

Foy and Daphne, intrigued by the tale, had visited Warleggan at the same time they had journeyed to Jamaica Inn. The village had stayed in Daphne's mind, not least because, while picnicking there, they had found themselves camped on a nest of adders, whose hissing had alerted the two young women to their presence. Already thoroughly unnerved, they had then walked round the barbed-wire fence until they came to the gate on which was a large bell. Greatly daring, they pulled the bell, whereupon about eight enormous dogs, wolfhounds and Alsatians, appeared from nowhere and sprang at the fence snarling and barking. Prudence, she said, overcame the spirit of adventure, and they beat a hasty retreat.

A year later they returned, in a car driven by an explorer who had travelled the world, including a crossing of Alaska. This time they all climbed the fence where it had fallen in somewhat, and found themselves within twenty yards of the mad vicar himself, looking like a figure from another time in a frock coat, green with age, and a nineteenth-century, black shovel hat. He saw them. They all froze and then the three young women, including the Alaskan explorer, made for the fence and home. After further years of solitude and silence, a party of villagers finally plucking up sufficient courage to go and see how he was, broke into the vicarage, and found him dead on the floor, the floorboards having been torn up for firewood.

When Daphne and Christian visited the vicarage years later, it had fallen into almost total disrepair, and had an atmosphere which froze both of them. After they had wandered about the deserted grounds and Christian had taken some photographs, they returned to their car to find another visitor. He was a man who had taken a lease on the place, only to find that neither his wife nor the rest of his family were prepared to live in it. He was merely checking up to see that all was well. Daphne told him of her past experiences and how she had once seen the Revd Densham himself walking up and down the overgrown path. '"He still walks," said the man, softly, "back there in the garden."' She wondered if the man turned up regularly, in the hope of seeing the unhappy shade, or if the Revd Densham had somehow infected the newcomer with his own strange eccentricity.

The story summarized here does give something of the flavour of the book, which is evocative of the romantic and legendary aspect of Cornwall. Her close association with Christian helped her tremendously during this bleak period of her life. She was also to relive the latter years with Tommy in her descriptions of how they had sought out the local associations with King Arthur, King Mark and Tristan and Iseult. She used too the information she had amassed on the Civil War in Cornwall, and drew on the research she had undertaken when she was writing her biography of Branwell Brontë, revealing the Cornish connection with the family for the first time to many of her readers. She reviewed legends of the real smugglers – or 'fair traders' – who had operated in the Fowey area in the eighteenth and nineteenth centuries.

Travelling around the county brought back other early memories, memories of holidays spent in Cornwall before the one that had changed her life, at the age of nineteen; a holiday at Mullion Cove when she was five, when Muriel had felt it necessary to take a nurse, a nursemaid and a holiday-governess along just to look after three little girls; how, during that holiday, after Muriel had left them so that she could accompany Gerald on a continental holiday, the children had been woken in the middle of the night by the excited nurses, wrapped up and rushed outside to see the great shoals of pilchards coming in, and how they had all watched, breathless with excitement, as the water boiled with fish as the fishermen battled to get them into the nets. She was lucky, for the heyday of the pilchards had already passed; such sights were rare even at the turn of the century.

Retracing her steps to Mullion Cove in 1966, she found it a dismal place, the beach covered with ice-cream cartons, cigarette packets, contraceptives and other rubbish, the ears assaulted as well by radios and barking dogs. One wonders what she would say if she saw Mullion now: it, and other beauty spots on the south coast, still covered with litter, to which has been added mountains of plastic detritus and raw sewage, not to mention the sounds of the ubiquitous ghetto blaster. Looking to the future of Cornwall, she ends on an optimistic note where sensible tourist policies march side by side with investment in, and revival of, indigenous industry. It is as well she never knew at the end of her life just how different it was to be.

Vanishing Cornwall was completed quickly and published in 1967. In that year there was a sad footnote to those early days at Ferryside. After Tommy's death, Daphne felt there was no point in keeping the boatyard now he was no longer there, and so she sold it. The Hunkins, who had been witnesses at her wedding to Tommy in Lanteglos Church all those years ago, lived in a cottage which was part of the boatyard property. Tom Hunkin had acted as caretaker and foreman for the Brownings for twenty-one years. In May 1967 the new owners sold the cottage, and gave the Hunkins notice to quit. The Hunkins were prepared to move, but found it impossible to buy a house in Polruan where property, even then, was high because of its popularity with second-home owners. Eventually the new owners took the Hunkins to court to get them out of the house, and the judge granted an order on the grounds that their tenancy was invalid and that they had lived there only on the 'whim' of Lady Browning, who would have been called as a witness had she not been abroad on holiday.

This stung Daphne into a rare appearance in news print when she contacted the *Western Morning News* to inform them that she had returned from her holiday a fortnight before and that she had never been told such a case was pending. The Hunkins, she said, had been the Brownings' rent-free tenants and were certainly not there on a 'whim'. Unfortunately, by the time she intervened, it was too late and the Hunkins had had to give up their home.

Daphne was now going back and forth to Kilmarth to oversee the conversion work and found, somewhat to her surprise, that it was her new home that was to provide the impetus for her final historical novel. She had already turned her back on the style of those earlier ones. She had lost interest, she told friends, in affairs of the heart, she had no desire to write another *Rebecca* or *Frenchman's Creek*, rereading them now she found they bored her.

The idea for *The House on the Strand* was triggered off by the history of the site, and that of Tywardreath parish, but also by the strange litter left in the cellar by Professor Singer – not least the pickled embryos and stained test-tubes. She discovered that the owner of the first house on that site had been a Roger Kylmerth who had lived there in the early fourteenth century. At the same time there had been a priory at Tywardreath, where the prior and monks had been involved in such scandalous behaviour that it had resulted, according to County Records, in a punitive visit from the famous Bishop Grandison of Exeter. According to Daphne, her researches showed that the older monks had encouraged pretty young men into joining the priory for homosexual orgies. The present-day churchwarden of Tywardreath Church says that women were involved as well, not least younger nuns from a nearby nunnery, and he is delighted to show you the carved tomb of the prior who presided over the goings-on at the time.

Daphne's detailed researches into Public, County and Parish Records revealed the history of the families who were the feudal overlords of the time – the Bodrugans, the Carminowes and Champernounes – at a time when England was riven with internecine wars between the effete Edward II and his Queen Isabella, and her paramour, Mortimer. She was particularly delighted when she found on the Lay Parish Roll for 1327 the name of Roger Kylmerth as one of the Commons possessed of goods 'to the sum of ten shillings or upward.'

The strands of the past – the corrupt monks and the families split by civil war (as in *The King's General*) – were woven in with those of the present day and with the old laboratory in the Kilmarth cellars, to which was added the current notoriety of the hallucinogenic drug LSD; there had been a number of well-publicised court cases in Cornwall in the 1960s, where the new drug had become popular, especially with the county's hippy community – Flower Power had hit Cornwall in general and St Ives in particular.

Once again she walked the countryside which would

feature so crucially in this particular story. Not, this time, the romantic creeks of the River Helford or the Malpas of Tristan legend, or the dramatic coastline of *Jamaica Inn*, but the back lanes and byways, between the small china-clay port of Par and Kilmarth house. In the fourteenth century that landscape would have looked very different, with a much wider estuary into Carlyon Bay. She explored the hamlets of Strickstenton and Treesmill, the lanes sunk deep beneath Cornish stone-hedges, where stunted oaks and bushes of blackthorn almost meet overhead. She worked out which modern settlements were based on the earlier medieval ones, how the place names had changed over the centuries. Dressed as ever in slacks, jersey and anorak, her dogs at her heels, she physically plotted out the strange journeys of her hero while he was under the influence of a drug, worked out where his guide and mentor, Magnus, met his death on the railway line between Trevarren and Par.

The result is something of a *tour de force*. For the last time she inhabits a male persona, this time that of a publisher who has always been overshadowed by his brilliant biophysicist friend Magnus, with whom he has had a relationship which has virtually cut him off from any other emotional entanglements. Then, in his forties, he marries a pushy American woman with two children. Magnus has been experimenting with a hallucinogenic drug and he persuades the narrator to go down to his house at Kilmarth, without the family, and try it out. The drug takes him back, without warning, into the fourteenth century where he finds himself inexorably linked with the fortunes of Roger Kylmerth and witnessing a tragic love story played out against a background of family feuds. The trips become an addiction, and he takes more and more of the drug, until he is warned by Magnus to stop before he damages himself permanently. But Magnus, on the way to Kilmarth to explain the drug's dangers, cannot resist taking it himself one last time and is knocked down and killed crossing a railway line which, of course, did not exist in 1327.

After that the narrator's experience mirrors that of Dr Jekyll, as eventually he finds himself changing without even having taken the drug; it all ends in disaster when, finally, he is transported back to find Roger dying from the effects of the Black Death that decimated the county in 1348. 'Again I think she was underestimated with regard to this particular novel. She handles the double timescale brilliantly,' says Rowse. He also felt she put into the mind of her narrator much of herself – 'the intolerable strain of waiting for unwelcome guests, anticipating that "dire" moment when a car appears on the drive.' There is much of the essential Daphne there, he feels. 'As for the fantasy world that is so exciting, it holds a fascination which is lacking in the world of today. The trouble is that daydreams,' he paraphrases her, 'like hallucinogenic drugs, become addictive; the more we indulge, the deeper we plunge.' Daphne only once seriously considered taking such a drug herself, and that was when she was researching Branwell Brontë. According to Angela, she had discussed her researches with a friend who was a doctor and he had offered to provide her with some laudanum, so that she might understand something of Branwell's experiences. She heated up a little milk, as she had been told, and put the laudanum into it; at which point she got cold feet, not least because she feared instant addiction, and so poured it all down the sink. Selective travel and research was sufficient to provide her with the stimulation she needed.

Meanwhile the fortune continued to roll in. Gollancz estimated, just before publication of *Vanishing Cornwall*, that her total sales – so far as could be reckoned – had topped 5,250,000 copies in the British Commonwealth alone, with a grand total of world sales standing at well over twenty million, including translations into thirty languages. To that now had to be added the copies of *Vanishing Cornwall* and *The House on the Strand*.

When the former went into Penguin paperback it was reprinted nine times, twice in the first year. But in 1972, three years after the publication of *The House on the Strand*, on the advice of her agent Curtis Brown, Daphne broke with Penguin and sold eight of her bestselling titles to Pan Books, for a contract worth over £100,000.

'We did not feel able to match it,' said Christopher Dolley, the then managing director of Penguin, 'even though we had published her books for years.' Daphne is quoted in *The Times* as saying that she was not transferring titles only for monetary reasons, but because she did not feel that Penguin had sold her well enough throughout the world . . . Given her staggering sales figures it is difficult to see how she could reconcile this with the facts.

She continued, meanwhile, salting it away, much of it into the family trusts and, indeed, told this writer in the summer of 1969 that she kept back only about £4,000 to live on, a modest sum in view of the expenses of Menabilly and the imminent move to Kilmarth. Over the next twenty years, as the vast sums continued to flow in, she was to live more and more frugally, even to the point of physical discomfort.

CHAPTER 25

Out of Eden

I n the early summer of 1969 the move to Kilmarth finally became a reality. In those last days Daphne wandered round the stripped and empty rooms, piled with packing cases, taking her leave of the beloved Menabilly on which she had lavished so much love; that splendid forty-five-foot 'Long Room', the smaller sitting room that Tommy had made his own, the panelled gallery and the Gatehouse, which had featured so prominently in *The King's General*, but which never had yielded up its secrets to her. When Pickfords' van came to remove the furniture, it stuck fast under one of the trees which had to be cut down with an axe. Daphne had loved the trees, most especially the lilac, and had let the shrubs grow as they would with only the minimum of pruning or cutting-back.

Moving house after twenty-six years, she wrote, was rather like facing a major operation; to a friend she said it was more like a second death, after losing Tommy. Browning's belongings were brought along too, including the remains of the first old *Ygdrasil*, which was beached in the grounds of Kilmarth, as it had been at Menabilly. While she had been prepared to let the Menabilly gardens more or less run riot, she planned that the overgrown garden in her new home should be cleared and put in order, blight-struck roses replaced, possibly the old tennis-court reclaimed for the grandchildren.

The grounds, she wrote, abounded with wildlife – badgers

and foxes, owls, jackdaws, swallows and martins and a host of butterflies. She even had the equivalent of the shed in the Menabilly garden, in the form of a summerhouse facing out across Carlyon Bay. A steep path led from the house across a field to the beach, easy to walk down, not so easy to walk up. She nicknamed the climb 'thrombosis hill'.

Physically she was active and fit, if underweight; mentally very lively. In the Queen's Birthday Honour's List of that summer she was given the accolade of Dame, and was duly invested at Buckingham Palace by the Queen, on 23 July. So she faced her new life without her mainstays, Menabilly and Tommy; yet, throughout the rest of her life, when she gave one of her increasingly rare interviews to the media, she would return continuously to those two events which had left so strong a mark on her – her first sight of Menabilly, and how Tommy had sailed into her life in *Ygdrasil* that summer long ago.

When she had poured out her feelings to Rowse about the move before she made it, he had told her she should look on it positively, that she might even find, in spite of everything, that it might act as an inspiration. In the event it had already given her *The House on the Strand*, which boded well, and which was published in the summer of the move. It was a strange friendship she and Rowse enjoyed in those latter years, a friendship which had grown from those early days of envy and jealousy on his side and fear of his academic ability on hers. Both of them were now living in large, isolated old Cornish houses, both with housekeepers and no other permanent residents; he at Trenarren, she at Kilmarth. He would regularly lunch with her, but she would never allow him to reciprocate her hospitality. She would not leave Kilmarth to lunch at Trenarren. It became a joke between them, carried on in letters and cards, in which she signed herself 'Madame Non-Non'. 'She always knew her own mind,' says Dr Rowse, 'and it was usually "non". Very occasionally she said "yes" to something, then I would call her "Madame Oui-Oui"; but she still never agreed to come here for lunch!'

So he would go over to Kilmarth where Esther Rowe would provide delicious food and where wine was always on offer, although neither of them would drink it, both sticking firmly to water. Daphne confined herself to a glass or two of Dubonnet when she was entertaining visitors who liked a drink. Over such a lunch or afternoon tea she would show the vivacity, coupled with a strong sense of humour, which so belied her public persona.

Gradually Kilmarth was put in order – the cartoons and pictures on the walls, the familiar furniture placed in the new surroundings. Although there was no 'Long Room', there was a large and beautiful drawing room, out of which opened first a dining room, and then her library, so that when the doors of all of them were left open she could see from one end of the house to the other, which created a sense of enormous space. The sitting room also had french windows, opening out on to the garden, so that in summer, with the sun pouring in, it became almost like a conservatory.

In 1970 there was an event which would no doubt have delighted Tommy. Their eldest daughter Tessa's marriage had broken down, and in that year she remarried. She could hardly have made a happier choice from Daphne's point of view, for she married the son of Tommy's admired Lord Montgomery, thus uniting the two families in an ever closer tie.

In 1971 Gollancz brought out another anthology of short stories, *Not Before Midnight*, later reprinted by Penguin under the title *Don't Look Now*. This story, from which the Penguin edition took its cover title, became one of the most financially successful film adaptations of any of her books, directed by Nicolas Roeg, and starring Donald Sutherland and Julie Christie. The plot of *Don't Look Now* had come to her when she was on holiday in Venice. One night while out walking in the city she had become lost in a maze of little backstreets and narrow, squalid alleyways, and had seen, running by the side of a canal, a figure she had taken to be that of a small child. When it turned round, however, she saw that she had been mistaken and that it was an unpleasant-looking dwarf. This, coupled with her continuing interest in telepathy and premonitions, resulted in the story of the couple who, visiting Venice on holiday and trying to get over the death of their child, have an inexplicable glimpse of what turns out to be their future, a future which ends in a brutal and meaningless murder.

All the stories in this anthology are bizarre. It includes that mentioned earlier, 'A Border Line Case', in which the young girl falls in love with, and beds, albeit unknowingly, her own father. There is also one that is among the most chilling in English twentieth-century short story-writing, 'The Breakthrough'. In this Daphne abandons Cornwall and glamorous locations in Europe for East Anglia, an area which has attracted a good many novelists and most especially crime writers such as P.D. James. She sets her story in the bleak Suffolk marshland in that strange area between the village of Dunwich, most of which has fallen into the sea, and the bird sanctuary of Minsmere.

Well away from home ground, she showed that she had not lost her touch when it came to a sense of place. 'The sandy track topped a rise and there below us, stretching into infinity, lay acre and acre of waste land, marsh and reed, bounded on the left by sand-dunes with the open sea beyond. The marshes were intersected here and there by dykes beside which stood clumps of forlorn rushes bending to the wind and rain, the dykes in their turn forming themselves into dark pools, one or two of them miniature lakes, ringed about with reeds.' There was also another reason why she chose that particularly bleak part of the Suffolk coast for it is over-burdened with military and nuclear establishments. In her story she posits that there is also another secret establishment, one which does not research into weaponry, but into the civil and military uses of telepathy and how it has got out of hand because the senior scientist has become obsessed with what happens to the human soul on death; whether there is a measurable release of energy that might prove the existence of the human spirit.

He thinks he has a way of finding out through one of his brighter subordinates who is dying of leukaemia. To hand is one of a pair of surviving twin children, a child who is severely mentally handicapped, but gifted with strange psychic abilities. The scientist proposes, by the use of a computer appropriately named Charon, to link the mind of the dying man with that of the idiot child, to see if it is possible to pass his consciousness into hers at the moment of death. Put baldly it sounds ridiculous, but the story is written with such power that it becomes compulsive. Eventually the unfortunate young man dies and it does appear that, indeed, the experiment has been a success, for some kind of energy force has left his body at the same time as the child finds a voice. But after that nothing goes as planned for the child speaks not only on behalf of the dead man, but of the twin who died at birth as well. With increasing force the child screams in agony, 'Let them go! Let them go!', until finally the scientist, still reluctant to spoil his experiment, is forced to turn off the computer which has linked the three entities together.

It would seem that in her resolution of the story, Daphne was coming to conclusions of her own regarding death. 'If intelligence survives,' says the scientist, 'If Force 6 (the life force) can triumph over matter, then it's not just one man who has beaten death but all mankind from the beginning of time. Immortality in some form or other becomes a certainty, the whole meaning of life on earth is changed.'

Yes, thinks the narrator – once again a young male persona – yes indeed, but to what end? 'The fusion of science and religion in a partnership at first joyous, then the inevitable disenchantment, the scientist realising, and the priest with him, that, with eternity assured, the human being on earth is more easily expendable. Dispatch the maimed, the old, the weak, destroy the very world itself, for what is the point of it if the promise of fulfilment lies elsewhere?'

She had more than enough time for introspection, as she continued her long walks in all but the worst weather, her solitary evenings eating supper in front of her television set. She frankly admitted in her later years that she had become something of television-addict, and no-one who saw any of the news or current affairs programmes of the early 1970s could have been unaware of the war in Vietnam, and the controversy surrounding it, or of the American attempts to justify their presence in South-East Asia.

It may seem the strangest of starting points for a du Maurier novel, but however true it might have been that Daphne cut herself off from world events (apart from the war, of course) when she was young and writing at Menabilly, she certainly kept well abreast of what was going on both nationally and internationally as she grew older. She had rarely expressed her views on anything remotely contentious, apart from the semi-mocking references to her admiration for Harold Wilson. The new book was to give her a platform for a range of ideas – ideas which left her loyal and devoted readership totally bewildered – for *Rule Britannia*, in many ways her most remarkable book, is totally unlike anything she had written before.

The horrors of Vietnam, portrayed nightly on the screens of the nation's television sets produced strong anti-American sentiments which had manifested themselves in large-scale demonstrations both in England and Europe. The Wilson administration had havered, fudged, and finally given America its luke-warm support, thus leading to a charge which would be made with even greater fervour in the 1980s: namely that when it came to foreign policy, we had become little more than a satellite state. The question of whether or not we should go into Europe, was also much in the air, as the succeeding Prime Minister, Edward Heath, battled to link the UK with the European Community. In Cornwall there was also growing antipathy to government at long distance from Whitehall and an upsurge in feeling which led to the formation of a small nationalist party, Mebyon Kernow – Sons of Cornwall.

Out of this Daphne forged *Rule Britannia*. It was the main

plot-line that upset so many people. Daphne puts forward a situation in which, strange prophetically, although Britain has become part of Europe and joined herself economically and financially to the EEC, there arises a fiercely nationalistic prime minister. He becomes disenchanted with the connection, just as the European nations have become tired of the American presence, and of providing military bases and establishments for them, and so the Europeans have called on the American government to take their forces home. This leaves only Britain as America's uncritical ally, to try and placate a jumpy American administration. So the country undergoes what might be termed an invited invasion, a British 'government of national unity', agreeing to the take-over. There has been no Parliamentary discussion, the deal is a secret one and so one morning the nation wakes up to discover that Britain is being run by the United States. At first it is the iron hand in the velvet glove, but gradually that glove is removed, dissidents are rounded up, internment camps established, rationing is imposed and punitive measures taken against anyone opposing the new regime.

The events are seen through the eyes of 'Mad' (short for 'Madam'), an eccentric actress of nearly eighty, her adolescent granddaughter Emma, and the household of homeless young people 'Mad' has adopted over the years. Daphne liked to deny that there was any similarity between her and 'Mad', saying she saw more of herself when she was a young woman in the character of Emma, but her views sing strongly out of 'Mad', along with a courageous, obstinate and humorous personality that is very like Daphne at the time she was writing the book; indeed, the descriptions of 'Mad' tramping round the woods of Kilmarth in her old jerseys, trousers, seaboots and cap fit exactly the Daphne of later years.

The plot details the growing resistance to the Americans which begins in Cornwall, and is fostered and given impetus by 'Mad', along with an admittedly unlikely premise that an army of resistance will be led by the young Prince Charles who is looked on by the inhabitants of Cornwall in much the same way as was his predecessor of the same name, at the end of the Civil War. 'Mad' dies after setting up a brilliantly successful sabotage operation, and giving stirring quotations from Shakespeare and Wordsworth over an illegal radio network, and we are left believing that, with the assistance of friends in Europe, it is just about possible that the Americans will finally be defeated and go home.

Rule Britannia did not only shock her usual readership, it left the popular media at a complete loss, a feeling summed up in the headline 'Yanks Go Home Says Du Maurier!' Reviewers appeared unable to come to terms with it at all, unable to understand why she should apparently become, 'so anti-American' and 'political', why she should abandon her 'romances' for something so 'completely different', tackling subjects which were obviously not her province.

She considered the book to be a satire, comic but with serious undertones though, 'I'm afraid a lot of people didn't see the point.' She felt *Rule Britannia* gave her that freedom to comment on current and contentious events denied to her in normal circumstances. It enabled her to ask just what it would be like to be taken over by the Americans, even with the best of motives, to try and imagine how ordinary people might feel. It also suggested that it was necessary for all of us to seriously consider the benefits – or not – of closer ties with Europe; to think about whether it might not be time for far greater devolution from the centre of government for Scotland, Wales and, indeed, for the far west of England; not least she looked at the role, or lack of it, of a monarchy in twentieth-century Britain. It is little wonder, therefore, that the book had the reception it did.

Read now it seems even more prophetic in an era where our old relationship with America, in spite of the Gulf War, is under scrutiny on both sides of the Atlantic, when for the first time our commitment to Europe has become a real political issue, and when there is growing concern over the increasing centralization of power from Westminster. It was an unlikely book on which to bow out from a long career as a writer of fiction.

She did not see it, of course, as the last novel and throughout the rest of her writing life she lived in hope that she would once again feel the imaginative inspiration needed for fiction. She was sixty-two when she wrote *Rule Britannia*, and eleven years later, in a rare BBC interview, she was still saying that she hoped and prayed that she might wake up one day and find her head filled with an idea for another novel; but it was not to be. The creative muse is a cruel and wayward force and she could never again call it back. She made one final attempt in 1980 when she resurrected her idea of a novel based on the Jacobite Rebellion and the Clan Macdonald, actually going up to Scotland on a family holiday in search of material; but nothing came of it, no story-line grew in her mind as had always been the case in the past, no amount of strolls in the Scottish countryside, trips to Glencoe or research into the history of the '45 made any difference. Sadly, it simply would not come.

Daphne had travelled a long way from the fortunate, cosseted and excited young girl, scribbling frantically away at Ferryside on her saga of three generations of a Cornish boat-builder's family, to the self-contained and rather isolated woman writing a political satire which shocked her fans. On one point at least the two met, that of dress; for Daphne now hardly ever moved away from trousers, well-cut trouser suits for entertaining visitors and going away, old corduroys, anoraks and seaboots for home – much the same dress as that worn by her younger self forty years earlier.

Only a handful of books remained to be written and after the last, the autobiography of her early years, she would put her name only to a collection of essays, many written years earlier, and a similar anthology of short stories.

Reading her essay on moving house, written after she had been at Kilmarth a little while, one might think that she had fully, indeed happily, accepted the change. She writes: 'The house I looked upon with misgivings before

I moved, wondering whether I should ever settle down in new surroundings, no longer gives me the somewhat dubious impression of a pleasant holiday residence, lent to me for a season by obliging friends, but is transforming itself, day by day, week by week, with familiar furniture and objects all about me, into the friendly warmth and comfort of a place well loved, where I am made welcome. In short, we are at one, and I am at home.'

No doubt, intellectually, that was all true; but the emotional reality was somewhat different. For the next ten years she was to haunt the woods and grounds of Menabilly like some unhappy ghost, reverting in a sad and curious way to the days of her youth, when she had prowled illicitly round the gardens of her magic house. How often the Rashleighs were aware of her visits, they do not say, but they cannot have failed to know of her brooding presence. She would set off across her own grounds at Kilmarth, intent on a trip to the beach or a brisk walk cross country, only to find herself drawn inexorably back, again and again, to Menabilly. From a distance she watched the efforts made to clear the gardens and cut back the shrubs, the demolition of the Victorian wing, and even the Gatehouse which had so intrigued her, made necessary because its structure had become unsafe.

Later she did visit the house again officially, although possibly her friends are right when they say at some deep level she never really forgave Philip Rashleigh; for in her mind he had turned her out of Eden.

CHAPTER 26

Golden Lads and *Growing Pains*

The early years at Kilmarth were fruitful ones. After *Rule Britannia*, Daphne was to undertake by far her most ambitious works of non-fiction, two books analysing the lives and times of Antony and Francis Bacon. She had been drawn to the subject in a number of ways, in part by reading James Spedding's mammoth seven-volume biography of Francis, but also by the memory of that eccentric uncle, who doggedly searched the bed of the River Wye for proof that Bacon wrote the plays of Shakespeare. While Daphne was never to go quite as far as that, she did incline to the view that either or both the Bacon brothers had had some kind of an input into the plays, or that Francis, at least, had had a direct influence on some of them.

Her capacity for research by this time should not be underestimated. The gentle schooling she had received at the hands of her governess and her time with Fernande in Paris had hardly equipped her for historical research. She was self-taught. The work she undertook herself on the Bacon family is quite remarkable and that part which, of necessity, she had had to put out to researchers, was meticulously overseen. On her behalf, Mrs St George Saunders and a team from Writers' and Speakers' Research, transcribed over three hundred original letters taken from the Bacon collection, many of which had never been transcribed previously. Others were found for her in the Folger Library, the Harleian and Cotton manuscripts in the British Museum and Lambeth Palace.

Most of the actual physical ground-work she embarked on herself, accompanied again by Christian, who could take the necessary photographs of pictures, places and documents, as well as acting as driver. She pursued the Bacons through their early lives at Gorhambury, where the present Countess of Verulam allowed access to papers and copies of family portraits, to Montauban on the Tarn, where Antony had spent crucial years of his life; to Bordeaux and the sites of the London houses of the Bacon brothers. The rarely reproduced pictures alone are fascinating, especially that of the father, Sir Nicholas Bacon, with his venal face and politician's eyes.

The first volume, *Golden Lads*, is much the better of the two, full of detail and written with great zest, but never losing sight of its main subject; it also has humour. Writing of Queen Elizabeth I's visit to Sir Nicholas, in his new mansion of Gorhambury, Daphne says: 'The Queen herself was said to be "highly gratified" by the visit, and by way of expressing her thanks to have sent her picture to hang in the long gallery. If the bejewelled, red-wigged, hook-nosed lady in the portrait that hangs at Gorhambury today is really Queen Elizabeth – and it bears small resemblence to any of her other well-known portraits – then Her Majesty insulted them by palming off on them an indifferent likeness that she evidently preferred to have out of the way.'

But it was while researching documents in Montauban, in the original sixteenth-century French, that Daphne was to come across material hitherto completely unknown, even to Elizabethan scholars. The knowledge that both the Bacons had homosexual tendencies was not new; what had not been known before was that Antony, while living in Montauban and supplying spymaster Francis Walsingham with information, had been publicly accused of sodomy, a charge which, if proved in the France of that day, required the offender to be burned at the stake. In fact a priest found guilty of the crime in a town not far from Montauban, had suffered that fate in

Cahors in 1563. Antony Bacon had lived for some years with a favourite, Thomas Lawson, and the household was full of pretty pages. It soon became apparent locally that there were homosexual relationships among the boys, not all of them entered into willingly; at least one boy who left Antony's service claimed, with corroborative physical detail, that he had been sexually abused by one of the older boys, and that this had been condoned by Antony. Eventually word got about that Antony himself seduced and abused his pages, persuading them into the performance of unnatural acts.

Daphne gives him the benefit of the doubt. She considers, from what is known of his character, that his involvement was emotional and affectionate, rather than physical (in fact towards the end of his life he told his doctor he had always remained a virgin); but be that as it may, the accusation was laid firmly at his door, and he only narrowly escaped prosecution and execution by the intervention of Henry of Navarre, who was his friend. It is remarkable, writes Daphne, that amongst the state documents of Queen Elizabeth for the years 1586–7, 'there is not a single one referring to the charge brought against Antony Bacon. If any ever existed it must have been destroyed.'

Her discovery shook Elizabethan scholars. 'She actually did make a genuine contribution to sixteenth-century English history when she discovered this archive,' says A.L. Rowse. 'It was a very remarkable achievement deserving wider recognition. She was very anxious that I should approve of the two books. She really worked at them; she didn't just rely on having good researchers.'

In *Golden Lads*, Daphne concentrated on Antony, weak and spendthrift, but clever – although never as bright as Francis. She also discovered rarely publicised, if not new, material on his last years, the years when he was so deeply involved with the Earl of Essex, and the rebellion leading to the execution of the man who, after the death of Robert Dudley, Earl of Leicester, was Queen Elizabeth's greatest favourite. Several of Essex's closest associates died with him, the aristocrats by the axe on Tower Hill, their far less fortunate colleagues, who were not ennobled, by hanging, drawing and quartering at Tyburn; but Antony, ill and crippled – probably with arthritis – remained out of sight and although his name was mentioned several times during the prosecution of Essex, a prosecution in which his brother Francis played a leading role, he was never arraigned. Within two months of Essex's death on the scaffold at Tower Hill, Antony Bacon was dead.

'How he died, where he died and where he was buried has remained unknown throughout the centuries until the present day,' writes Daphne. But a search in the Harleian manuscripts at the British Museum led her to the register of St Olave's Church, Hart Street, and here she found the entry – 'unnoticed for centuries' – of Antony's burial. 'May 17th, 1601 Mr Anthonye Bacon buried in the chamber within the vault.' There is no other entry of his death anywhere, no will was ever proved. Was he in the circumstances, she wondered, buried secretly at night? As the other close associates of Essex confessed their guilt – or not – and met their deaths, he must have wondered if he would soon be following them. Did he therefore decide to cheat the gallows and die by his own hand? Or, ill as he was, did he just lose the will to live once his beloved Earl was dead? It is a fascinating puzzle most likely destined to remain insoluble.

St Olave's Church had been bombed in 1941 and, when the site was cleared, the coffin of Samuel Pepys was found in a vault beneath the communion table in the chancel. Daphne could find no record of any others mentioned as having been discovered at the same time, and the area was sealed over again when a new church was built on the site. As an odd footnote, when she visited it in October 1973 and was sitting silently in the peaceful building, the organist began softly playing the old air, 'Greensleeves', the tune 'sung by courtier and commoner alike, known to Henry VIII, danced to by his daughter and surely strummed upon the virginals by Antony Bacon himself.

'Just as suddenly as it began, the music ceased. The quest that had taken the intruder to Montauban, Bordeaux, Gorhambury, Redbourne, Twickenham and through many a dusty document, had ended too. The caged bird was at rest.'

Her second volume, on the life and times of Francis Bacon, is not so successful, full of well-researched detail, to the point where you lose the thread of the argument. Once more she attempted to trace resemblances between Bacon's life and work and Shakespeare's plays, an attempt which led to heated, but friendly, arguments with A.L. Rowse, arguments their friends remember with amusement and pleasure.

She obviously found working on the Bacon books both absorbing and highly enjoyable, the addictive searching through archive material, the journeys around the English countryside and to Montauban and Bordeaux chauffered by Christian; then back again to Kilmarth to write, her year punctuated by visits from her growing grandchildren whose Wellington boots, in descending order of size, stood in a row in the converted wing waiting for their arrival. Between this growing younger generation and herself was a warm and affectionate bond and there is no doubt they loved their visits to Kilmarth where they could play out adventures to their hearts' content.

Golden Lads was published in 1975 – a prodigious feat, for the book was still being researched in October 1973. The second volume, *The Winding Stair*, followed in 1976. Both, said Gollancz, were received with 'respectful acclaim', by reviewers.

But by 1976 Daphne was already deep into another book. For years she had been pressed to write her autobiography, something she had steadfastly refused to do. Eventually, for whatever reason, she agreed to write a book dealing with her early years. She had kept diaries from her teenage years until her marriage, and so had this material on which to draw. The book would come to an end with her marriage, when the diaries ceased.

She began on her voyage of rediscovery with the early years at Cumberland Terrace, followed by the move to Cannon Hall. It is, of course, impossible to know how accurately she portrays her feelings and thoughts throughout her childhood and adolescence, when she was actually experiencing them, and how much was written with hindsight, but what does come across strongly from both *Growing Pains*, and her sister Angela's *It's only the Sister*, is how totally self-absorbed both girls were throughout their early lives, how removed from ordinary life, how unreal it all seems.

Daphne charts her emotional life, her intense crush on Fernande, her sensual awakening by Geoffrey, the relationship with Carol Reed, who is called only by his first name; but there are only a few flashes of self-revelation, such as her hysteria as a child whenever she saw her mother with her hair down, and how she and Muriel finally turned to each other for the first time in their lives, on Gerald's death. There is also the curious comment, in view of the strong affection in which she held Fernande, that possibly Fernande would never have made such a favourite of her, had she not been a du Maurier. Nor do we learn anything more of the real Gerald from the coy references as to how she saw herself, Geoffrey and Gerald in their roles of Lucretia, Cesare and Alessandro Borgia, or how he came the heavy father over her relationship with Carol. There is nothing in *Growing Pains* of the Gerald of the biography, written in such white heat after his death, that biography which was so desperately honest in its attempt to show him warts and all.

Although the book is sub-titled *The Shaping of a Writer*, there is little in it that gives any clues as to how this came about, nothing to make the reader feel, as they wade through the endless accounts of trips abroad, holidays, social events and family parties, that she had ever felt an all-consuming compulsion to write; about what had moved her, influenced her or motivated her. All we know is that, over a number of years, she wrote short stories, an activity which she appeared easily to be able to put aside, at will, in order to go off on yet another holiday and that then, quite suddenly, she felt able to sit down and write a historical novel about the family who owned the local boat-yard. There is no sense that, welling up inside her, was a force so overwhelming, so essential to her provenance as a person, that when it finally disappeared years later, it destroyed her. *Growing Pains* remains the story of an indulged and wealthy young girl from a famous family, one who writes a little, has a couple of emotional entanglements and then, after a whirlwind romance, marries a handsome young soldier with whom she sails off into the sunset to live happily ever after. As a writer who always defended herself against the charge of being a romantic novelist, she would scarcely have used such a plot in one of her own novels.

Yet, however disappointing the book might be for the reader, it was for her a poisoned chalice. It forced her to sit down and relive a past she had shut away, totally outside a ring fence of fiction, to compare herself and her own life with the personalities and lives of those heroes and heroines through whom she had lived, vicariously, over so many years. It also brought back the dead – so many dead; dead family, George and Gerald and Muriel, Arthur and Sylvia Davies, along with four out of five of their 'Lost Boys'; Geoffrey, with his trail of broken marriages and failed relationships, dying an impoverished chicken farmer (she could not remember where or when); Tommy and, of course overshadowing them all, Gerald. It reminded her of those early days in Paris with Fernande, who had died of leukaemia, and of the intensity of her feelings towards her. She relived her love affair with Carol Reed and that first meeting with, and subsequent marriage to, Tommy; and it brought back her passionate quest for Menabilly and her determination to live there at whatever cost.

Although she stopped her autobiography at the point where she and Tommy sailed away to Frenchman's Creek, following their marriage at Lanteglos Church, finishing the book at that point did not prevent her from reliving what had happened afterwards, most particularly those years safe inside Menabilly, totally absorbed in the writing of fiction. Whatever she might have seen or felt when she looked back, which might have given us a real insight into her as both a woman and a writer, she cut the story off abruptly when she reached the age of twenty-five.

Perhaps there was more in those original diaries than the edited and sanitized account of her life given in *Growing Pains*; perhaps what is in the book is truly all she felt she had to reveal. Whichever way it was, the actual writing of it had a profound effect on her. It forced her, according to Dr Rowse, to face up fully to just how much she had been in love with Gerald, and how it had haunted her subsequent emotional life.

The end of the book marks the cut-off point, after which no more would be revealed, the point at which in real life she had retreated into her world of fantasy, a retreat from which neither childbearing, nor even the war, would force her out.

But the effort of going even that far had unforeseen consequences. 'She told me,' says Dr Rowse, 'that writing even that much about herself had given her a terrible – and final – "writer's block". She had put so much of herself into the protagonists of her novels, had lived through them so intensely for years, that when she had finished looking inward to write about herself as she really was, somehow there was nothing left.'

She had admitted, after Tommy's death, that she had always managed to keep the real world at bay behind the walls of fiction. She had then had to face up to life outside the magic garden of Menabilly. Finally, there had come the self-searching required for *Growing Pains* – and that last was to prove fatal.

CHAPTER 27

Arnhem Revisited

U p until the publication of *Growing Pains* in 1977 Daphne's life had a definite pattern, centred around writing, even if that writing was no longer fiction.

Mornings would be spent in research, writing or responding to 'unnecessary' letters. Afternoons, in all but the most impossible weather, out walking, accompanied when she first moved to Kilmarth by her dog, Moray, then, after his death, by his two successors. She described herself as she set out for such a walk on a stormy day, as being dressed 'like Tolstoy in his declining years', in a fur cap with ear flaps, padded jerkin, and knee-length rubber boots. She would trudge across the lanes and fields, turned into a 'muddy Passchendaele' by the inclement weather, mud which would remind her of the horrors Tommy had had to endure in the trenches during the First World War. She also describes how, on several occasions, she had taken shelter crouching with the dog behind a hedge, to get out of the wind and rain, in a place known locally as Little Hell, bringing to her mind Harrison Ainsworth's description of the cell in the Tower of London known, during the sixteenth century, as 'Little Ease'. She would make a note of the birds she saw on these expeditions, always looking out for the rare stranger blown in by the gales.

She describes cheerfully how sometimes she would return

home to find the wind had blown her fire out, leaving the lounge full of smoke. If it happened to be Esther Rowe's day off, then she would go down and fetch logs from the cellar and try to start the fire again herself, often, she reported, unsuccessfully. When this happened she would resign herself to drinking her tea beside a cold grate, her eyes protected – somewhat strangely – from the smoke by sun glasses!

Her meagre supper would be eaten on her knee in front of the television set, in a room full of Gerald memorabilia – photographs, pictures, portraits and small effects. A tub in the hall outside contained a vast collection of his canes and sticks, some quite bizarre, including swordsticks of various kinds, canes with jewelled heads and one topped with a carved ape. Out in the hall and up the stairs were other shades of the family past, the cartoons of Mary Anne, framed drawings by George. At the end of the evening she would go down to the basement to let the dog out, 'unafraid of the dead of six centuries', before going upstairs to bed where she would say good-night to Tommy's portrait, before kneeling, as they had both been used to do, to say her prayers before settling down to sleep.

Sundays were only a little different, in that she had to cook her own lunch. She always refused invitations either to visit or be visited. In the morning she would read the appropriate Catholic Mass for the day, although she had still not followed Jeanne who had been received into the Catholic Church some years before. After lunch, black coffee, and the inevitable cigarette, she would again set off for a walk. That she lived frugally, to the point of physical discomfort, is obvious as she freely admitted how she would lie in bed on a rainy night until she felt an 'ominous' drip of water on the pillow, putting up with it until it was sodden before doing something about it. She would not use another of the many bedrooms, the beds in them were usually unaired and not made up, there was no heating used in them unnecessarily and many of the lamps did not even have light bulbs in the holders. So she would wrestle with the bed, pulling and tugging it until she managed to get it into a part of the room where the rain did not come through the ceiling from the leaking roof. At that point she could still laugh at herself saying that, apart from the lack of Tommy's companionship, she would not change her lot for the world.

She had often been referred to as a 'recluse', although she did not see herself in such a light. Her family visited her regularly and she visited them. She invited friends – such as Rowse – to meals at Kilmarth. She travelled abroad on holiday, and in order to research her books, and she still paid visits to London. But after *Growing Pains* there was only one real flurry of activity, before the abortive trip to Scotland, after which she did truly become a recluse in the proper sense of the word.

'I was on my way to Holland to play a small role in Richard Attenborough's epic war film about the Arnhem disaster,' writes Dirk Bogarde in his own autobiography, *An Orderly Man*, '(although I had sworn never to play featured bits or cameo roles), but I had reversed that decision – unwisely as it turned out, persuaded into joining the massive band of superstars and lesser mortals gathered together to recreate one of the most appalling defeats the British had had to suffer in World War II, one at which I had personally been present, not in the city but just across the river.' So writes Dirk Bogarde on Richard Attenborough's film of the Cornelius Ryan book, *A Bridge Too Far*. He is still not sure why he agreed to do it, except that he had a longstanding friendship with both Sheila and Richard Attenborough, going back to his early years in Rank pictures.

It was fortunate he did not know what was to come, for Attenborough's film was to cause a furore, not only over the main thrust of its story-line (although it suffered from all the defects of such a heavily financed feature film, stuffed with international stars and aimed at the world market), but over Bogarde's own portrayal of 'Boy' Browning.

Before commencing filming, Attenborough sent copies of

the script, which had been written by William Goldman, to all the main figures who took part in the Arnhem affair and who were still alive, including General Robert 'Roy' Urquhart, who played such a prominent role. In deference to Browning's involvement, he sent a copy to Daphne, which she read and passed on to Sir John Hackett, a close family friend and the Commander of the Fourth Parachute Brigade at Arnhem.

Later Richard Attenborough went on record saying that at this stage Daphne had two main objections, one minor, the other not. The first related to what Tommy had worn. The script had him flying a glider in kid gloves, a description from the book, but Daphne disagreed, writing to Attenborough: 'He was always well dressed, I grant you that. He thought it was part of discipline. But the little scene there sounded frightfully stupid. No mention of the fact he'd trained as a para. the hard way.'

Attenborough at once agreed to take it out, if she found it objectionable. Next she told him Tommy had been shown wearing a 'pantomime' uniform, although in fact it had been copied from a real one in a glass case in the Airborne Museum. Her other criticism was more valid, indeed crucial, in some respects to the entire story. In Ryan's book, Browning makes the quote from which it took its title – that, tactically and practically, Arnhem might prove to be a 'bridge too far' – right at the beginning of the story, when he gave the opinion to Montgomery on being told of the latter's proposal to attempt the taking of all five Rhine bridges. Afterwards, as we know, he gave the plan his whole-hearted support, but it is essential to know that he said it when he did. Ryan's source was Urquhart, who was there; but in Goldman's script Browning said it at the end of the film, after the disaster, apparently with hindsight. Daphne demanded Attenborough put the comment back in where it was originally made, before the Arnhem Drop. She pointed out the importance of this in a statement to *The Sunday Times* on 23 October 1977: 'My husband said to Monty "Don't you think we're going a bridge too far?" In the film this is cut out completely and Dirk Bogarde only says it after the battle in a stony-faced way. I can't remember what I actually said to Attenborough but I think it was "put it back at the beginning".'

Attenborough's memory was clearer. His recollection was that he spoke to Daphne on the phone and agreed to an important script alteration, where there is an exchange between Bogarde and Sean Connery, who was playing Urquhart. Instead of Bogarde merely saying, 'It was a bridge too far', he was then made to say, 'I always thought it was a bridge too far'. It was also made clear, throughout the film, that Browning was acting on Montgomery's orders. Finally, just before he went to Holland to begin filming, he received a letter from Daphne, addressed 'My dear Dickie', saying 'Many, many thanks for your letter. I truly appreciate the immense trouble you have taken with the script and Boy's part in it.' That, thought Attenborough, made everything all right.

In June 1977, *A Bridge Too Far* went on release, at which point for Attenborough the sky fell in. Daphne was enraged and she was prepared to make full use of the friends she had in high places. She was also adored by the surviving officers who had been at Arnhem with Tommy. Although she had not seen the film, and would steadfastly refuse to see it, she became convinced that Tommy's sacred memory had been desecrated. She wrote to Mountbatten, Tommy's old commander in the Pacific, and asked him to tell her after the charity, gala-opening, what he thought of Bogarde's portrayal of the role. After which a flood of letters began in *The Times*, commencing with one from General Sir John Hackett himself on 25 June, in which he starts by saying he cannot imagine it possible that 'Sir Richard Attenborough (would be) unkind, unthinkable to find him lacking in regard for the truth. But it must be said, however, that the portrayal of the late Sir Lieut.-Gen. Sir Frederick Browning is both untruthful and unkind.

'Untruthful because it shows a superficial, shallow, heartless person who is uncaring – flippant even – about the fate of the brave men committed to his charge and displays instead of strength of character, a petulant obstinacy born of weakness. He was not like that at all and could not have commanded such widespread loyalty if he had been.

'It is unkind not only because it will affront very many men who knew Browning well and, though some might say he had faults (and who has not?), gave him their admiration and respect, but although he is dead there are those living who were closer to him still and knew him better and these will be deeply hurt and unnecessarily wounded.' There was a great deal more in the same vein.

The letters of some of those who wrote on Browning's virtues verge on hagiography. Colonel Frederick Gough, writing on 7 July, ended his letter saying: '. . . long after the film is dead and forgotten, the survivors of Arnhem and the families of those who fell will be sustained by Sir Winston Churchill's moving words – "Not in vain may be the pride of those who have survived and the epitaph of those who fell" – Without the magnetic inspiration of "Boy" Browning, our founder and leader, those words could never have been uttered.' Alastair Tower wrote: 'He was tall, erect, immaculately dressed. He looked you straight in the eye with a cheerful smile. He was filled with fire, enthusiasm, energy and inspiration. He excelled at every sport he set himself to master. He spoke only of attack when others spoke of defence. He believed that alertness and discipline went hand in hand. He had the quality of superb leadership.

'His contemporaries recognised his genius for command. He fully understood his troops. That is what he was like. That is why he received such widespread loyalty. During my life I have been privileged to measure his tributes from British and American servicemen of every rank. If there was ever a man *sans peur et sans reproche* "Boy" Browning was that man.' One is left wondering how anyone could live up to such a reputation.

The offence caused to the Browning family was made crystal clear to Attenborough, a double one since Tessa was now married to Montgomery's son. He was also informed that the Queen Mother herself had entered the lists and at a reception she had given at Clarence House had expressed her full approval for the letters in *The Times* and *The Sunday Times* as they continued to flow in. Military men who had not been at Arnhem and did not know Browning entered the fray and two even laid a wreath on the Cenotaph in his memory, after writing a fulminating letter to Attenborough. And still Daphne refused to see the film.

A reporter who rang up and asked her why not said she told him that Ryan had never portrayed Tommy in such a vicious way in the original book, and that people had rung her up in horror at the film version. She had not seen the film and did not want to, she no longer went to London, and even if it came to the local cinema in St Austell she would still not go.

The man in the eye of the storm was the unfortunate Dirk Bogarde, one of the finest screen actors in the British cinema, a man who had decided to give up acting altogether and who had had to be heavily persuaded into playing the part.

'Alas,' he writes, 'my performance caused an uproar when the film was finally shown. There were cries of fury and distress from the widow and family of the man I was representing, and anger was expressed, so I was reliably informed, from Windsor Castle to Clarence House. Letters were even written to *The Times* (of all papers) complaining of my interpretation. I was crushed with dismay.

'I didn't see the film so I'm not qualified to make any comments, or judge where – or if – I went wrong. I had known the officer I played in Normandy and Holland: the very last thing I would have dreamed of doing was to defame his character or reputation, but both of which I was told I had; God knows how. Such distress did this cause me that I considered making an apology in the press and sending my salary to an army charity. It wasn't much, as it happened, but I was determined not to retain one farthing.

'After 30 years of working in the cinema and 60-odd films, this was the harshest blow I'd had to take. And it taught me, for the last time, never to go against my sense of order again. At least in the cinema. However, my hysteria simmered down after two trusted people had seen the film at my request and instructed me to make no apology but just shut up. My work, I was informed, was professional, straightforward, military and cold. "Which," as one of them said, "I suppose is what Generals were meant to be". So that was a relief; but it took a long time to set aside. Forgetting, however, was different.' There is a very real irony that Bogarde, so well known for his meticulous research into the fictional characters he played, had actually based this interpretation not only on a real person, but on one whom he had known personally, and it is worth noting here that Bogarde himself had no mean war record.

The film did not, on the whole, please the regular film critics either. 'So muddled is the final impression left after nearly three hours . . . and so curious the portraits given of several of the senior British Officers, that I can only assume something other was being attempted than a clear account of the battle . . . It was a serious misjudgement,' wrote Patrick Gibbs in the *Daily Telegraph*. 'A reel too long,' was the heading in the *Sunday Mirror*. 'In this story any resemblance to persons living or dead is not coincidental – because the dead can't sue,' said Bernard McElwaine. More pertinent was Alexander Walker's comment in the *Evening Standard*. 'I really doubt if anyone any longer wants movies that turn some horrifying human disaster into the stuff of visceral entertainment or try and celebrate the tens of thousands of unknowns who died and at the same time assign roles to famous faces who glorify the Hollywood star system.' Would that it were true – the film was a tremendous success throughout the world, not least in Japan where, the man who put up the money, Joe Levine, is quoted as saying 'there they like to see white men killing each other, business is *sensational*.'

Yet, setting the film and its critics on one side, there is a point to be made. It is impossible to know just how Browning came across in person at the press conferences he gave after Arnhem, but the accounts do make chilling reading, and there is one statement which appeared in every newspaper report of the time, that already quoted in the earlier chapter: 'If one or two things had gone right we should have got to Arnhem Bridge. That is a tragedy of war and a lot of first-class men were lost. Otherwise I have no regrets.'

Tommy Browning, when Daphne either writes or talks about him, remains a singularly lifeless figure, seemingly preserved like a fly in amber as he was when she first met him, when he was thirty-five years old. She was still describing that first meeting, in almost exactly the same words, when she was over seventy, as if a needle had become stuck in an old gramophone record, or as if that record had been scratched and so kept repeating a single phrase, over and over again. She might occasionally refer to his brave army service, the methodical way he organized the early household moves, his love of boats, but there is nothing of him as a lover, a father or a grandfather, as the lively personality he so definitely was. The only time she actually wrote about their companionship in a way that brings him to life, is when she was describing their expeditions together, in search of Tristan and Iseult.

Tommy would always remain, in her public utterances, a man apparently without any human faults, apart from her painful single admission, long after his death, that his infidelities had hurt. There are a number of examples of how what she said actually measured up against the reality, but one will suffice. She would always tell journalists that, 'Tommy never drank'. She continued saying it even after he had been involved in a spectacular local court case in Cornwall.

Two days before the Christmas of 1963, Tommy Browning pleaded guilty at Truro and West Pydar Magistrates' Court, to driving a car while unfit through drink or drugs. He was first seen driving his Alfa Romeo erratically towards Truro, by a following motorist, frequently on the wrong side of the road. When he found himself behind a long line of standing traffic, he proceeded to pull out and pass it.

His car 'narrowly missed the leading vehicle,' said the police prosecutor, 'which was a van and it struck a glancing blow to the second vehicle, which was a truck. At the time of the collision with the truck, his tyre was heard to burst, but instead of stopping, the defendant's car went on, being driven with a flat tyre, still pursuing an erratic course.'

He continued: 'When it (his car) was approaching the ambulance station there was again a line of traffic, this time coming from Truro, and owing to the way in which his car was being driven, that line of traffic had to stop suddenly, with the result that there was a collision between two vans and a motor-cycle. One van ran into the back of another and the motor-cycle ran into the back of the second van, the motor-cyclist being thrown off his machine sustaining head injuries and a fractured wrist.' A motorist tried to stop the car, giving it a 'slow down' signal, 'but Sir Frederick overtook him and went on towards Truro.' Finally a police patrolman on a motor-cycle caught up with Tommy and brought the car to a halt. By that time it was being driven on the rim of one wheel, the tyre being completely missing. The driver, continued the police prosecutor, 'did not seem to be aware that he had been in an accident or to know how he had lost his tyre.' A blood test revealed an alcohol content the equivalent of eleven whiskies, and there was a half-full bottle of Scotch on the back seat which Tommy admitted he had been drinking, although he did not usually do so.

The Lieutenant-General had behaved throughout, said the prosecutor, with the utmost courtesy. In defence, his solicitor said that although he had not been asked to mention the Lieutenant-General's distinguished war record, he could hardly avoid doing so, given his service to the nation. He blamed pills that the defendant had been taking for the state he was in, pills whose side effects had not been known either to him or to his doctor. He also opined that there was a great deal of doubt, quoting no lesser source then the distinguished pathologist Sir Keith Simpson, as to the level of alcohol in the blood at which judgement might become impaired. Finally, the family doctor was called, who confirmed that he had prescribed tablets for which he had received no warning of possible side effects and possibly, therefore, it was 'one of those drugs of which side effects are constantly being discovered. The general drank only small quantities of alcohol on rare occasions.'

The court found Tommy guilty, fined him fifty pounds with costs and disqualified him from driving for twelve months; but so far as Daphne was concerned, whatever those who remember him might say, Tommy never drank!

To return to his portrayal in *A Bridge Too Far*, it is unlikely that, for Daphne, *any actor*, however talented and conscientious, could adequately have portrayed Tommy. One can only speculate as to what might have been her reaction to an actor who might have had the temerity to attempt to put Gerald on to the stage or screen . . .

CHAPTER 28

'Old Evil, loose my chains and let me rest . . .'
Another World, Daphne du Maurier

Some ten years or so after Daphne moved into Kilmarth, there was a rapprochement between her and the Rashleighs. Hearing that a member of the family was unwell, she called in to enquire how they were, bringing with her some apples from the Kilmarth apple trees. She was invited in.

Obviously things had changed. The Rashleighs were in the throes of demolishing the Victorian wing, their own pictures were on the walls, their own furniture in the rooms. Yet Daphne, when she returned to Kilmarth, said that she could not recall a thing, she saw Menabilly still as it was when she had lived there herself, so all pervasive was the image in her mind.

However, the ice having been broken, she became a regular visitor to Menabilly, going over for tea at least once a week. She also asked if she might have a bunch of lilac from her favourite tree each year on her birthday, and this Veronica Rashleigh happily agreed to do – although the weather did not always make it strictly possible. Her visits would pass pleasantly and the Rashleighs have happy memories of Daphne and another guest, Dr Rowse, arguing hotly about the provenance of Shakespeare's plays over the sandwiches. 'But although our house did mean so much to her and featured in some of her books – especially *The King's General* – we were only ever peripheral to the story of her life,' says Veronica Rashleigh.

Throughout Daphne's last years she and Angela, depending on their relative states of health, would visit each other at Kilmarth and Ferryside, usually weekly, although when one was more severely indisposed than the other, then the one who could get about would ensure that, so far as was practical, the visits were kept up. Throughout the rest of Daphne's life the two kept in touch by telephone, conscientiously ringing each other at nine o'clock every morning.

'Life at Kilmarth was often bizarre,' wrote Michael Thornton after her death. 'The royalties absolutely pouring in from the twenty-five books made her one of the richest writers in the world, yet she lived like a church mouse, dressed in old fishermen's jerseys, sou'westers and Wellies, pushing her bed around the room to miss the drips from the leaking roof.' The chronic fear that had gripped her years earlier, that somehow the golden flow would cease, became obsessional, fuelled no doubt by the fact that she had found herself unable to write. It was not that she was miserly – she was generous to a fault where her family were concerned – but that she seemed unable to bear to spend any money on herself, even necessary money, or eventually on Kilmarth.

When she had first moved in, it was a truly delightful place. The way the rooms opened out one from another and the long windows in the sitting room meant that on a fine day the sun poured in along the whole length of the house. The walls, as at Menabilly, were crowded with portraits, pictures and cartoons, the portrait of herself at sixteen, painted by Harrison Mann, having pride of place over the mantelpiece – a picture which shows that extremely determined chin.

The sitting room was a particularly comfortable room, not at all grand, but pretty and lived-in, with its deep sofas and pastel curtains, a room where Daphne would sit and talk and dispense tea. But gradually, during the last seven years of her life, Kilmarth became more and more run down and neglected, as she lost interest in it.

For over ten years she had tried her best to fight off depression. There is presently a certain amount of argument among

295

psychiatric experts as to whether or not chronic depression can be a hereditary condition. Certainly it had assailed members of her family, as we know, in at least four previous generations, but clinical depression can descend upon anyone, no matter what their circumstances and however courageous they might be. Daphne seemed just able to keep going for about two years after the abortive trip to Scotland, and when she was seventy-three she was still saying, in that BBC radio interview, that she hoped and prayed every day that she might wake up one morning and find that she had not lost her inspiration, that she would be able to write at least one more novel. It never happened.

'The life of the imagination had been everything, when that went, everything went,' says Rowse, 'because she really didn't have anything to fall back on. It was the source of awful unhappiness to her and throughout the rest of her life she was to become increasingly miserable and depressed. In those last years life became increasingly hopeless for her, it ceased almost to be bearable. She became a truly desperate woman. I tried to get her to write something, anything. She'd always loved animals so I suggested she wrote about her much loved dogs, but she refused. She was an obstinate woman, you know, look at her portraits and note that chin – a very firm chin. She just wouldn't hear of it.'

This was confirmed by Michael Thornton in the *Observer* after her death: 'A black depression descended upon her and grew. For the first time in her life she wrote despairing letters which alarmed her friends, so utterly unlike her did they sound.'

In 1982 there was a crisis. Exactly what happened is unclear. Both her doctor and Esther Rowe described it as a severe nervous breakdown, but it seems to have been more than that. Others have suggested the onset of Alzheimer's disease or a slight stroke which left her physically unimpaired, but mentally confused. Whatever it was, her old friend Rowse says: 'After that everything folded up. She wouldn't see me, she wouldn't see anyone – often she didn't even want to see her own family.' Nobody seems to know precisely what happened, perhaps it was a combination of things, perhaps just that terrible state that can descend on an elderly person which those of us who have had to experience it within our own families know only too well – when the parent one has known and loved becomes not only so despairing and depressed that life is a burden to them, but they also appear to suffer a sea change of personality so that they become, quite literally, someone else.

Certainly those last years were deeply unhappy ones. She would still walk the grounds of Kilmarth with her dogs, but she only rarely ventured further, either to Menabilly or Ferryside and as time passed, so she became increasingly confused.

In October 1982 Gollancz had formally announced that there would be no more du Maurier books. Said Livia Gollancz, daughter of the firm to whom Daphne had remained loyal throughout her working life: 'It's very sad when someone like that comes to the end of the line but it comes to us all.'

In 1980 the firm had published the last anthology of Daphne's short stories, under the title *The Rendez-vous*. They had been collected from all periods of her life, the title story being one she had written as a very young woman after one of her trips to Paris in the 1920s. In her foreword to it she explained once again how virtually all her ideas had come to her in those incidents observed when travelling, at home or abroad, although some had been inspired by conversations overheard in Gerald's dressing room, or over lunch at Cannon Hall. People seemed disappointed, she wrote, when she told them that none of the people in the stories was 'real' that the incidents were all 'made up'.

'Made up . . . my father Gerald made up his face to become another man upon the stage. Whereas I sit in front of a seedy hotel in the Boulevard Montparnasse and imagine what happens inside it . . .'

The last book she worked on herself was *The Rebecca*

297

Notebooks and Other Memories. She described it to many people as 'the scrapings of the barrel'. It consists of the notes she made when she was plotting *Rebecca*, notes found in the notebook returned to her from Doubleday and a small collection of essays written between the years 1946 and 1976.

Perhaps here is the time to mention, briefly, the book which appeared in the September after her death. *Enchanted Cornwall*, says the blurb, is the last book to have been *written* by Daphne du Maurier. It was published not by Gollancz, who had published all her work except for her first two novels, the tract for Moral Rearmament and *Castle Dor*, but by Michael Joseph, the firm founded by her first literary agent. It has proved the subject of great contention. It is edited by Piers Dudgeon, described as her 'Devon editor' and was given the imprimatur of Christian Browning. It is a handsome volume full of beautiful photographs and over Christmas 1989 it sold heavily.

However, readers found it extremely puzzling. There are long extracts from Daphne's Cornish novels, suitably illustrated, along with linking passages which the publicity material leads one to believe were written by Daphne during that last year of her life. 'The last book of that legendary novelist, Daphne du Maurier,' said the Michael Joseph publicity. 'Completed shortly before her death,' wrote one reviewer, 'it represents a victory over infirmity, loneliness and old age.' This prompted a fellow writer to say that 'in reality it represents a victory of hyperbole over fact. For Daphne, who died in April, did not actually write the book at all.'

As Michael Thornton says of it, her severe depressive illness got worse and worse during those last years and 'her inability to write made her utterly miserable and in almost every letter she sent me there was the same lament: 'I have tried and tried to write more stories, but it's no good. I find I just cannot'. Asked about the provenance of the book, Christian Browning told the media that in it were a lot of extracts from her Cornish novels pasted together,

298

interspersed with various thoughts she had written down and taped over the years, also interviews she had given . . . and there was some unused material from a television film he had made for her seventieth birthday. Piers Dudgeon said that he had found 'ghostly inspiration' in studying Daphne's work and that 'in a sense' Daphne had written everything in the book. Later, Michael Joseph said that the book was based on material given to Piers Dudgeon.

In fact all the linking passages in the book can be traced to other du Maurier books, rewritten and edited, and the way this has been done does no service to Daphne. One crucial example is worth picking out. In an essay she wrote in the 1960s entitled 'This I Believe', she says: 'In my end is my beginning. The "I" who writes this essay lives and dies. Something of myself goes into the children born of my body and to their children and to their children's children. Life, in whatever shape or form it takes, goes on, develops, adapts.'

This appears in *Enchanted Cornwall* as a foreword signed by Daphne in the highly ungrammatical form: 'I, who writes this, lives and dies, but something of myself goes into the children born of my body and into their children . . . Life in whatever form it takes goes on and is truly eternal.' The claim that Daphne 'wrote' *Enchanted Cornwall* (apart from the extracts from novels), certainly assisted its sales, but if it is taken to mean that she wrote the book in the same way as she wrote, for example, *Rebecca*, it is not an interpretation with which any literary purist, any writer, or most of her readers, would agree. She deserved better.

Eventually Daphne became so confused and frail that a nurse was employed to live in and assist Esther Rowe in looking after her. For months before her death she seemed virtually unaware of what was going on around her. Writing, either her own or that of other people, meant nothing to her. Whatever conflicts she might have experienced with regard to a religious faith, she seems, towards the end, to have found visits from the local vicar, Canon Oatey, comforting. He was one of her last visitors.

On the morning of 19 April 1989, Esther Rowe went in to wake Daphne as usual, to find she had died peacefully in her sleep. No-one who loved her or knew her as she used to be would have wished her to linger on; the last years must have proved extremely distressing, particularly for her family.

The line quoted at the beginning of this chapter is from a poem called 'Another World' which she wrote in 1947, a time when everything was blooming for her. Tommy was home from the war, the children happy, the creative flow in full spate and money rolling into the bank from royalties and film rights; yet it is prophetically bleak. It ended:

> Old Evil, loose my chains and let me rest
> Where I am best,
> Here in the muted shade of my own dust.
> But if I must
> Go wandering in Time and seek the source
> Of my life force,
> Lend me your sable wings, that as I fall
> Beyond recall,
> The sober stars may tumble in my wake,
> For Jesus' sake.

Tributes poured in from all over the world, from those who had known her, and from those in their tens of thousands who had never met her, but who had remained her devoted readers throughout the years. By a strange irony an adaptation of the novel so closely associated with Menabilly, *The King's General*, opened at the Theatre Royal in Plymouth the following night.

By her own request she was cremated. A memorial service was held for her in the little chapel on the Menabilly estate, an event attended by only her family and a handful of invited friends. The date and time were deliberately kept secret. There was no celebration of her life, with a national memorial service; there was not even a local one for those

300

who had known her, and among whom she had lived for so many years. Her ashes were scattered on the land she loved, mourned not least by the devoted Esther Rowe, who had provided her with so much loving support and care over thirty years. The confusion and depression that had descended on Daphne meant that she had not made any provision for Mrs Rowe in the event of her death, a matter of some anxiety, as Kilmarth had long been her home as well as Daphne's.

Daphne left nearly half a million pounds in her will, the rest, mostly royalties from books, had long been settled in family trusts. In September members of her family put a selection of items from Kilmarth into a local auction sale. They included a William IV writing desk, and a mahogany Sheraton Revival writing table, on which it was thought Daphne had written both *Jamaica Inn* and *Rebecca*. There were also the two special chairs assigned to Tommy and Daphne for the Coronation, and given to them by the Queen afterwards. Evidence of the frugality of her life at Kilmarth was apparent in the state of most of the objects, the surface of the Sheraton writing table was so badly damaged that in the picture in the catalogue taken for the sale it is shown covered with books. Nearly everything of any size was worn, or badly affected by damp, anything with a flat surface marked with rings made by hot tea or coffee cups; even the seats of the Coronation chairs were badly stained with mould and damp. But none of this deterred the fans who descended in their droves for the auction.

Prices for Daphne memorabilia proved to be staggering. The Sheraton Revival writing table was valued at between £800 and £1200; in the event it fetched over £8,000 and was bought, not inappropriately, by the owners of Jamaica Inn. Everything went, from the Coronation chairs to a mahogany curtain rail which was sold for £40! Such was the devotion she had inspired in her fans, they were happy to buy just about anything which had had a direct connection with their idol.

*   *   *

Daphne du Maurier lived through a period of enormous change, from the brief, golden Edwardian age to that of the Cold War, the nuclear bomb and modern technology. Two devastating World Wars were fought, the map of the world altered, Britain lost an Empire and society was turned upside down. Yet she remained outside all of it.

It is hard to think of another twentieth-century writer so cut off from the world and the rush of events. At first she was protected by wealth and family position, later by her retreat behind the walls of Menabilly, where even the events of the Second World War only impinged when they directly affected Tommy. Finally there were the years as a recluse at Kilmarth. Hers was also a life singularly without the struggle experienced by virtually all writers; the struggle to be published, for recognition and, above all, to earn enough to live on while continuing to write.

'Obstinate', 'tenacious', 'loyal', 'underestimated', 'talented' – all these are adjectives used by those who knew her. 'She was,' says A.L. Rowse, 'a much nicer person than I could ever be. She had a good sense of humour and of irony and she was self-mocking – all of which are endearing characteristics.'

Her reclusive image tends to suggest that she was cavalier in her treatment of people, inhospitable perhaps or unwelcoming, but that was not so. She did not suffer fools gladly, and she never made any secret of the fact that she disliked socializing for its own sake, but to those she favoured with invitations into her home, she could be immensely kind. She remained, almost to the last, a physically attractive woman enhanced by those remarkable eyes and she gave off an air of an older and more elegant world, even down to her enunciation, so like that of the Queen; and she certainly did have a most remarkable charm, a lasting legacy from Gerald to his favourite child.

'Du Maurier Country', of course, never did exist. It is a Cornwall fashioned from her romantic imagination; but what she did was to write so evocatively of the physical beauties of the county, that she made countless readers, who never had and never would set foot there, see it as she did herself, so that for them, too, it became a dream world. It is ironic that this in itself has helped bring about some of that despoilation which concerned her so much when she wrote *Vanishing Cornwall*, and pondered what she had set in motion when, long before, she had written *Jamaica Inn*. For even in 1976, when she was musing in print what part she might have played in helping to commercialize Cornwall, more and more reliance was being placed on tourism to prop up the county's ailing economy as, one by one, the remaining traditional industries succumbed to market forces, unable to compete in the harsh climate towards the end of the twentieth century.

But even her ironic imagination would have found it difficult to contemplate an era when the whole nation was encouraged to become one great theme park, where 'du Maurier country' became a place on the map, squeezed somewhere between Arthurian Magic Lands and 'Poldark' mines, Tunnels in Time and a whole range of gimmickry designed to attract the tourist; somewhere to make for after a quick tour of 'Hardy's Wessex' and 'Lorna Doone's Exmoor'.

None of this harsh reality, however, is likely to affect those thousands of readers whose vision of Cornwall will always remain that of Daphne, a lotus land like Lyonesse or Avalon, which will never die.

Local people nowadays are ambivalent about Daphne and 'Du Maurier' country; perhaps they always were. There has been no hesitation in cashing in on the name of the author and her best-known books. Boat trips advertise 'Daphne du Maurier's cottage' and 'The Real Manderley', although Menabilly cannot be seen from the sea, even if the description were accurate. Jamaica Inn has its 'Joss Merlyn' bar, restaurants are named 'Frenchman's Creek' and 'La Mouette'. She has, inadvertently, done local businesses proud.

The ambivalence comes at the mention of Daphne herself. After her death, the local vicar was not alone in expressing his surprise that there was no memorial service, no celebration of her life, that could be attended by neighbours and admirers of her work. It was accepted that she had always 'kept herself to herself', whether through shyness or because she felt a very definite distinction between the du Mauriers and the rest (apart from the landed gentry); but that she should be kept so removed even in death was much remarked. Older residents remember her as a courteous figure, dropping in now and then, to do a little shopping in Par, or how the Queen and the Duke of Edinburgh took tea with the Brownings long ago; but the most common reaction is 'of course, she never mixed much', 'never showed much interest in local activities'.

The cautious attitude to Daphne is best summed up, when the question of her success is raised, in the phrase 'well, she made an awful lot of money out of her books about Cornwall, but what did she actually *do* for us?' This is followed by two particular stories.

Towards the end of the 1950s, a local farmer put a number of caravans in one of his fields and let them out to holiday-makers. The site was a prominent one, the caravans considered an eyesore, and his action was certainly not popular with local people. On this occasion, for once, the Brownings took a prominent role in the opposition, both Daphne and Tommy complaining that the caravans spoiled their view of the coastline when they were out sailing in their boat. Eventually, the site was closed down, Tommy taking much of the credit for this. Shortly afterwards, in 1961, he stood for the Conservative Party in a local council by-election in this deeply Conservative constituency and, to his surprise, he lost. The somewhat muddled reason given was that, while many people had agreed with him that the caravan site had been a mistake, they were against the part he had played in its closure, seeing it as a case of wealthy people stopping a local man from earning some money, just because it offended their eyes when out in their yacht!

The second story compounded the matter. Not long afterwards it was announced that a local property developer was in negotiation for a series of fields on which he planned to build expensive housing. The fields were on the skyline, above Fowey, on the coastal stretch, which links the outskirts of the town to the Rashleigh land surrounding Menabilly, where it goes down to the sea. It seemed that the only way to prevent such despoilation was by buying the land for the same amount, or more, than the developer was offering. Local residents set about trying to raise the necessary cash by the usual methods of jumble sales, coffee mornings and a variety of other fund-raising activities. A tentative approach was made to Daphne to see if she might become a major contributor, but she did not respond.

'At the price land was then, she could have bought it for the town ten times over and not even noticed it,' remembers the owner of a local business, whose family has lived in Fowey for generations. 'You'd have thought she'd have wanted to keep that stretch of coastline free from houses and roads, because not only can you see it from anywhere, it was right slap bang up against Menabilly land. But she didn't do anything.'

In the event, a Mr A.J. Allday, who had made his money in the motor trade, bought the fields and gave them to the people of Fowey in perpetuity. A modest stone records the fact with an inscription. They are now known as 'Allday's Fields' and form part of the National Trust coastal footpath. Nor is Mr Allday alone. Right behind the du Mauriers' Ferryside at Bodinnick, is 'Hall Walk'. The first part of this tract of woodland was left for future generations by a similarly civic-minded gentleman (Mr Hall), at the end of the sixteenth century, and the 'pleasant walk' is mentioned by Richard Carew in his 1602 *History of Cornwall*. At the end of the last war, Hall's Walk, was added to by Lieutenant-Colonel Peter Shakerley RA, who gave the rest of it, and the cliffs below, in joint memory of the men from the area who died in the 1939–45 War and of Sir Arthur Quiller-Couch, 'Q', whose monument, like that of a celtic chieftain, stands at the highest point, looking westward.

There are no 'du Maurier Fields', nor a 'du Maurier Walk'. There is only 'du Maurier Country', a romantic dream.

Epilogue

There was to be no shortage of literary obituaries following Daphne's death. They ranged from those which praised extravagantly everything she had ever written, to the dismissive, in which she was written off as just another romantic novelist, albeit an extraordinarily successful one. The commonly known facts of her life were repeated endlessly – her place in an already famous family, the purchase of the ferry house in Cornwall, her discovery of the long-neglected Menabilly, her marriage to 'Tommy' Browning; the massive success of *Rebecca*, and her reputation as a recluse.

Although all together she had written twenty-five full-length books and several collections of short stories, over a period of fifty years, it was the same handful of titles which appeared in the serious broadsheet newspapers, the tabloids and the magazines: *Rebecca, Jamaica Inn, Frenchman's Creek* and *My Cousin Rachel*, the so-called 'Cornish' novels, on which she had built her reputation as a popular novelist. *The House on the Strand* and *Rule Britannia*, while also set in Cornwall, were only rarely mentioned.

Although the first few books had been written easily and rapidly, one straight after the other, she was not, in point of fact, a prolific author, and the rate at which her novels appeared became slower and slower, until they ceased altogether. Both her publishers and her readers would have taken far more from her, but she always refused, quite rightly, to force the pace.

Will her work last? Only time will tell; but it is now possible to look objectively at both her weaknesses and her strengths. There is no doubt whatsoever that she had a fortunate and cushioned start in her chosen avocation, heavily assisted by the du Maurier name; but there is no way this would have carried her along indefinitely for, while Gerald was certainly a household name when she began writing novels, he had long since ceased to be, by the time she had become a best seller. The cachet of the du Mauriers was certainly crucial in enabling her initially to find both a good agent and a publisher with such ease, but even her first book, *The Loving Spirit*, though naive in style, retains a great deal of charm.

Considering her weaknesses first then, the two novels subsequent to *The Loving Spirit* expose them in good measure. *I'll Never Be Young Again* has them all – unbelievable characters, unlikely experiences, lack of vocabulary and, in this instance, dreadful dialogue as well. It is not even all that interesting as a period piece, as there are plenty of far better novels on the theme of the Bright Young Things of the 1920s. It also showed her apparent strange and ambivalent attitude to sex at that time, a kind of prurience, allied with a desire to shock, but without any sense of deep emotional intensity, passion, or even straightforward desire.

These criticisms apply even more strongly to *The Progress of Julius*, this time with incestuous love thrown in for good measure, and there can hardly have been a more unpleasant fictional Jew since Dickens' Fagin or, earlier, Barabbas in Christopher Marlowe's *Jew of Malta*.

If she had stopped then, after *The Progress of Julius*, it is unlikely that she would have ever merited any more today than a line or two in a biography of Gerald. As it is, the current edition of *The Oxford Companion to English Literature* dismisses her entire career in seven lines, mentioning only *Rebecca*.

The dialogue in all her books is stubbornly middle class, a limitation of which she must have been well aware, for her attempts to cope with writing in dialect, even Cornish dialect, are usually unsuccessful, while the language of her few, working-class characters is quite unreal. This is no doubt the reason why few ordinary working people appear in her books, and when they do so in her plays they are stock characters, such as jokey family 'treasures' of the 'Lor' luv yer, Missus' variety. Equally unreal, as has been mentioned before, is the Cornwall of the historical novels (apart from *The House on the Strand*), the promotion of a highly romanticized picture of a countryside peopled with spoiled beauties, evil parsons and dashing Frenchmen, all presided over by wealthy county families living in substantial comfort. Whatever she might have said to the contrary, these *are* romantic novels. For a more authentic glimpse of what life must really have been like in the Cornwall of the late eighteenth and early nineteenth centuries, then the first four novels of the *Poldark* series by Winston Graham come far nearer to reality, with their carefully researched descriptions of struggling tinners, half-starved labourers and rough squires, all battling for survival in a harsh, if beautiful, environment.

Turning now to her non-fiction, this improved steadily once she finally began to discard her previous method of mixing often well-researched fact, with imaginary situations and dialogue; while she had been able to get away with unlikely or unreal dialogue in her fiction, it certainly does not work when it is put into the mouths of people who really existed.

Daphne was always very honest about what she recognized as her own shortcomings, not least the trouble with spelling and grammar, which lasted throughout her professional life, and it is obvious that she did owe a great deal to good and sympathetic editors, and to the assistance of people such as Oriel Malet.

However, having rehearsed her weaknesses, what about

her strengths? As she proved with her first truly popular novel, *Jamaica Inn*, she was, first and foremost, a formidable story-teller and to say that this is more in the mode of the nineteenth century than that of the twentieth, is intended as a compliment. The reason why *Rebecca* has had such an enormous success, in spite of the fact that, taken at face value, its characters are frankly unbelievable and a synopsis of the plot might look absurd, is because it is told with such vigour that it sweeps the reader along regardless, as indeed does *Jamaica Inn* which preceded it. Almost all her novels, in fact, introduce a colourful cast of characters which remains in the mind, even if they are not fleshed out as are, say, the Revolutionary narrator of *The Glass-blowers*, the fictional Honor Harris of *The King's General* or the actress-turned-guerrilla-leader, 'Mad', in *Rule Britannia*.

Anyone who has ever read *Rebecca* remembers the enigmatic Maxim de Winter and the sinister Mrs Danvers; likewise who can forget Joss Merlyn or the albino vicar in *Jamaica Inn*, the beautiful, ambivalent, and possibly murderous Rachel of *My Cousin Rachel*, or the wicked Lord Rockingham in *Frenchman's Creek*?

As well as this gift for story-telling and for evocative descriptions of the countryside, she had another very real strength; she was never a formula writer. It would be quite wrong to class her with writers of routine, endlessly-repeated, historical novelettes, or as little better than a purveyor of one or other of the six plots of a Mills and Boon romance. However successful one book might have been, she rarely followed it up with another which was similar, although she was probably at her best when there was a mysterious element to her stories as in *Rebecca*, *My Cousin Rachel*, or *The Scapegoat*.

Her work also developed and matured over the years but, partly as a result of her early success, the development shown in her later writing was underestimated. For example, in *The House on the Strand*, she pulled together the threads of much of her earlier work – recreation of past centuries, descriptions of the countryside, and a mystery – and made out of them a haunting book. In *Rule Britannia* she showed a satirical and sharp edge, in both the story and in the writing, that she had only revealed before in her short stories, and her short stories do contain some of her very best work. *The Infernal World of Branwell Brontë* is very praiseworthy, and *Golden Lads*, as has already been pointed out, contained entirely original research. Compared with the rash of hyped, formula books which are piled in heaps at supermarket checkouts, the so-called 'creepy-weepies' and 'sex-and-shopping' paperbacks, the novels of Daphne du Maurier stand, quite genuinely, in a class apart. It remains to be seen how she will be regarded fifty years from now, whether she will be remembered much as Jeffrey Farnol is today, as a once popular novelist now very much out of fashion, or as a consummate story-teller, like Robert Louis Stevenson, whom she adored.

There is a strange thread running through the three generations of the du Mauriers – George, Gerald and Daphne. It is as if, at their birth, all three of them had been given one of those gifts so beloved in fairytales, a gift which grants great success or wealth, or both, but which carries with it a hidden price. The 'gift' granted to the du Mauriers manifested itself in three different ways.

It came first to George and he, alone of the three, desperately wanted recognition as a serious artist, studying in Paris at the height of the Impressionist flowering. He was certainly a considerable draughtsman. Yet he made his name, fame and fortune, drawing cartoons for a popular humorous weekly magazine and with the melodramatic novel, *Trilby*.

When the gift descended to Gerald it was of a different nature. It was that of a very real, theatrical talent, but it does not seem that he wished it had been other than it was, for he never appeared to want to stretch himself by attempting the great roles. (He would, of course, have been the perfect Maxim de Winter.) It was left to the up-and-coming Oliviers and Gielguds to break new ground in classical acting.

By the time it reached Daphne, the gift had changed

again, this time appearing as a talent for story-telling. Her considerable achievement was to write extremely popular books which reached an enormously wide readership, making her one of the wealthiest and most successful novelists of her day.

They were, all three of them, talented, accomplished, middle-brow and tremendously financially successful. But then came the price which had to be paid for all that artistic skill, theatrical flair and ability to write. It was chronic depression, coupled with a feeling of insecurity, and a fear that the talent, along with the financial reward it brought, would dry up. The depression was a trait which had come down the generations from Robert and Louis Busson du Maurier. All three of the creative du Mauriers suffered from it, Daphne most acutely of all; but it was remarkable, that gift which flowered for those three generations. It is also one that appears to have died with Daphne.

But even if that is the case, then the legacy she left behind was that she gave pleasure to, literally, millions of readers, a pleasure which is still experienced by those who come to the best of her work for the first time as well as those who reread their favourites, such as *Jamaica Inn* and *Rebecca*, with continuing enjoyment. It is no mean achievement.

BIBLIOGRAPHY (GENERAL)

Barker, Felix *The Oliviers*, London, Hamish Hamilton, 1953
Birkin, Andrew *The Lost Boys*, London, Constable, 1979
Bogarde, Dirk *An Orderly Man*, London, Chatto & Windus, 1983
du Maurier, Angela *It's only the Sister*, London, Peter Davies, 1950
Harding, James *Gerald du Maurier*, London, Hodder & Stoughton, 1989
Lean, Gareth *Frank Buchman, A Life*, London, Constable, 1985
Millar, Hoyar *George du Maurier and Others*, London, 1937
Morley, Margaret *The Faces of Laurence Olivier*, London, LSP Books, 1978
Rowse, A.L. *Friends and Contemporaries*, London, Methuen, 1989
Ryan, Cornelius *A Bridge Too Far*, London, Hamish Hamilton, 1974
Wapshott, Nicholas *The Man Between*, London, Chatto & Windus, 1990

BIBLIOGRAPHY (DAPHNE DU MAURIER)

The Loving Spirit, London, Heinemann, 1931
I'll Never Be Young Again, London, Heinemann, 1932
The Progress of Julius, London, Heinemann, 1931
Gerald *, London, Gollancz, 1934
Jamaica Inn, London, Gollancz, 1936
The Du Mauriers *, London, Gollancz, 1937
Rebecca, London, Gollancz, 1938
Come Wind, Come Weather, London, Heinemann, 1940
Frenchman's Creek, London, Gollancz, 1941
Hungry Hill, London, Gollancz, 1943
The King's General, London, Gollancz, 1946
The Parasites, London, Gollancz, 1949
My Cousin Rachel, London, Gollancz, 1951
Mary Anne *, London, Gollancz, 1954
The Scapegoat, London, Gollancz, 1957
The Infernal World of Branwell Brontë, London, Gollancz, 1960
Castle Dor (with Sir Arthur Quiller-Couch), London, Dent, 1962

The Glass-blowers *, London, Gollancz, 1963
The Flight of the Falcon, London, Gollancz, 1965
Vanishing Cornwall *, London, Gollancz, 1967
The House on the Strand, London, Gollancz, 1969
Rule Britannia, London, Gollancz, 1972
Golden Lads *, London, Gollancz, 1975
The Winding Stair *, London, Gollancz, 1976
Growing Pains *, London, Gollancz, 1977
The Rebecca Notebooks *, London, Gollancz, 1981

* = Non Fiction. *The Glass-blowers* is semi-fiction

PLAYS

Rebecca, 1939
The Years Between, 1946
September Tide, 1948

SHORT STORIES

Daphne du Maurier's short stories were published in a number of collections – the same collections sometimes appearing under different titles. Below they are given in the first edition in which they appeared.

The Apple Tree, London, Gollancz, 1952
The Breaking Point, London, Gollancz, 1959
Not Before Midnight, London, Gollancz, 1972
The Rendez-vous, London, Gollancz, 1981

Index